"Paul Lakeland's *Church: Living Communion* seizes t[...]
the brink of change and points the direction forwar[...]
realistically through its marks, and leads us through the scho[...]
external challenges to its authentic witness. Attentive to the laity, he then
builds a practical strategy for moving beyond survival to revival. All this in
limpid accessible prose: brilliance in simplicity. This authoritative book will
appeal to everyone who has a stake in the Catholic Church in North America
today."

Roger Haight, SJ
Scholar in Residence
Union Theological Seminary

"This is a teaching moment in the Church and this is a teachable book on the
Church. In this eminently readable book, Paul Lakeland offers his readers
only what they need to know to think and talk intelligently about the identity
and mission of the Church. With honesty, he describes the challenges facing
the Church that perplex and polarize in a way suitable for debate in the
classroom and in reading groups. He invites his readers to develop an
inductive approach to ecclesiology, and in the process he promotes the
cultivation of practical wisdom that can help communities respond to these
challenges with genuine hope."

Bradford Hinze
Professor of Theology
Fordham University

"Paul Lakeland's brilliant account of ecclesiology may well come to be
recognized as the first truly twenty-first-century analysis of the Church.
His study addresses the events and insights of the last decade and then
transposes into a new key historical-critical readings of the New Testament,
themes from Vatican II, ecumenical consensus statements, Lonergan's
methodology, and postmodern concerns. In an engaging, refreshing style,
he also faces up to the Church's failings in hard-hitting language, marked by
stark realism. Finally, he gently poses ten challenges to the Church, which he
deems eternal."

Michael A. Fahey, SJ
Professor
Boston College

Series Advisory Board

Church

Living Communion

Paul Lakeland

Tatha Wiley, Series Editor

A Michael Glazier Book

LITURGICAL PRESS
Collegeville, Minnesota

www.litpress.org

A Michael Glazier Book published by Liturgical Press

Cover design by Ann Blattner.

1   2   3   4   5   6   7   8   9

Library of Congress Cataloging-in-Publication Data

Lakeland, Paul, 1946–
    Church : living communion / Paul Lakeland.
      p. cm. — (Engaging theology)
    Includes bibliographical references and index.
    ISBN 978-0-8146-5993-9 (pbk.)
      1. Church. 2. Catholic Church—Doctrines.   I. Title.

BX1746.L28 2009
262'.02—dc22

                                                      2009015091

To Elizabeth and Selwyn Palmer

For welcoming the stranger, and all that followed.

CONTENTS

Editor's Preface

In calling the Second Vatican Council, Pope John XXIII challenged those he gathered to take a bold leap forward. Their boldness would bring a church still reluctant to accept modernity into full dialogue with it. The challenge was not for modernity to account for itself, nor for the church to change its faith, but for the church to transform its conception of faith in order to speak to a new and different situation.

Today we stand in a postmodern world. The assumptions of modernity are steeply challenged, while the features of postmodernity are not yet fully understood. Now another world invites reflection and dialogue, and the challenge is to discover how the meanings and values of Christian faith speak effectively to this new situation.

This series takes up the challenge. Central concerns of the tradition—God, Jesus, Scripture, Anthropology, Church, and Discipleship—here are lifted up. In brief but comprehensive volumes, leading Catholic thinkers lay out these topics with a historically conscious eye and a desire to discern their meaning and value for today.

Designed as a complete set for an introductory course in theology, individual volumes are also appropriate for specialized courses. Engaging Theology responds to the need for teaching resources alive to contemporary scholarly developments, to the current issues in theology, and to the real questions about religious beliefs and values that people raise today.

Tatha Wiley
Series Editor

Preface and Acknowledgments

A book about the Church could be a book about a number of different things. It could be about church architecture, but the building is not the Church. It could be about bishops or the clergy or the pope, but none of those is the Church. It is, of course, about us, because we are the Church. The Church is the community of believers down through the ages, and the Church today is the living members of the community, including but not exhausted by Church leaders. In conversations among Catholics "the Church" is too often the "them" with whom we disagree or who are telling us what to do or who are somehow objectified. We need another name for that portion of the Church, because the whole Church is the Church. For the great majority of laity, for whom over the centuries it has been hard to say "Church" and think "us," the time has more than come when we have to say "Church" and mean "us," with all that this implies for taking responsibility, insisting on accountability, and assuming adulthood. Becoming subjects of our own history, with all that this means for adults, is long overdue for the Catholic laity. It is in this spirit and with this Church in mind that this book is written.

The approach to ecclesiology adopted in this book is therefore resolutely inductive. That means that our starting point will be with the grassroots experience of Church, and that in its turn means that the book cannot be anything other than specific to a particular context. It is one of the marks of inductive method, perhaps the most important, that it begins locally, though of course the implications of local reflection can be profoundly important for the universal Church. It was Henri de Lubac who pointed out that ecclesiology is that branch of theology where we are talking about ourselves. In this book that is exactly what we will be doing, and this brief preface exists simply to explain a point or two about what this focus on "us" means and then to offer the customary but no less sincere thanks to a number of people.

The book begins with an updated reading of the marks of the Church—oneness, holiness, catholicity, and apostolicity, together with an additional, fifth mark of eternity—which puts the Church of today into the context of tradition. In the second and third chapters we focus on the American Catholic Church, because you cannot do inductive theology from an abstract, universal standpoint. Of course, it goes without saying that catholicity means that many other local ecclesiologies will enter into dialogue with and correct that of North America, and that together all these theologies form the rich tapestry of Roman Catholicism. So the second chapter examines some challenges facing American Catholicism today, both internally and in terms of its mission beyond itself, confident in the knowledge that what we learn in our context will be as valuable to the rest of the Church as what happens in Africa and Asia is for us. The third and final chapter makes a brief foray into an American inductive ecclesiology for the twenty-first century. Borrowing its structure from some principles first enunciated by Bernard Lonergan, it focuses its attention on the need for conversion, for adulthood, and for accountability, and it offers four images to consider as a basis for ecclesial reflection. Three—pilgrim, immigrant, and pioneer—are drawn from the American experience. A fourth and perhaps startling image, that of hospice, I owe to the Catholic moral theologian Bryan Massingale, though I take full responsibility for the way it is used here. I ask the reader to be patient with this difficult image, and it will reveal its power and potential.

Because of the commitment to an inductive method, much of what the reader might expect to find in a Catholic ecclesiology will be missing. There is very little here that is purely informative about the history of the Church or its major doctrines. The emphasis is on Church, that is, on the shape of the community of believers, at this time and in this place. Of course, historical depth is a necessity for a full understanding of where the Church came from and what it is today. Some of this is provided in the first chapter, much of the rest of it will be found through following up on the notes, which I have kept brief and primarily bibliographical. It is there that the reader will find the suggestions for further reading that will augment and expand on what is here.

Principal among those who deserve thanks are those theological ancestors and current colleagues from whom I have learned so much. My ecclesiological ancestors include Yves Congar, Henri de Lubac, Karl Rahner, and Bernard Lonergan. My colleagues happily still with us, some of them relatively young for theologians, include Joseph Komonchak,

Roger Haight, Richard Gaillardetz, Bradford Hinze, and Gerard Mannion. I have learned, like so many, from the writings of Elizabeth Johnson, and I wish she would write an ecclesiology, but I suspect she will not. I am grateful too to Tatha Wiley, the series editor for Engaging Theology and herself no mean theologian, who combines tact, charm, and being a pest into a well-nigh unstoppable force; and Hans Christoffersen of Liturgical Press, a model of patience and fortitude. As always, my colleagues in the Religious Studies Department at Fairfield University have provided me with help both direct and indirect, and I am particularly grateful to John Thiel and Nancy Dallavalle. My wife Beth and my son Jonathan are to be commended for keeping out of the way and pursuing their own equally important careers while letting me get on with mine. But the inspiration for this approach to ecclesiology has come to me above all from the many fine people I have met in traveling around the country these past few years talking to church groups, especially those associated with Voice of the Faithful. An inductive approach to ecclesiology is one that taps the wisdom of concerned and active laity such as these. I hope that this book will be some small return to them for all the energies and hopes they have placed in the future of the Roman Catholic Church in America.

Chapter One

The Marks of the Church

From ancient times the Church has been characterized by the four "marks" of unity, holiness, catholicity or universality, and apostolicity. These identifiers were added to the Nicene Creed, originally fashioned in 325 CE at the Council of Nicea, by the bishops at the Council of Constantinople in 381. Catholics and most other Christians today thus find themselves reciting their profession of faith in "one, holy, catholic, and apostolic Church." They are four distinctive characteristics of early Christianity, which most if not all Christian faith communities have maintained in their own traditions up to the present day. The Catholic Church, perhaps more than others, has not only consistently seen them as marks of the Christian Church but in times of polemic it has used them as indicators of where the one, true Church of Christ is to be found, namely, in the historic Roman Catholic Church. To borrow a phrase or two from ecumenical theology, most churches other than the Catholic Church would see the marks as objectives, destined to become realities on the day when we are all *united*. The Catholic Church has tended to see them as real marks of itself, to become perfected on the day when all Christians are *re-united*.

As ways of talking about fundamental characteristics of the Catholic Church that do not immediately lead to invidious comparisons with Orthodox or Protestant traditions, the marks of the Church are hard to better, though they need interpreting. They speak truths about the Church recognized by Protestants, Orthodox, and Catholics alike. All believe the Church is in some sense one, that it bears the characteristics of holiness

1

and universality, and that it is faithful to the apostolic tradition and witness. For this reason it seems wise to choose the marks as an approach to exploring how the Church understands itself. But they cannot just be taken at face value. What is the true meaning of oneness when there is division? What is holiness in the light of the sinfulness with which the Church has at times aligned itself and from which it has never been entirely free? How is the Church universal if there are many forms of church and many places where it is not present? And what does it mean to claim to stand in the apostolic tradition?

In this chapter readers will encounter a fifth mark that is not part of the tradition and that would probably not be acceptable to most traditions other than the Catholic and the Orthodox, namely, the eternity of the Church. The other four marks are all introduced here as answers to the questions, *what, who, where* is the Church, and *what* is the Church *for*? To them, then, we add the related question, *when* is the Church? There are many other candidates too. Charles Curran has recently written that a fifth mark of the Church is its sinfulness, Michael Himes has suggested that conciliarity is another, and Dolores Leckey argues for the role of the laity as a further defining characteristic.[1] Cogent as all these are, here we will take up only five. They offer answers to the five most fundamental questions we can ask about the Church and provide a framework for our task here in this first chapter, to examine anew the Catholic tradition's understanding of the Church.

Holiness, or "What is the Church?"

When we approach a topic as vast as that of the worldwide Church, it makes sense to begin by making sure we are in agreement about what we mean by "Church." For one thing, and most of us will not need telling this, we are not using the term to refer to the building in which Catholic Christians worship. For that purpose, we employ the subtly different term "church." But "the Church," ah, that is so much larger and wider and more interesting a phenomenon, not always as beautiful as that ancient Gothic cathedral, nor as colorful or bizarre as some German rococo or Italian baroque edifice, but immeasurably more complex and alive than a mere building.

So "Church" refers to the whole religious family, in this book in the first instance that of the Roman Catholic Church, though other Christian

---

[1] In William Madges and Michael J. Daley, eds., *The Many Marks of the Church* (Mystic, CT: Twenty-Third Publications, 2006).

churches are never far from our considerations and will occasionally be addressed directly. It is as geographically wide a descriptor as the entire world, at least for now (it could get bigger with space travel or missionary outreach to life-forms out there in the universe that we have not yet discovered), and as historically extensive as a couple of thousand years. It includes the holy and the not so holy, the pious and the relatively secular, the regular churchgoers and the "Christmas and Easter Catholics." Doubtless, as we proceed, we will want to make some qualifying judgments about inclusiveness and exclusiveness, but the term "Church" as a term denotes all those who would recognize themselves somehow or other as members of the Catholic Church.[2]

While agreement about the meaning of the word does not even begin to scratch the surface of an answer to the question, "What is the Church?" it does bring before us the important initial challenge of determining how we would go about seeking an answer. If we were to build on the thoughts in the preceding paragraph and produce a detailed picture of what the Church looks like, describing the various places and historical moments that have made up its contemporary countenance, reviewing the types and numbers of peoples within its ranks, explaining its practices, and so on, we would not have definitively answered the question, because we would not have broached the issue of meaning. If, on the other hand, we were to turn immediately to a theological or philosophical question about meaning, we would be in the opposite danger of being way too abstract for what the Church on the ground is actually like. In other words, we can adopt neither an exclusively inductive nor deductive approach. Both the concrete reality of the Church and theological ideas about the Church will factor into a measured and helpful response to the question, "What is the Church?" However, the almost exclusively deductive approach of classical ecclesial reflection has to give way to a stronger orientation to bottom-up approaches, if only to restore some balance.

The question about the nature of the Church has most often been answered in a deductive or Procrustean[3] fashion, defining either abstractly or—at best—unhistorically what the Church *is* as if this is what

---

[2] This way of identifying Catholics by personal affiliation rather than conformity to an external set of requirements will be consistently applied throughout this book, showing a preference for an "inductive" (bottom-up) rather than "deductive" (top-down) approach to ecclesiology.

[3] Procrustes, the giant who trimmed or stretched his sleeping victims to fit the bed on which they lay, is a symbol of the distortions of deductive thinking, when real people and situations are forced to measure up to abstract ideas.

it always *was* and probably always *will be*. One of the biggest problems with this approach is that it is so unself-conscious about the historical positioning of the answer being given, and of the historical subjectivity of the one offering the answer. It is, moreover, quite blind to the organic nature of the Church. Like any other body in history, the Church is always in a certain sense the same, but always equally truly in a constant process of change. The analogy to the human body is instructive. The continuity of my identity as me or yours as you is not guaranteed by the physical identity of the body I had ten or fifty years ago and the body I have now. It is, rather, the memory that maintains continuity in the process of constant physical change. Not even my self-consciousness now can guarantee that it is the same self-consciousness as was exhibited in this physical body at some prior time, without the string of memory to connect the two moments. Moreover, memory itself is a tenuous process, subject to forgetting as well as remembering, both intentional and accidental. On such a fragile thread hangs the identity of the Church, and a bold confidence in abstract universals fails because it does not respect this essentially historical reality.

The problems with a deductive approach to the identity of the Church can be illustrated by looking at one of the most successful efforts to employ it, the classic work by Avery Dulles, *Models of the Church*.[4] In a certain sense Dulles has already stepped beyond deductive approaches in preferring a multiplicity of models to the one definition preferred in recent centuries of the Church as a visible, perfect society here on earth. However, when we ask about where the models Dulles identifies and explains are derived from, we find them almost exclusively drawn from the work of specific theologians or Church leaders. Obviously enough, all theologians determine their personal ecclesiological orientations in dialogue with Scripture and the writings of the great thinkers of the early Church. But when a model proposes itself solely because of its scriptural origin, the result must be that it will be employed therapeutically with respect to the actual living body of believers at any one time. Ecclesiology understood this way then becomes a corrective to Church practice, seen probably as always more or less errant—because human—from the perfection of an ahistorical idea of Church derived somehow from biblical and patristic evidences. However, what one person sees as a necessary correction, another may well perceive as a distortion of the living reality.

---

[4] Avery Dulles, *Models of the Church* (Garden City, NY: Doubleday, 1974; New York: Doubleday, Image Books, 1991).

While we would be foolish to discard biblical and patristic sources in our search to understand what the Church is, we should be on firmer ground by beginning with the actual historical reality of the Church in the times in which we live. There are many consequences of this more inductive approach to ecclesiology, not the least of which is that it is ineluctably contextual.[5] The Church seen from North American or African or Asian perspectives will evince different histories, cultural characteristics, and (perhaps) political alignments. The danger of this approach, though, is that it can lead to fragmentation, and to avoid just such a possibility it has to be combined with some overarching common understanding of its nature and purpose. Just as we said that it is memory that binds the Church now with the Church of bygone ages, so we need to search out the theological glue that holds together the many and various versions of the Church around the world. The tendency to identify the glue in terms of authority should be avoided, though it is far too common. While there is a kind of unity in all being in communion with Rome or having many liturgical practices in common, these are extrinsic signs of unity. Figuring out what the Church *is* will require a successful hunt for a common feature of ecclesial life that, wherever we find it, will be intrinsic to the sense of the community about what it is to be Church.

When we say that the Church is a community of faith, we are making a claim that is both banal and significant but one that will lead us quite a way along the path of answering our initial question, "What is the Church?" Initially, the statement that the Church is a community of faith seems quite minimalist. Where is the beauty, richness, and glory of the story of Roman Catholicism? How stark and simplistic this description seems and, indeed, to how many other religious groupings around the world it can be applied. It is surely true that Mormons and Baptists and Buddhists and Jews could all assent in some way to the accuracy of this description as applied to their own situation. On the other hand, to make this general kind of statement our starting point helps us avoid the single biggest pitfall of the history of religions in general and the self-understanding of Roman Catholicism in particular, namely, to define ourselves by our differences from others. So often in ecumenical dialogue among Christians someone makes the observation that "what we have

---

[5] On this topic see especially two books by Robert J. Schreiter, *Constructing Local Theologies* (Maryknoll, NY: Orbis, 1985); and *The New Catholicity: Theology Between the Local and the Global* (Maryknoll, NY: Orbis 1997). See also Clemens Sedmak, *Doing Local Theology: A Guide for Artisans of a New Humanity* (Maryknoll, NY: Orbis, 2002).

in common is so much more than what divides us." For Christians, at least, this is surely true and perhaps even truer than we imagine in the wider world of interreligious dialogue. But it comes as a surprise only because we tend to begin from our differences instead of from a more generic foundation of common purpose and understanding, dare one say, of common faith.[6]

To return, then, to our foundational assertion that "the Church is a community of faith," we need to spend a little time unpacking the meaning of the three nouns "Church," "community," and "faith," but proceeding in reverse order and approaching the task inductively. First, the faith that binds the community we call Church has to be explained by looking at the actual practice of Christian believers at the present and at any chosen moment in the past. There is always a temptation, of course, to short-circuit the project by turning to "the Faith" that we as Roman Catholics are supposed to be committed to, and to trot out a series of definitions from the Nicene Creed or the *Catechism of the Catholic Church* as if they represent what is permanent and religiously satisfying in our experience of God. But this more deductive approach involves presenting a template to the Christian, inviting acceptance as the mark of possessing "the Faith," though among this list of beliefs there may be some with which we have genuine difficulty and there are certainly a few that we could not readily explain. In fact, creedal formulations or sets of beliefs taken from catechisms of one kind or another correspond to religious life only as grammar corresponds to the living language. One can speak a language and speak it grammatically without ever studying grammar. And grammar always follows after the living language, a fact with which grammarians have never been entirely comfortable. Indeed, grammar is quite dependent upon the way the language itself is spoken, and is always playing catch-up. It has its importance, but that importance lies in its explanatory potential, not in some presumed normative role it exercises relative to actual speech. In similar fashion, theology follows after religious life and experience; it does not precede it.

The analogy between faith/the Faith and speech/grammar requires us to begin by examining what is constant in the faith that two millennia of Christians have found at the center of their lives. It is heartening,

---

[6] Ormond Rush has argued persuasively that in ecumenical dialogue the practice of explaining our positions to one another needs to give way to that of explaining how each tradition understands its faithfulness to the ancient apostolic Church. See *Still Interpreting Vatican II: Some Hermeneutical Principles* (Mahwah, NJ: Paulist Press, 2004).

though unsurprising, to find that kernel of faith in *the experience that the loving care of God for us is supremely available in our intimacy with the story of Jesus Christ*. If any element of this description is missing, then we are only dubiously Christians; so if we do not believe in God or our God is not loving and caring, or we do not find the story of Jesus to be the way in which we come closest to God, then we may be good and even religious people, but we are probably not fully incorporated into a Church that claims to be "a community of faith," whose faith rests upon the experience that the loving care of God for us is supremely available in our intimacy with the story of Jesus Christ.

This more inductive approach to determining the identity of the Church begins at the heart of what it is to be a believer and puts doctrines and creedal formulations in their proper and secondary place. Theology or religious reflection has a very important function in exploring and explaining the implications of our religious experience, but only so long as it retains appropriate humility. Again, the analogy with the role of grammar is instructive. Religious reflection functions properly when it protects the integrity of religious experience, just as grammar's proper role is to ensure that speech communicates clearly, that it does what it is supposed to do. But religious reflection functions inappropriately when it tries to tell us what our religious experience is or must be, just as grammar oversteps its mark when it insists on real speech following rules that make it harder for people to understand one another. A particularly good example of religious reflection overstepping its bounds can be seen in the long parade through Christian history of efforts to identify the historical Jesus as opposed to the Christ of faith, or to determine the essence of Christianity, or indeed to organize the books of the Bible into those that are more important and those that are less so, in search of some "canon within the canon" that will correct and corral the wild and lively world of individual religious experience. When religious reflection becomes unhinged from the experience of God that it is meant to be subject to, it can turn literally deadly. No heretic was ever burned at the stake for her or his experience of God; they all went to their deaths because they understood their experiences of God to be primary and doctrinal formulations to be secondary. Their judges were the theological grammarians.

A person of faith as we have just described it, or indeed a multitude of such persons, does not of itself make a Church, and so we turn to exploring the meaning of the second term in our description, "community." In ordinary American parlance, "community" is almost as overused a word as "family," and often equally sentimentalized. The Church is rarely referred to as a family, and given the dynamics of all too many families, this is a blessing.[7] But the Church is commonly and rightly referred to as a community, so we have to get clear what we mean by this. We certainly do *not* mean that its members are necessarily alike, or like-minded, or all agree with one another on everything, or feel that they have to socialize with one another, or wear the same uniform, or cheer on the same sports teams. We don't even have to like one another all that much.

In the first instance, to say that the Church is a *community* of faith is to assert that we are bound together by the common possession of an outlook on life, its purpose and destiny, grounded in the experience that "the loving care of God for us is supremely available in our intimacy with the story of Jesus Christ." The Church, then, is not a club we join because we like what it offers or find the people congenial; it is a community we find ourselves a part of because each of us, individually, has encountered and been touched by the love of God in Christ. In responding to the call of Christ we find ourselves, perhaps to our surprise, shoulder to shoulder with a host of other human beings, past and present, dead and alive, who differ from one another in many ways but have heard the same call and responded to it. We did not choose them and they did not choose us. Think of it in the manner of Jesus' calling of his disciples. Jesus saw something in each of the Twelve, and they "left their nets and followed him." They did not get along with one another particularly well, they squabbled at times and remained a pretty fractious bunch throughout his public ministry, but these personal idiosyncrasies are dwarfed in importance by the common work they did of leading the young Church they built on Jesus' foundations.

If we may be permitted to call our common life within the community of faith our "ecclesiality" we can borrow a pair of terms from John Paul II's thinking about collegiality and describe our ecclesiality as possessing both an *affective* and an *effective* dimension.[8] The affective aspect of our ecclesiality is the human bond between us, grounded in our common commitment to Jesus Christ. While we may not like one another, the fact that our lives and our world are rendered meaningful because of our

---

[7] The family, curiously enough, is often spoken of as "the domestic Church." See *Lumen Gentium* 11, though the term goes back to patristic times.

[8] See Paul Lakeland, "John Paul II and Collegiality," in *The Vision of John Paul II: Assessing His Thought and Influence*, ed. Gerard Mannion (Collegeville, MN: Liturgical Press, 2008), 184–99.

common link to Jesus truly does bind us to one another on a human level. This is true quite trivially for fans of the New York Yankees or Manchester United or Bruce Springsteen, all of whom, despite being as varied as the human race in its entirety, have this one thing in common to bind them into a discernible community. It is true at a much deeper level for members of religious communities because—though baseball, soccer, or rock music fanatics might disagree—the call to which members of religious communities have responded is so much more comprehensive. Even Yankee fans have to put their allegiance aside at times, to go to work or to negotiate with a spouse who may not share the same fascination, and most of them find they can balance these different dimensions to their lives. But the Buddhist or the Christian has to include all the dimensions of her or his life within their foundational identity as a follower of Jesus or the Buddha. Hence the affective bond between Christians is at a much deeper level than that between Grateful Deadheads or the Daughters of the American Revolution.

If the affective dimension of our ecclesiality is strong because of the claim made upon us, the community is only the more united because of *effective* ecclesiality. The effective dimension of the community of faith is what is more commonly called its apostolicity. To be an apostle is to be sent, to be a "missionary," which itself means someone who is sent. Effective ecclesiality, then, is the common work of the Church as it fulfills the mission that Jesus Christ left to it. Another way we identify this aspect of our life as Christians is as discipleship. Our task is to be "other Christs" for the world in which we live, somehow to transmute the message of Jesus so that the changing world can continue to hear it clearly. And, as anyone knows, there is no better way to build a community out of a plain bunch of people than to give them a common task. Together, the affective and the effective work feed off and sustain one another.

This discussion of ecclesiality brings us to the third term in our description, that this community of faith is the "Church." More precisely, let us recall, "the Church is the community of faith grounded in the experience that the loving care of God for us is supremely available in our intimacy with the story of Jesus Christ." The world knows many communities of faith, each of which is distinguished from the others because of the particular character of its founding experience and the insights to which this experience leads. Formally speaking, the Church is no different from the others. But materially it is quite distinct. "Faith" has one character for Buddhists, another for Muslims, another for Christians, and while some religious traditions share a lot in common (the

Abrahamic traditions of Judaism, Christianity, and Islam, for example), others may be quite irreconcilable.

Communities all have at least some patterns of behavior and common structures, perhaps leadership models and even rules and regulations. Successful communities are those in which this organizational culture has grown organically out of the grounding experience upon which the community's affective and effective ecclesiality is based. In other and simpler words, first Jesus who is the Christ, then the community of disciples, then the Church. So, as we explore the term "Church" here we are turning for the first time to what in many other places is where ecclesiology begins, with structures. In this text, structures come after, and while in human terms it is pretty logical to think that first we have a group and then it develops structures to assure its own continuity, integrity, and effectiveness, to put things in this order when talking about the Church is more controversial than we might imagine. For one thing, it subverts the common assumption that the Church was fully developed in the mind of Jesus Christ while he lived and taught on earth. It does not, of course, challenge the belief that there is a discernible line of continuity between Jesus of Nazareth and the Church of the second or twelfth or twenty-first centuries. But it does suggest that the outline of that continuity is a whole lot clearer looking backward than it could ever have been looking forward. [9] The parallel in our own lives is clear; when we are young we rightly imagine all kinds of possibilities and may have strong hopes for a particular future, but only later in life can we discern a pattern of any kind, because the pattern becomes clear only in retrospect.

As we think in a preliminary way about the meaning of "Church" we can neither anchor it in the distant or recent past nor see the entirety of its meaning only in the present form that it takes, and we have to be able to distinguish between which of its features are time-conditioned strategies for the better proclamation of the Gospel and which are essential. The Church in any and every age, let us recall, is that community of faith distinguished by the experience that the loving care of God for us is supremely available in our intimacy with the story of Jesus Christ. If we could travel back in time to any century in the last twenty, we would find the Church where we found such a community. We would

---

[9] On a retrospective theory of tradition see the magisterial work of John E. Thiel, *Senses of Tradition: Continuity and Development in Catholic Faith* (New York: Oxford, 2000), esp. 84–94.

not always find the Church if we went looking for features of our present-day Church such as celibate clergy or permanent deacons or diocesan finance councils or cardinals or Gothic cathedrals. These things and many others have emerged at different points in our history as the Church has sought to be effective, and occasionally they have waned in importance or even disappeared, and sometimes even reemerged (as happened in the case of permanent deacons). None of these things on this list is essential to the Church, though some of them have been very important in its history. If they disappear, it will be because affective and effective ecclesiality is not as well served by them now as it once was. But there are other ecclesial phenomena that it is not so easy to imagine disappearing. What would the Church be, for example, without the Eucharist or without the Bible? These are fundamentals because although one could imagine a community of faith that had neither—and there are a number of Christian communities that pay little or no attention to Eucharist—it would not be *this particular* community of faith. Scripture and the Eucharist are fundamental to the experience that the loving care of God for us is supremely available in our intimacy with the story of Jesus Christ.

A more traditional way of approaching an answer to the question, "What is the Church?" is to explore the history of images that have been employed to describe or even define it. This, indeed, was the method used by the Bishops present at the Second Vatican Council (1962–65) as they put together their major document on the theology of the Church, usually known by the first two words of its Latin text, *Lumen Gentium* (LG).[10] The first chapter of this critically important document, "The Mystery of the Church," assembles a whole set of images for the Church drawn from the pages of the Bible: a sheepfold, a flock, a cultivated field, a vineyard, the house of God, the holy temple, the Holy City, that Jerusalem which is above, our mother, the body of Christ, the bride of Christ. It then concludes this list with a reference to Christ who established "his holy Church, the community of faith, hope and charity, as a visible organization through which he communicates truth and grace to all men," and identifies this "sole Church of Christ" as one that "subsists in the Catholic Church, which is governed by the successor of Peter and by the bishops in communion with him," though of course "many elements of

---

[10] This translates as "light of the peoples," but we have to remember that the light it refers to is Christ. The Church, say the council fathers, reflects that light in the world.

sanctification and of truth are found outside its visible confines" (LG 8).

The second chapter of *Lumen Gentium* is titled "The People of God." Much has rightly been made of the council's decision to reorganize the sections of the document (from what had been presented in an earlier version) and place this chapter before the discussion of the hierarchical element in the Church. However, what is equally important though less commonly observed is that the discussion of the Church as the People of God belongs here precisely because it addresses the puzzle with which the first chapter has left us. Having said that "the one Church of Christ . . . subsists in" the Roman Catholic Church, but having added that "elements of sanctification and truth" are found outside it, the council fathers have to find a way to talk about the Church that places the Catholic Church at its center while at the same time relating all other believers in whatever religious traditions to its central saving role in God's design. It is the determination to be Catholic without being exclusive, in fact, to be "catholic," that drives them to an examination of the Church as the People of God.

We will turn to a fuller exploration of the image of People of God in the section "Who is the Church?" But here we need briefly to consider some other important facets of *Lumen Gentium*, for this document is after all—whether we are more liberal or more conservative in the way we read it—the single most authoritative Church statement on ecclesiology of recent times, perhaps ever. It represents a concerted effort of all the Roman Catholic bishops in the years of the council, aided by the best theologians, to draw together the witness of Scripture and the voice of Tradition[11] into a comprehensive picture of what it means to be the Church of Christ. It is not, and cannot be, the last word on the topic, because history is not like that. Times change and perceptions change with them. But it is, for now, the clearest utterance, under the guidance of the Holy Spirit, of the meaning of our community of faith. So let us draw this section of our chapter to a close with a brief glance at important dimensions of the conciliar vision of the Church, aspects to which we will return frequently in the pages that follow. There are three we should attend to particularly closely, namely, the unity of the Church, the holiness of the Church, and the historicity of the Church.

---

[11] Throughout the text the word "Tradition" is capitalized when it refers to the living memory of the Church as the second source of revelation, after Scripture, in the Catholic vision of things.

The choice of the governing image of the Church as the People of God attests immediately to the critical importance of stressing the unity of the Church. To begin, as had originally been planned, with a discussion of the hierarchy before turning to other sectors in the Church, would not only have perpetuated the mistaken assumption that the clergy/laity divide was somehow fundamental to the Church's being but would also, and perhaps even more unfortunately, have left any discussion of unity looking like an afterthought. If you begin with the parts, you are left with the question of what it is that holds them together as one. But if you start with an organic principle of unity—a people—you are well positioned to relate each role in the Church to the good of the whole community.

A fine example of the way in which the bishops employed the organic image to good advantage can be seen in their treatment of infallibility. Their immediate inheritance in this regard was, of course, Vatican I's dogmatic definition of papal infallibility, and if they were going to approach the subject of infallibility again it was clear that they would have to do so in line with what had been said at that late nineteenth-century gathering.[12] Vatican I, though, was a notoriously incomplete council, hastily suspended after Rome came under siege. If the bishops in 1870 had intended to say more on the subject of authority, they were unable to get to it. Vatican II clearly set out to correct this lack in the earlier council, and the bishops chose once again to explore the notion of infallibility in the context of the organic unity of the Church. Having placed it where it belonged, as an action of the Holy Spirit as guardian of the Church's continuity in truth, they went on to identify three ways in which the Holy Spirit guarantees that the Church remains in truth, and so three ways the Church expresses infallibility. The first is the very same as Vatican I had identified, in the pope's role as the focus and symbol of unity of the entire community and the consequent responsibility that he has to clarify the faith of the Church, for the sake of its unity and its permanence in truth. Second, they located a similar exercise of infallible teaching in the entire college of bishops (always including the pope), not only when they are gathered in a council like Vatican II but even when—united in faith—they are dispersed around the world but teach with one

---

[12] Defined on July 18, 1870. For a good brief discussion of the notion of infallibility and the relation of its treatment in Vatican I to that in Vatican II, see Richard R. Gaillardetz, *By What Authority? A Primer on Scripture, the Magisterium, and the Sense of the Faithful* (Collegeville, MN: Liturgical Press, 2003), 81–88.

voice. Third—more striking still—the bishops see what we might call a performative infallibility vested in the entire community of faith when they are united in their belief, the so-called sense of the faithful (*sensus fidelium*).[13]

The matter of holiness pervades the whole document but is discussed most directly in chapter 5, "The Call to Holiness." While this chapter has its flaws, particularly the way in which holiness is discussed following the classic pyramidal image of the Church, starting with the bishops, then moving to priests and deacons and so on, it is prefaced by an important statement that the call to holiness is universal, as "all Christians in any state or walk of life are called to the fullness of Christian life and to the perfection of love." "By this holiness," the council continues, "a more human manner of life is fostered also in earthly society" (LG 40). At the end of this chapter of the present book we will be answering the question of the purpose of the Church, what the Church is *for*. Right here, we can see that holiness is *for* mission, and that mission is oriented to the humanization of society. So when the bishops move on to discuss how holiness is manifested in the lives of bishops, clergy, laity, and even religious, it is always placed in this context. Holiness is not primarily or even significantly a matter of private piety. Holiness is always apostolic.

Finally, the council is at pains to indicate the historicity of the Church, that is, its dynamic presence within history, growing and changing and struggling with new circumstances and different conditions. While this topic is one of the central issues in that other great council document *Gaudium et Spes*, the "Pastoral Constitution on the Church in the World of Today," in *Lumen Gentium* the bishops broach the subject in their surprising little meditation on the Church as a "pilgrim" (LG 7). "Pilgrim," in fact, is a wonderful compromise image for a body of bishops not all of whom want to take history all that seriously. So, on the one hand, the chapter orients the Church within history toward its final consummation and fulfillment in the reign of God at the end of time. As a meditation on the communion of saints and the symbiotic union between what is sometimes called the "militant" and the "triumphant" Church, its theological content is deeply traditional. On the other hand, the very choice of the term "pilgrim" to describe the Church within history suggests an open and hopeful passage through time. The much-

[13] The discussion of the respective roles of pope and bishops in the exercise of infallibility can be found at various points in sections 18–24 of LG. The proclamation of the infallibility of the whole community is to be found in section 12.

quoted reference of the council to the importance of "reading the signs of the times," an emphasis above all of *Gaudium et Spes*, has its theological justification here. "[T]he final age of the world is with us and the renewal of the world is irrevocably under way," yet "until there be realized new heavens and a new earth in which justice dwells (cf. 2 Pet. 3:13) the pilgrim Church, in its sacraments and institutions, which belong to this present age, carries the mark of this world which will pass, and she herself takes her place among the creatures which groan and travail yet and await the revelation of the sons of God (cf. Rom. 8:19-22)" (LG 48). As a worldly pilgrim, the Church points beyond itself. Christ established his Church at Pentecost, say the bishops in this chapter, by sending his Spirit on his disciples to set up the Church as his Body, "as the universal sacrament of salvation." In and through its sharing in the vicissitudes of the historical condition, in and through its imperfections, the Church points beyond itself to the reign of God. As a pilgrim, it travels hopefully, but it has not yet fully arrived at that toward which it points.

Eternity, or "When is the Church?"

While the council fathers at Vatican II were clear that the Church *is* the People of God, they seem to have left it to subsequent reflection to determine all that this might mean about its structure and ways of carrying out its mission. Alongside the theological reflection in *Lumen Gentium*, there are also several quite distinct sets of assumptions about how the Church came into existence. At times, the bishops tie its continuing existence to some set of essential characteristics in the mind of Christ, whom they consider its founder in some quite literal sense, while at others they see its origin in Christ's post-resurrection gift of the Holy Spirit to the disciples, which places the "founding" of the Church at some point after Jesus of Nazareth is no longer bodily present in history.[14] At still others,

---

[14] Compare the picture of the Church in sections 3–5 of LG with the quite different flavor of section 8. In the earlier passage the Church is inaugurated in Jesus' preaching of the kingdom but coming more clearly or more fully into existence after his death and resurrection, through the power of the Holy Spirit. Here it is "the kingdom of God now present in mystery." In the later passage, however, where the bishops are struggling with identifying the Roman Catholic Church as the one true Church, there is a quite different emphasis on an identity between the mind of Christ and the actual structures of Roman Catholicism. So the Church is established by Christ "as a visible organization. . . . Structured with hierarchical organs," principal among them the office of Peter and the apostles.

they seem to think that historically conditioned details of Church history are somehow essential characteristics of the community of faith.[15] Each of these ideas, and all of them together, lead us to different responses to the question, *"When* is the Church?" Does the Church come into existence with the birth of Jesus or with the calling of the disciples? At the moment at which Jesus breaks bread and blesses it and tells his disciples to do the same in his memory? At his crucifixion, resurrection, ascension into heaven? At Pentecost? When the followers of the Nazarene first accept the designation of "Christian"? Or at that precise moment, lost in time as it must be, when Jesus' disciples first said in faith, "Jesus *is* the Christ"?

It is neither possible nor useful to pinpoint the moment at which there is a Church of Christ. Historically speaking, it must be related to the life and death of Jesus, and it cannot exist before Jesus, though there are theologians who have thought it was somehow anticipated in the history of Israel. Theologically, the existence of the Church is not necessarily tied to the history of Jesus of Nazareth. Just as theologians sometimes talk of the "preexistent Christ," the Word of God from all eternity (most notably in chapter 1 of the Gospel of John), so the Church as part of the divine plan for the salvation of the world can be thought of as existing from all eternity too. Just so long, that is, as we do not make the mistake of thinking "eternity" means that the Church was "there" in history three or four thousand years ago, or even at the beginning of time. Our question, however, is one about the worldly history of the Church, not about its preexistence, and as a worldly reality its origin cannot be tied to a particular moment. It is not as if the early followers of Jesus held a meeting to draw up a constitution for their new society of friends, and we could date it as we can date the Augsburg Confession of the Lutherans or the Thirty-Nine Articles of the Church of England. And even if they had, it would surely be possible to argue that the "real" Church had come into existence with the faith of those who eventually saw the need to draw up a formal constitution, rather than with the constitution itself.

While we cannot pin down the precise historical moment at which the Church comes into existence, we can certainly provide a rule by which we can identify *if* there is a Church in existence at any particular moment. We can say, as we did in the last section, that there is a Church

---

[15] It is one thing to represent the Petrine office as a primary characteristic of the Church, but it is quite another to insist upon its late nineteenth- and twentieth-century modes as definitive ways of exercising that office.

when there is an identifiable community, however small, bound together by the common experience that the loving care of God for them is supremely available in their intimacy with the story of Jesus Christ. To say that there is no Church until there is an identifiable community means that there is no Church just because Jesus planned to found a Church, if indeed he did. There is only a Church when the teaching and person of Jesus has led a group of individuals to form a community somehow focused upon his person. For those who favor a "low Christology," stressing the humanity of Jesus and his slow growth into knowledge and understanding of the implications of his mission for his identity, this is not a difficult idea. But even if you prefer a higher Christology, one that understands the historical Jesus from the beginning as the Son of God present in history, it is a mistake to think of the Church as real because Jesus Christ intended it. Low Christology or high, the Church as a historical reality depends upon the free, faithful response of ordinary human beings to the meaning of Jesus Christ. You can put it a little more strongly and say that without the human response in faith to Jesus, his status as Savior remains hidden, if it happens at all. True, Jesus sends the Holy Spirit into the world, but the Spirit of God cannot compel faith. Salvation is an offer of divine grace, not a manacle. Just so, there is no Church without disciples, and disciples freely respond to the offer of grace. Here, we might say, we see the courage of God, who subordinates the divine will to human freedom. A God who becomes incarnate has to pay this price.

While we can clearly discern in the first followers of Jesus an identifiable community gathered around him, this in itself is not sufficient to determine that the Church exists within the time of Jesus' public ministry. They must also somehow have a common experience of what Jesus means for them. But the gospels make it pretty clear that during their time following Jesus in his preaching and teaching and healing there was little or no unanimity among these followers about what and who Jesus was. In fact, they show every sign, despite having been captivated by his person, of people who are trying to figure it all out and often getting it wildly wrong. They fight among themselves about who will be greater in the kingdom of heaven, they do not or will not hear his clear predictions of his passion and death, they fall asleep in the garden of Gethsemane, and they flee in fear when Jesus is taken captive. Peter, their leader, is so confused that at one point Jesus says to him, "Get behind me, Satan," and his flight when Jesus most needs him is compounded by a threefold explicit denial of any connection to his Lord and master. As in so many other human situations, the women appear to be a good deal more constant than the men, but taken overall it seems quite impossible to believe that this distinct community of followers has any kind of shared experience that grounds their fellowship, beyond the personal charisma of their leader. They follow him, but there is no clarity at all at this point about why they are following him, still less about the full implications of his mission. A puzzled and conflicted fascination does not qualify as faith.

The common experience of Jesus' first followers that will begin to change this group of individuals from an association of people captivated by the personality of Jesus into a community of faith will have to wait on the encounter with the risen Jesus. While Jesus preaches the coming of the reign of God, he himself is not the object of faith. In Mark's gospel Jesus appears from the beginning with the message, "Repent and believe in the good news, the reign of God is at hand" (see 1:15). The faith he calls for is faith in the reign of God, not faith in himself. In the synoptic gospels of Mark, Matthew, and Luke, Jesus during his brief years of ministry consistently points away from himself and toward God and God's reign. If he draws people to him, as he surely does, it is because of the power of his teaching and healing as testimony to the coming reign of God. It is not because he himself becomes the object of worship. That will begin to occur only when the event of his death and the experience of his resurrection shift the attention of his disciples from the content of his preaching to the identity of the preacher himself. This genuine paradigm shift that makes faith *in* Jesus possible is the direct work of the Holy Spirit, occurring—as it always does—through human creativity.

If it is indeed the case that faith in Jesus must await the experience of the resurrection, it seems there cannot be a Church during Jesus' earthly life. For, while the teaching of Jesus certainly brought his followers to a greater awareness of the loving care of God for them, the proclamation of the advent of the reign of God is not enough to form a Christian community of faith. For that to happen, the early community must identify the story of Jesus himself, not his preaching of the kingdom, as the key that unlocks the meaning of history. Jesus himself has to be received by them as the perfect revelation of the saving love of God. Or, in the words of our working description of the Church, as making God "supremely available" to them. Before his death and resurrection they do not have the data to make such a confession of faith possible. However, even after these events they depend on further help from the gift of the Holy Spirit, without which they would have remained cowering in their hiding place, despondent and afraid.

The events of Pentecost are most often singled out as the key moment in the coming-to-be of the Church. Fear is replaced with courage, despair with confidence, and the disciples complete their transformation into apostles. When they encounter the risen Jesus, the Holy Spirit comes upon them in order to confirm them in their mission, to send them out to preach, as indeed they do according to the account in the Acts of the Apostles. These men, whom Jesus gathered around him because he saw something in them and they in him, are sent (an apostle is one who "is sent") in the power of the Spirit to preach something that Jesus did not preach, namely, himself as the content of the message. It is, of course, probable that at the time of their initial preaching the apostles did not fully comprehend the message they were preaching and had not entirely plumbed the depths of its religious implications. Since we have not yet fully explored the meaning of Jesus Christ, we should not be surprised to learn that they had not done so either.

When the apostles began to preach Jesus in the power of the Holy Spirit, they were unaware that they were about the business of laying the groundwork for a new community of faith, but this does not mean that a new community was not in the process of formation. Looking backward from our historical vantage point we can see lines of develop-ment, both before and after Pentecost, that show the slow emergence of the Church of Christ. From within the events themselves, it is not at all as easy to see what is happening. But from where we stand there is no doubt that Pentecost was a decisive, if not the decisive, moment in the formation of the Christian Church. The beginning of Jesus' public min-istry (Mark 1, Luke 4) is consequent upon his being filled with the Holy Spirit, just as it was for those Peter addressed in Acts 2. The parallels are instructive about the development that is taking place, even allowing for the poetic license of the evangelists:

> Jesus came into Galilee, preaching the gospel of God, and saying "The time is fulfilled, and the kingdom of God is at hand; repent, and believe in the gospel." (Mark 1:14-15)

> And Peter said to them, "Repent, and be baptized every one of you in the name of Jesus for the forgiveness of your sins; and you shall receive the gift of the Holy Spirit." (Acts 2:38)

While the Church has subsequently become clearer that something decisive happened at Pentecost, it is true that much remained to happen before it could be said that the early followers of Jesus had developed a full awareness of the meaning of their emerging community. While the apostles at Pentecost were engaged in something profoundly new, they could not foresee all that their preaching would lead to. The communal self-consciousness that was necessary before the community would begin to see itself as the Christian Church and to refer to itself in that way only developed over the course of the first century. Many elements contributed to this growing awareness: the preaching of the apostle Paul, the resolution of the Council of Jerusalem after which circumcision and inclusion in Judaism was no longer considered a requirement for becoming a Christian (around the year 50 CE), the destruction of the Jerusalem temple (70 CE), the writing of the gospels (around 70–100 CE), and the fierce but sporadic persecution that the early community experienced. The most important factor does not appear on this list and is largely hidden from history, namely, the continuing experience of the risen Jesus. For some forty years before there were gospels, the Christians gathered together to break bread and bless and share wine in memory of Jesus Christ. By degrees this memorial meal became ritualized into the sacrament of the Eucharist. It was the Eucharist, finally, that made the Church.

Some readers may be disconcerted by the above discussion of the slow emergence of a self-consciously Christian community, since the gospels themselves present a picture that at times looks as if the Church is very much in existence even during Jesus' life. The apostles are chosen and sent on mission, Jesus preaches his own resurrection, Jesus appoints Peter to be the rock on which he will build his Church, and so on. We can never forget, however, that the gospels themselves are written from the same retrospective vantage point as we occupy. Looking back at what must at the time have been much less clear, the gospel writers imposed a pattern upon those events that was not apparent to those who lived through them. In the light of history all seems clear; at the time, we live—at best—in hope. Consequently, the fact that the evangelists write from a distinctly post-resurrection perspective explains a lot of the conflation that leads to words and attitudes inserted into gospel texts that are expressions of a significantly later faith experience.

As we suggested earlier, pinpointing a precise time when the Church came into existence is neither profitable nor possible, but this very fact explains the occasional language about Jesus as its "founder." While we have determined that there is no Church, indeed there can be no Church, so long as Jesus himself is alive and preaching the coming reign of God, it does not follow that there is no connection between Jesus and the Church, or that a kind of ecclesial kernel was not somehow present in his teaching. The point can be illustrated by analogy with the Roman Catholic position on the status of the human fetus. Faced with the question of when precisely in the passage from conception to birth a human fetus becomes a human being, many answers have been offered at one point or another in history: at implantation, at the moment when the growing fetus becomes able to survive outside the womb (viability), after one or two trimesters, at birth, and even, to be honest, sometimes at some point after birth. The Church maintains that the moment of conception is the only acceptable answer to this question, not simply because it makes it easier to maintain a consistently pro-life ethic and certainly not because it knows that the answer is correct, but because on a continuum it is wholly impossible to pinpoint a moment of certainty. Just such a historical continuity exists in the growing Church as we can see in the development of embryo, fetus, and child. Just such an answer is provided by the Church. There is no point in history at which we can say "aha!" now we have the Church. It grows in continuity with Jesus' determination to reform elements of Judaism. At Pentecost or at the Council of Jerusalem or in Corinth or in Rome around 66 CE when Peter and Paul die in the persecutions of Nero, we are tantalized by elements of Church. We see it peeking out from the mists of history, but if we could clear the mist we might be surprised by how much is not yet "the Church." Pentecost, sure, but what did they really preach at Pentecost if the early followers of Jesus were promptly offered a little corner of the temple where they could worship? Yes, it was the Church, but yes, it was also a group within Judaism, in the view of the Jewish community and in their own self-understanding. The child, they say, is father of the man. But the child is equally not yet the man. When your child grows into a woman, you can look back and see decisive moments at which she began to emerge. But at the time she was just a cute kid or a pushy adolescent.

This entire discussion of the historical development of the early Church forces us back to the consideration of historicity that we began in the previous section, and it requires us to resist the inclination to exempt the Church from the historical process. There is a naive reading of the Church's development that sometimes emerges in theological but more commonly in pastoral circles. One of its most notoriously unhelpful expressions occurs in the Anti-Modernist Oath that was established in 1910 as a way of stamping out what Pope Pius X had identified as "modernist" tendencies in the Church. All priests were required to affirm "that the Church, the guardian and teacher of the revealed word, was personally instituted by the real and historical Christ when he lived among us, and that the Church was built upon Peter, the prince of the apostolic hierarchy, and his successors for the duration of time."[16]

The fundamental problem with all such approaches to the history of the Church is one of a misunderstanding of the way in which we should be reading the sources of our tradition. Today, scholars do not treat Scripture or early theological writings as if they somehow escape the historical condition. (This, of course, is one of the "modernist" sensibilities that Pius X was so concerned about.) The truth they contain—in the case of Scripture, the inspired word of God they offer—is accessed by treating them as texts with a history that might be as complicated as any other historical document. What we encounter in Scripture is not a set of blueprints that can always be read as true in some naive fashion that ignores their history but, rather, writings whose saving truth emerges in history as the human mind in this or that historical moment examines them in a careful, respectful, and scholarly fashion.

Explaining the great sea change that came over Catholic theology in the mid-twentieth century, the Canadian Jesuit Bernard Lonergan wrote that "[t]heology has become an empirical science in the sense that Scripture and Tradition now supply not premises, but data."[17] When we go from thinking of theology as deductive to seeing it as empirical, dramatic changes occur in the way we utilize the tradition. For a long time (perhaps even in some circles still today) the Church thought of the vocation of the theologian as proving the truth of what Scripture and Tradition had already declared. While Christian theologians got around some of the problems of explaining the Old Testament through what was called "typological exegesis," that is, understanding a person or thing in Hebrew Scripture as foreshadowing or anticipating an aspect of the New Testament (so Noah's ark is a "type" of the Church), their treatment of Christian Scripture itself had necessarily to be much more literal. What was there was there because it actually happened in just this way. And theologians employed highly sophisticated philosophical systems and logical strategies to defend the literal truth of the Scriptures. To treat Scripture and Tradition as data rather than premises makes the theolo-

---

[16] See William J. Schoenle, *The Intellectual Crisis in English Catholicism: Liberal Catholics, Modernists, and the Vatican in the Late Nineteenth and Early Twentieth Centuries* (New York: Garland, 1982), esp. 229. The full text of the oath can be found at http://www.franciscan-archive.org/bullarium/oath.html.

[17] Bernard Lonergan, *A Second Collection*, ed. William F. J. Ryan and Bernard J. Tyrrell (Philadelphia: Westminster, 1974), 58.

gian much more objective, much less of an apologist.[18] As Lonergan put it, "Where before the step from premises to conclusions was brief, simple, and certain, today the steps from data to interpretation are long, arduous, and, at best, probable. An empirical science does not demonstrate. It accumulates information, develops understanding, masters ever more of its materials, but it does not preclude the uncovering of further relevant data, the emergence of new insights, the attainment of a more comprehensive view."[19]

As Lonergan develops his discussion of this change in the theological task he makes many important points, but one in particular is of value to us in our consideration of the Church. Because religion is about the relationship between God and the human person in the human community, says Lonergan, "any deepening or enriching of our apprehension of man possesses religious significance and relevance."[20] Classically, he continues, the tradition analyzed the human person as body and soul, but today we add "the richer and more concrete apprehension of man as incarnate subject." So a developing understanding of the human person and community changes at least one of the terms in our theological equation. And since the Church is fundamentally a community of faith, a gathering of human persons across history, Lonergan's point is particularly important. Indeed, it is quite helpful for our considerations to employ Lonergan's term of "incarnate subject" analogously in reference to the Church. The Church is made up of a multitude of incarnate subjects, but the Church itself can be seen as a kind of collective incarnate subject. People are understood differently as human knowledge of their complexity grows; just so, the People of God is understood differently too.

In looking for a foundation for the newly historicist and subject-centered approach to religion and theology that he has identified, Lonergan turns to the idea of conversion and discusses it in a way that converges nicely with the picture of the Church we have been developing. Conversion is an experience that affects individuals, a "radical transformation . . . on all levels of living." While it may be sudden or take a lifetime, conversion means that the subject sees everything differently, because the subject has become different. It is a product of experience

---

[18] See Marie-Dominique Chenu, *Is Theology a Science?* (London: Burns & Oates, 1959).

[19] Lonergan, *A Second Collection*, 59.

[20] Ibid., 60.

and while in essence it is private, yet "it can happen to many and they can form a community to sustain one another in working out the implications, and in fulfilling the promise of their new life."[21] Just such conversions are visible in the effect of the Spirit upon the disciples at Pentecost, and the emergence of the Church in the years that follow is an excellent example of the formation of a community to sustain individuals in their changed attitude to reality.

Lonergan's discussion of the shift from classical to historicist, or deductive to empirical theology, and his recognition of conversion as the foundation of theological method in the new scheme of things are enormously helpful in making a more sophisticated response to our question, "When is the Church?" While there are undoubtedly a few well-documented examples of the Damascus-like dramatic conversion experienced by Saul of Tarsus, most of us are more likely to undergo a far more attenuated conversion experience. Taking a lifetime, perhaps, or stretching over many years, it may be marked by moments of consolation, insight, and growing love for God and God's world. But it will also, because we are human, demonstrate the contrary, times when our sinfulness will be evidenced in turning inward to protect ourselves from the insistent demands of ongoing conversion. When, then, are we finally "converted"? Even the saints have their failings, and the centrality of human freedom requires that we recognize that no one, short of the moment of death, is beyond change, even change for the worse.

What we have said about conversion in the life of the human incarnate subject can be repeated analogously with reference to the Church, the community of those who celebrate and yet struggle with the daily demands of conversion to Christ. There is no blinding Damascus moment for the Church, no time when the Church suddenly became "converted to Christ," no "before" of sinfulness and certainly no "after" of saintly progress through history. When we look at the Church as a historical phenomenon and utilize Scripture and Tradition as data rather than premises, we become aware that the conversion of the Church of Christ to Christ himself is an ongoing process in which generosity is in tension with self-centeredness, and the freedom and confidence granted by the Holy Spirit must struggle against the timidity and fear of "the old Adam." Because conversion to Christ can be undergone only at great personal cost, individually and collectively we will not always embrace it whole-

---

[21] Ibid., 65–66.

heartedly. And yet this fallible human community, Christians believe, is also God's chosen vehicle for reflecting the saving light of Christ in the world.

At this point we might usefully return to our working description of the Church and regroup. The Church, we said, in any and every age is that community of faith distinguished by the experience that the loving care of God for us is supremely available in our intimacy with the story of Jesus Christ. It would be quite accurate if too lapidary to rephrase this description: the Church is the community of the converted. And promptly add that the converted are always in the process of conversion. Two things follow immediately. The first, which we have already touched upon, is that where there is no conversion to Christ, there is no Church. Before conversion was possible, the Church was not possible. There was no empty structure or institution, waiting to be populated. The second, new to our discussion, is that if the ongoing conversion of individuals often includes moments of backsliding, then the Church seen analogously as the communal incarnate subject of the converted is also not immune from sinfulness. In recent decades, with particular though not exclusive reference to the Church's failures toward the Jewish community during the Holocaust, popes (especially John Paul II) have offered public apologies in the name of the Church for the failings of its members, but they have resisted the suggestion that the Church itself sinned. The reluctance to call the Church itself sinful is occasioned by a conviction of its divine origin. In Catholicism, the Church is not simply a community of those who gather together in virtue of their common conversion to Christ but also a part of the mystery of God's salvific intent. Without wishing to contradict that perception, we need also to recognize that when we treat Scripture and Tradition as data rather than premises, we have to recognize that when there were no Christians, there was no Church. In history, the Church comes into existence when two or three are gathered together in their common experience that the loving care of God for them is supremely available in their intimacy with the story of Jesus Christ. And so it seems reasonable to say that "Church" is empty without Christians. And if Christians sin, how can the Church not sin, since without sinning Christians, it would not exist?[22]

---

[22] On this question of the sinfulness of the Church, see Bradford E. Hinze, "Ecclesial Repentance and the Demands of Dialogue," *Theological Studies* 61, no. 2 (June 2000): 270–94.

Whether or not we are comfortable with the notion of a sinful Church, or simply want to settle for the certainty of sinners within the Church, the fact of sin within the Church leads us to another dimension of the question, "When is the Church?" We have already said that from a historical perspective there was a great deal of time—most of human history—when there was no Church, however much we may also want to say that the Church was "always" part of God's design. No Christians, no Church. But if this is the case, then do we not have to say that the Church itself *could* come to an end before human history itself comes to an end? As a purely historical judgment we would surely have to say that a time could come when faith in God's Church had disappeared from the world, and at such a moment there would no longer be a Church. Is the Church a reality like the Shakers, so that when the last few have disappeared, they are no more? Or is the Church somehow a dimension of what it is to be human, so that so long as there are human beings in the world, somehow there is the Church? To answer this question one way would mean we would have to say that there is, in a sense, always a Church, and this not only into the distant future, but also into the distant past. Earlier in this section we touched on how the Church is a part of God's design for salvation. As such, it is eternally present in the way that eternity is always present to each moment in time. We talk colloquially about "eternal truths." The Church would then be such an eternal truth and, like other eternal truths, not depend for its truth on whether people know it or accept it when it is put before them. Perhaps we might want to say that the Church is always present in history, but sometimes hidden, and that it was hidden for a very long time before it became apparent in the life and death of Jesus Christ—which might leave us with the interesting thought that the historical Jesus did not so much found the Church as unlock the door that revealed the hidden Church of the eternal incarnate Word. But then we are getting into deep theological water indeed!

God is eternal and we are time-bound creatures. Because we are destined ultimately to return to God, there is something eternal about us, surely, which is traditionally called the soul, but here in our human lives we deal in beginnings and endings, in knowledge and ignorance, in good and evil. We know the past somewhat dimly, the present as it flashes by, and the future not at all. If we are religious people, however broadly we understand that term, it means we do not see the meaning of history wrapped up in itself, but somehow beyond. Human history, of course, works itself out through strange combinations of chance and planning, but its ultimate meaning, like that of anything including our-selves, lies somehow beyond it. In the end, this is what it means to have faith or to be religious, to believe in a meaning that transcends everyday reality. The word "God" is not a name, but what Paul Tillich called an "empty symbol" of that eternal reality upon which every moment in time depends for its meaning and, indeed, for its very existence. The eternity of God means that whatever is in God is present to us in every moment, though present in mystery precisely because from the vantage point of history we cannot see eternity clearly. We see now "only as through a glass, darkly." One day, says Christianity, we shall see clearly.

The Christian Church and the Catholic Church in particular believe in the presence of the Holy Spirit, guiding the Church into all truth. This gift of the Spirit was promised by Christ in John's gospel, and it is a mainstay not only of Catholic understandings of papal and ecclesial infallibility but of all Christian confidence in God's guidance through history. Fundamentally, this means that somehow the eternal God is present in the historical process. Christians believe that God was present in an especially concrete way in the life and death of Jesus Christ but also that God is present in the world even after Christ has gone to his Father. And when we look around for the Spirit, it is in human beings and human activity for the good in history that we find the Spirit present. This is clear in Vatican II's *Lumen Gentium*, which states that the gift of the Spirit to the Church is found in the person of the pope, in the college of bishops, and in the whole assembly of the faithful. The Spirit is not out there somewhere, but in here somewhere.

When St. Augustine suggested that we should look for God within he was neither suggesting that God is synonymous with the human person nor arguing that the Spirit of God somehow lurks within some of us and not within others. His point was really one of philosophical anthropology, that is, he was making the claim that the human person as a human being is somehow attuned to or connected to God, even if this connection is damaged by sin.[23] And if this is the case, then it is the

---

[23] "Enter into yourself, leave behind all noise and confusion. God speaks to us in the great silence of the heart," and, "Where so ever you are, where so ever you may be praying, He who hears you is within you, hidden within, or He who hears you is not merely by your side, and you have no need to go wandering about, no need to be reaching out to God as though you would touch him with your hands" (*Homilies on the Psalms* 38:13).

case whether we know it or not or even, knowing it, we believe it or not or, believing it, we act on it or not. That is to say, openness to the presence of God within us comes to be a kind of structure of the human person, what the twentieth-century theological giant Karl Rahner called a "supernatural existential."[24] Openness to God does not have to be articulated in the language of Christianity or theism, and the word "God" need not come up. But openness to God as openness to transcendence, to the idea of the more that lies beyond the everyday, to ultimate mystery, is constitutive of what it is to be a human being. That is the Christian claim about the nature of human being, and this openness is not restricted to those with "faith" in a narrower sense.

Now we are in a position to close out this discussion of "when" the Church is, and to proceed to ask *who* the Church is. For there is sense to the claim that the Church always is, or that it "was in the beginning, is now and ever shall be," though the poetry of this phrase returns us to that before and after of history in which the Church was not, is, and hopefully will be. The language in which this issue is negotiated is often that of "the plan of God." The Church, we are told, is God's plan for the salvation of the world, continuing the loving presence of Christ in the world, in the power of the Holy Spirit. Certainly, in the mind of God that lies outside time, the Church is part of the grand design. But in the hands of God's agents in history, the Church must be nourished, protected, allowed to grow and change, understood as a dynamic historic reality. There is an element of human contingency about the Church, coupled somehow to the divine necessity of God's design.

Seeing the Church as eternal because of its role in God's eternal design for salvation means that every moment in time is somehow related to the Church, even those moments when, from a purely historical point of view, there was yet no Church. Some may find it helpful to talk about this earlier time as preparation for or an anticipation of the coming of the Church. This would fit well with that allegorical exegesis of Hebrew Scriptures that makes all the patriarchs and the great events of the early history of biblical Israel into foreshadowings of Christian history. But it may be more helpful to think of this prior time as the time when the People of God had not yet come fully into focus. We are all, in the words of Vatican II, from the most devout Catholic to the angriest atheist, somehow related to the People of God. The most fundamental meaning of

---

[24] See Karl Rahner, "Concerning the Relationship between Nature and Grace," in *Theological Investigations*, vol. 1 (Baltimore: Helicon, 1961), 297–317.

"people of God" is "the human race." The coming of Christ and the Church that bears his name gives focus and definition to God's will for the salvation of all people, but that will—as eternal—is not made real by the existence of the Church or the actions of Christ. It is made better known, it is made more effective, it comes into its fullness in history, but it is ever-present to the eternal God.

Oneness, or "Who is the Church?"

The question of *who* the Church is raises the issue of membership, of who is "in," and who is "out." This is a different kind of discussion, one that shows us once again just how historically conditioned our community of faith actually is. While we always want to say that the "whatness" of the Church has not changed over the centuries and is somehow in direct continuity with the teaching of Jesus, there is no way to say that the Church has always maintained the same notion of its ecclesial "whoness." The changing responses to the question of who the Church is can always be measured against our working understanding that the community of faith is bound together by the common experience that the loving care of God for us is supremely available in our intimacy with the story of Jesus Christ. But that joint conviction has not prevented there being a whole series of understandings of who, exactly, the Church actually is.

This question about who is in the Church clearly relates, then, to our immediately previous discussion about when the Church comes to be. The more willing we are to allow for a kind of preexistent Church based upon the natural openness of the human person to the transcendent, the happier we will be being more rather than less inclusive about "who" is in the Church. At the same time, however, we do not want to fall into the trap of telling people who are perfectly content in their own religious traditions that they are really somehow members of the Church. And so our problem comes into focus: Because we have defined the Church narrowly and, for most of its existence, over against those who are not part of it, have we perhaps created conditions that make the process of evangelization that much harder? And could it also be the case that we have misunderstood evangelization as the effort to draw others into a Church that stands over against that which is not the Church?

There is a current and highly controversial technical theological debate that tries to get at the truth of who is and who is not part of the Church. Sometimes it goes by the name of "the question of religious pluralism," and sometimes it comes dressed as "the theology of religions." Behind its surface concern about the relationship between the truth of Christ and the truths of other religions lie even more profound issues about the nature of the Church and the workings of God in history. If, as Christians believe, God wills from all eternity (which means in every actual historical moment, not "at the beginning") the salvation of every single human being, then either God is pretty hopeless at making what God wills happen, or God's will is not tied to some claim that only inside the Church is salvation possible, or at least much easier. God's will to the salvation of all means that the design is larger than the Church, though this is not to say that the Church is not essential to that design. Vatican II supports this point by making clear, on the one hand, God's will for the salvation of all while saying, on the other, that "the Church is necessary for salvation" (LG 14). That is, the existence of the Church, not necessarily belief in or membership of the Church.

The religious pluralism debate has most commonly been conducted by identifying three basic attitudes to the relationship of the Church to other religious traditions. First, there is an *exclusivist* attitude, which essentially argues that the Gospel of Jesus Christ and the salvation it brings is not shared at all by other traditions. At its worst this has meant at different historical moments for both Catholics and Protestants that "outside the Church there is no salvation," though it is pretty safe to say that most Christian believers today do not take such a harsh attitude to other faiths. Indeed, in surveys conducted in the last few years, 85% of Catholics asked said that so long as you believe in God, it really doesn't matter what religious tradition you belong to.[25] A second position, more or less that of Vatican II, is labeled *inclusivist* because while it extends the possibility of salvation way beyond Christianity, indeed to the whole human race, it understands all salvation somehow to occur through the saving actions of God in Christ. Third, a *pluralist* position goes beyond the generosity of the inclusivists to a view that is essentially relativist, arguing that Christianity is one way among many that human beings try to give structure to their natural drive to transcendence. This discussion often becomes more complex, but however it is conducted there are always three understandings of the Church under consideration. The exclusivist sees the Church over against other religions, the inclusivist sees the Church in some mystical sense embracing them, and the pluralist

---

[25] William V. D'Antonio and others, *American Catholics Today: New Realities of Their Faith and Their Church* (Lanham, MD: Rowman & Littlefield, 2007).

sees the Church standing shoulder to shoulder with them. Christians today can be found in all three camps, and most Catholics in all probability fall into the second group, though they have some sympathy, to the horror of their leaders, with the relativist position of option three.[26]

While our background awareness as we continue our discussion of the Church must be the conviction that God's design is so much larger and more mysterious than our knowledge of it, our concern must be with the Church in a somewhat narrower sense. We can perhaps call the Church that sector of the People of God with more focus and definition, characteristics that come not from the virtue of its members but from the fact that it is this group of people who are the recipients and guardians of God's revelation in Scripture and, above all, in the person of Jesus Christ. This relates quite closely to the working description of the Church we have employed earlier, and which it would be good to recall once again. The Church, we said, exists when there is an identifiable community, however small, bound together by the common experience that the loving care of God for them is supremely available in their intimacy with the story of Jesus Christ. As we go forward here, our questions will be about who is actually part of this narrower Church.

Two final preparatory thoughts before we move on. First, to be part of the People of God in the wider sense does not require being the member of a distinct community, or a claim to have experienced the love of God, or any awareness of the central role of Christ in making the love of God more fully present and more efficacious in the world. And second, even this narrower understanding of Church with which we are largely concerned here is much broader than many Christians throughout history have thought, and perhaps broader than we too have usually imagined.

The dominant response over the centuries to the question about membership of the Church is one that relies on visibility. Because the Church itself has been thought of over the same period primarily as a "perfect society," its members are those "who profess the same faith, participate in the same sacraments, and who are subject to the same pastors," especially to the pope. This description, drawn from the writings of the sixteenth-century Cardinal Robert Bellarmine, was insisted on as late as the First Vatican Council (1870), which also proclaimed that

---

[26] For a classic exposition of this whole issue see John Hick, *God and the Universe of Faiths* (Oxford: Oneworld, 1993).

"we must believe that the Church of Christ is a perfect society."[27] The idea of perfection, it need hardly be said, does not mean that the Church is a morally perfect society, for it is surely a Church of sinners. Perfection here refers to its completeness. That which is perfect, according to the schema *Tametsi Deus* (never voted on) is "that which is complete and independent in itself, fully sufficient in its own order to attain its proposed end, and not subject to any other society in those things which pertain properly to it."

Once we commit ourselves to seeing the Church as a perfect society, however carefully defined, it inevitably happens that we come to see it over against the world, in contrast both to secular society and to all those religions beyond it. The rest of humankind is defined negatively, as those who are "non-Christians" or even, at times, "non-Catholics," either hopeless sinners or ignorant or both. Evangelization is not so much proclaiming the Gospel as it is drawing converts into the Church, the community of the saved. Moreover, faith itself rapidly becomes a matter of assent to a series of propositions that operate as a sort of constitution for the Church. Faith, in other words, becomes "the Faith," and membership of the Church is worn proudly as a badge of identity that distinguishes us from them. My parents used to tell me stories of leaving their Catholic elementary school every afternoon in the England of the 1930s, to fight in the streets with the little children from the Protestant school across the way. In a childish reenactment of the horrors of religious wars, they fought other children because, well, they were them and we are us. The English musical comedy duo of Michael Flanders and Donald Swann used to bring the house down at their concerts with a rendition of their song, "The English, the English, the English are best!" Tongue in cheek for them and most of their audience, of course, but the Catholic Church of the nineteenth and twentieth centuries, especially in Europe and North America, would have proudly sung its own version, "The Catholics, the Catholics, the Catholics are best," as testimony to the ecclesial triumphalism that marked the period.

The emphasis on the Church as a perfect society and the concomitant identification of Church members by visible criteria is to a high degree explicable in historical and even sociological terms, and this truth is evident in the discussions at Vatican I over the preparatory schema in which the quotations about a "perfect society" appeared.[28] The majority

[27] *Supremi Pastoris* 10.

[28] Patrick Granfield, "The Church as *Societas Perfecta* in the Schemata of Vatican I," *Church History* 48, no. 4 (1979): 431–46.

of the council fathers at Vatican I were solidly in favor of understanding the Church as a visible society, but there was a significant minority who preferred to employ the concept of the "Mystical Body of Christ." While the minority lost out, they show that behind the facade of the council a different, more biblical and more theological account of the Church was beginning to emerge.[29] The emphasis on the perfect society version of the Church was dominant from the Council of Trent to Vatican I, precisely the centuries when the Church was at its most embattled, though the idea of the Church as a "society" can be traced back to St. Augustine's *City of God*. Yet even some of its advocates recognized its limitations, making distinctions between those who belonged to the body of the Church (visible criteria) and those who belonged to its soul (much less clear).

Between Vatican I and Vatican II the preferred image of the Church came to be that of the Mystical Body of Christ, which has profound implications for the question of who is or is not a member of the Church. Though it was really only at the later council that the idea of the Church as a perfect society was definitively sidelined, studies of the Mystical Body appeared much earlier.[30] In turning to this image there is a definite preference for a theological rather than a sociological treatment of the Church. The Church as the Body of Christ is a favorite theme of St. Paul, who tells the Corinthians that they "are the body of Christ and individually members of it."[31] Paul does not use the word "mystical," and in any case it seems to add little to the Pauline idea that all believers are members of the body, and Christ is the head, so that we are somehow joined together with him in an organic unity. Paul also uses the term to indicate that the members of the Church, like the members of a body, may have different responsibilities but all work together for the good of the whole, under the leadership of their head, who is Christ. Pope Pius XII in 1943 wrote a major encyclical letter explaining and extolling the beauties of the Mystical Body, so setting a kind of seal of approval upon the work of theologians over the previous century and confirming this image as the preferred *theological* model for the Church.[32] However, this did not

---

[29] A similar point could be made about the legitimate differences of opinion at Vatican I over the wisdom of defining papal infallibility, differences that of course did not and could not show up in the final documents.

[30] Probably the most influential was *The Theology of the Mystical Body*, by the Belgian Jesuit Emile Mersch, published originally in 1944 (New York: Herder, 1958).

[31] 1 Cor 12:27. See esp. 1 Cor 12:12-31 and Eph 1:22-23.

[32] *Mystici Corporis Christi*, available at http://www.vatican.va/holy_father/pius_xii/encyclicals/documents/hf_p-xii_enc_29061943_mystici-corporis-christi_en.html.

mean the immediate demise of the more *sociological* model of perfect society.

To call the Church the Mystical Body of Christ does not immediately open the door to an idea of invisible members, and it was not employed in that way by St. Paul. His objective was simply to clarify the relationships between Christ and the Church on the one hand, and among the members of the Church on the other. Curiously enough, given subsequent history, the body image employed by Paul undercuts any preference for a more extrinsic unity like "society," perfect or otherwise. We *join* or *are incorporated into* a society, but we *are* a body. The latter is part of our being, the former a conscious choice. Separating ourselves from a body to which we are physically joined is hazardous to our health; leaving a society may be more or less traumatic, but it is probably not terminal. The preference for the nonscriptural and somewhat arbitrary image of the Church as a perfect society was born in controversy, insisted on in face of the threat of the Protestant reformers. Yet, even more curiously, the idea of the Church as a society, if not a perfect one, is much more congenial to the Protestant understanding of Church as a human construction than it is to the Catholic conviction that it follows organically from the life and death of Jesus Christ.

The strength of the Mystical Body image and its papal seal of approval in 1943 is testimony to its value as a counterbalance to the excessive emphasis on visibility in a "perfect society," and it inevitably draws attention to the question of invisible membership in the Church. Historically, that question had been asked with reference to the just who had died before Christ. What were we to say of the eternal destiny of Adam and Eve, of Abel (if not Cain), of Isaiah and Jeremiah and so on? Were they in hell, in limbo, or somehow "mystically" incorporated in the Church of Christ, and so in heaven? And if the case could be made for the greats, what about all the other righteous people who preceded the birth of Christ? And if they could somehow be included, then what of all those who have lived subsequently, but through no fault of their own never heard the saving word of Christ, though they lived good lives according to their own understandings and the voice of their consciences? If any of these are saved, and for most of its history the Church has been able to say that some, at least, are in that condition (who wants to condemn Noah to eternal damnation?), then the question arises of their relationship to the Church even while they were alive. So long as you can entertain the idea of an eternal Church, such as we discussed in the previous section, living *before* the historical Church is not in itself exclusionary, but the question has most relevance to the here and now. The Christian Church has always deferred to God's mercy and our ignorance when difficult questions about the eternal salvation of others arise (for example, is Adolf Hitler definitely in hell?—answer, we don't know). But it has felt much readier to address the condition of the living, whether to anathematize them as heretics in the past or in more recent times to consider their relationship to the Church more benignly.

A substantive and balanced response to the question of membership of the Church has to await a clearer articulation of its identity. Who-ness is relative to what-ness. This in itself explains the emphasis on visibility in the years of ecclesial paranoia brought on by the twin challenges of the Enlightenment and the Reformation, and clinging to that image when the advent of the movement for Italian unification and the discovery of the historical-critical method drove the late nineteenth-century Church to the narrow defensiveness of Vatican I and the follies of the crusade against the straw men of modernism. If the theology of the Mystical Body was an important component in bringing intellectual Catholicism out of these dark ages, the less fearful papacies of Benedict XV, Pius XI, and Pius XII made for a more confident and thus humbler Church than that of the previous century. In less than a century the Church went from thinking of itself as a perfect society to proclaiming its character as a pilgrim people; in the same century, it opened itself up to the world, rethought its relationship to the world, and so was forced to a consideration of how the world is related to the Church. All this came to a head at Vatican II under the leadership of that most confident and optimistic of popes, John XXIII.

Returning now to Vatican II's central document on the Church, *Lumen Gentium*, and expanding on the brief consideration earlier in the chapter, "who-ness" follows smoothly upon decisions made about "what-ness." The first of seven chapters in *Lumen Gentium* is focused on biblical images for the Church that support the central concern to link the Church to the kingdom of God. So the Church is described as "the kingdom of Christ already present in mystery" (3), distinguished by virtues of "charity, humility and self-denial," with a mission to proclaim the coming reign of God and an identity as "on earth, the seed and beginning of that kingdom" (5). A multiplicity of biblical images adds richness to the picture: the Church is a sheepfold, a flock, a cultivated field, God's building, "the spotless spouse of the spotless lamb" (6), and many more. The images give way to an extended discussion of the Mystical Body (7); in the context of the proclamation that redemption comes to all human beings ("redeemed man and changed him into a new creation"), the council fathers say that "Christ mystically constitutes as his body those brothers of his who are called together from every nation" (7). Only after this is mention made of the Church as a "visible organization," though not as a "perfect society," and important qualifications are immediately added. "The visible society and the spiritual community . . . form one complex reality" with "a human and a divine element." And while this Church "subsists in" the Roman Catholic Church, "many elements of sanctification and of truth are found outside its visible confines" (8).

These important considerations in chapter 1 of *Lumen Gentium* set the stage for the even more remarkable discussion of the council's preferred central image for the Church, that of "People of God," which occupies the whole of chapter 2. Such an enormous amount has been written about the image of People of God, even some of it arguing that it is really "communion" and not People of God that is the heart of the conciliar vision of Church.[33] This is not a fruitful discussion, nor is it a controversy into which we are going to delve very deeply, except insofar as it has consequences for our concern about membership of the Church. Instead, we need an overview of what the document says about the People of God, which will lead to a focus on two issues in particular, the renewal of attention to baptism and the consideration of the boundaries of the People of God. As promised, we are going to find here a much more inviting sense of Church than had been employed for at least the previous four centuries, if not much longer.

Chapter 2 of *Lumen Gentium*, "The People of God," develops in three steps. First, the bishops establish that the People are God's people, chosen by God first in the covenant with Israel on Mount Sinai, then continued in the New Israel now called "the Church of Christ." Second, they present the entire Church as a priestly and prophetic people, in light of baptism, a community in which all are called to live holy lives, to participate in worship, and to bear witness to Christ. Third, they offer a quite remark-

---

[33] Communion ecclesiology is best approached first through Dennis Doyle's book of the same name, *Communion Ecclesiology: Visions and Versions* (Maryknoll, NY: Orbis, 2000). The controversy over the respective weight of "People of God" and "communion" both at the council and in the postconciliar Church is discussed most fully by José Comblin in *People of God* (Maryknoll, NY: Orbis, 2004). There is also an excellent article by Edward P. Hahnenberg comparing the Aristotelian and Platonic approaches to the parallel images—as he sees them—of Mystical Body and Communion. See "The Mystical Body of Christ and Communion Ecclesiology: Historical Parallels," *Irish Theological Quarterly* 70 (2005): 3–30.

able meditation on the Church as sacrament and sign of the unity of the whole human race, all of them somehow God's people. In all three moments in this extended theological presentation, unity and connections are highlighted, not—as in the past—division and opposition. Moreover, in selecting this image of "people" the council fathers beautifully finessed the challenge of balancing visibility and invisibility. They move smoothly between the language of "church," where visibility is always paramount, and "people," which is much more porous and distinctly fuzzy around the edges.

From the beginning of the chapter God's will "to make men holy and save them" is understood to entail the creation of a community or a new people, but in the context of a prior recognition that "at all times and in every race, anyone who fears God and does what is right has been acceptable to him" (LG 9; cf. Acts 10:35). Covenant, Church, and People of God all speak of God preferring community over individuality. God's design for "a people who might acknowledge him and serve him in holiness" produces a historical narrative beginning with Israel and leading to "that new and perfect covenant which was to be ratified in Christ." The destiny of this people is the kingdom of God, "begun by God himself on earth" and to be brought to perfection at the end of time. Though not including all people and sometimes seeming "a small flock," it is "a most sure seed of unity, hope and salvation for the whole human race." It is "the instrument for the salvation of all . . . the light of the world and the salt of the earth" (9). This People of God, then, this "Church" is born in the context of God's universal love, growing and changing through history, and commissioned to be a sign and instrument of the coming of the reign of God. Because it is part of God's design for salvation, its meaning is always to be found in relation to the divine will for the salvation of all people. The Church does not exist for the sake of its members, so much as for those who are not its members.

Because the meaning of the Church is directly related to its task as a sign and instrument of salvation, it is a priestly people. Christ the high priest, says *Lumen Gentium*, made the Church "a kingdom of priests to God, his Father." This common priesthood or priesthood of all the baptized is the fundamental characteristic of the Church, signaling its role as a community that stands somehow in a mediating role between God and the entire human race. The whole faithful people must offer themselves as "a spiritual sacrifice" to God, that is, as a gift to God to do with whatever God wills. They are charged to go throughout the world to "bear witness to Christ and give an answer to everyone who asks a reason for the hope of an eternal life which is theirs." While the priest-hood of all the baptized differs "essentially and not only in degree" from the ministerial priesthood, yet in virtue of their priesthood all the faithful share in offering the Eucharist and exercise their priesthood "by the reception of the sacraments, prayer and thanksgiving, the witness of a holy life, abnegation and active charity" (10).

In the context of discussing the priestly character of the People of God, the sacrament of baptism is rediscovered for the Church. For so long it had come to be merely a sacrament of initiation. Perhaps the confusion arose from the preponderant Catholic practice of infant bap-tism, and it has not been helped by the meaninglessness of the sacrament of confirmation—the "other half" of baptism—in the current under-standing of many Catholics. For too many, if baptism is entry into the community of faith, confirmation is their early exit in the midst of ado-lescence. *Lumen Gentium* dramatically corrects this picture, though it has to be said that the correction has largely not filtered down to the Catholic population. The council recognizes, of course, that baptism is a sacrament of incorporation, a new creation. But because of this the baptized "must profess before men the faith they have received from God through the Church." They are "true witnesses of Christ, more strictly obliged to spread the faith by word and deed" (11). The Holy Spirit also "distributes special graces among the faithful of every rank," by which the Spirit "makes them fit and ready to undertake various tasks and offices for the renewal and building up of the Church" (12). The whole faith community is called to active apostolic work because the community into which they are incorporated is not something turned in upon itself but a priestly community oriented to God's design for the salvation of all people. We will return to this "call to mission" in the last section of this chapter when we will consider the question, "What is the Church *for*?"

Having established that all the baptized are called to apostolic activity in the world, the council turns back to the point at which it began chapter 2 and considers in some detail the relationship between the baptized and the rest of the human race. Everyone, they declare, is "called to belong to the new People of God," which is "present in all the nations of the earth." The "catholic unity" of the Church "prefigures and pro-motes universal peace," they say, once more seeing the Church as both a sign of a greater divine reality and an instrument of achieving the end of the divine design, namely, the incorporation of the whole human race into the People of God. In the present moment, however, we are not on the brink of unity, and in recognizing this fact the bishops make a remarkable statement about the essential universality of the People of God. If the Church as the People of God is indeed the sign and sacrament of unity, then "in different ways to it belong, or are related: the Catholic faithful, others who believe in Christ, and finally all mankind, called by God's grace to salvation" (LG 13). Catholics are "fully incorporated" and understand the necessity of the Church for salvation. If, having faith, they rejected it, then "they could not be saved" (14). The harshness of this condemnation is reserved for those few, presumably, who formally reject what they know to be true. In earlier times this would have been called "selling your soul to the devil," abandoning belief for some immediate and selfish gain. The rest of the human race is treated much more gently, including other Christians to whom Catholics are joined through baptism and in a large measure of common faith, and to "those who have not yet received the Gospel" but who are "related to the People of God in various ways" (15, 16). Jews and Muslims are mentioned first, then those religious peoples from beyond the Abrahamic traditions, who "seek God with a sincere heart" and are moved by grace to do God's will "through the dictates of their conscience." Finally, divine providence gives grace necessary for salvation to unbelievers who "strive to lead a good life." All this is "preparation for the Gospel" (16), and the work and prayer of the Church is so that "into the People of God . . . may pass the fullness of the whole world" (17).

While this conciliar picture of the relationship between the Church and the whole human race may not satisfy the more radical proponents of a theology of religions, it has much to recommend it and was in itself a huge step beyond what had gone before. There is no more negative language about those outside the Church. Vatican II pronounces no anathemas, though the nearest it comes is its severe judgment on the faithful who formally reject what they know to be true. Of course, like the conditions for eternal punishment, there is no judgment that anyone has actually met them, and the responsibility for this judgment is left to God. And while the council insists that the Church itself is necessary for salvation, they evidently do not believe that conscious or visible membership in the Church is necessary. It is enough to be "related," and relationship occurs not in any intentional act of belonging or association but only in responding to the grace of God as it is received mysteriously in the lives of nontheists, unbelievers, and atheists.

The key to this picture of the Church as the People of God is the fundamental Christian conviction that Jesus Christ is the one Savior sent by God, and the Church is an essential element in God's design, since

Jesus somehow bequeathed his Church to humanity as the continuation of his saving presence in the world. God's eternal design is for the world to be saved, to live through and through in the knowledge and love of God, and Jesus Christ is God's chosen instrument. The Church is the sign and effective continuing presence or "sacrament" of salvation. Making this clear at the very beginning of *Lumen Gentium* the council declares that "Christ is the light of humanity," and the Church as "a sign and instrument" reflects that light into the world. For this if for no other reason the visibility of the Church will never disappear entirely from ecclesiology. But its visibility is in the manner of a mirror reflecting the love of God. A mirror is always there, but if it is doing its job properly, what we see is what it reflects, not the mirror itself. If it is not reflecting something other than itself, it is not a mirror.

The remarkable insistence of *Lumen Gentium* upon seeing all human beings as somehow related to the People of God follows from the Christian conviction that Christ is the unique Savior and that it is God's will that all people be saved. This "inclusive" understanding of Christianity, to use the term we identified earlier, is an insight that the council owed to Karl Rahner more than to any other single theologian. It was Rahner who worked out in most explicit fashion a kind of syllogistic argument for the universal efficacy of redemption through Christ. "God wills the salvation of all people through the redemption wrought by his Son, Jesus Christ, but most human beings, through no fault of their own, do not know or have not heard the message of Christ," so goes the first premise. "But God's salvific will cannot be frustrated," comes next. Then the punch line: "So they must receive the saving grace of God through their own religious traditions sincerely held, or through their own convictions in conscience about the nature of the universe and how to live a good life."[34]

The council's conviction that all salvation is through Christ also requires a focus on redemption as some kind of metaphysical act, some cosmic reordering of the universe to heal the alienation of the human race from God, and while theologians will never deny this, there are certainly some competing interpretations. The Church has fought vigorously to defend the traditional interpretation of the atonement against those, for example, who see redemption more as Christ showing the way to God and the reign of God. Here, the proponents of a lower Christol-

[34] Rahner, "Observations on the Problem of the Anonymous Christian," in *Theological Investigations*, vol. 14 (New York: Seabury, 1976), 289–94.

ogy (one that emphasizes the humanity of Jesus as the starting point for belief) stress Christ's life and death as God's way of indicating our path to a fuller union with God. You can probably have both interpretations and do not need to choose between them, but the reason to consider this here is that the decision to see Jesus more as showing the way to God than as effecting a change in the order of nature is that it radically alters the estimation of other religious traditions. If Christ's death and resurrection restores humanity to relationship with God, then the salvation of anyone and everyone is accomplished through him. But if he shows the way to God, while Christians might want to insist that he does this in by far the best way possible, it is not impossible to see other religions and the founders of other religious traditions as somehow leading their followers toward the truth, even if neither they nor their coreligionists could or would express "truth" in Christian terms. Indeed, Rahner himself may have hinted at the less orthodox interpretation, though for the most part he explicitly endorsed the inclusivist version. In his famous essay on Vatican II as "the coming of the world Church," he refers to the generous words of *Lumen Gentium* on the salvation of unbelievers who follow the voice of their consciences and says that they imply "the possibility of a properly salvific revelation-faith even beyond the Christian revelatory word."[35] Perhaps Rahner let his famous guard down a little here, since he definitely seems to be suggesting that not all of God's grace has to be seen as mediated through Christ. Later theologians have paid a high price for similar observations.

It is critical in the end to see that the development of Church teaching on membership in the Church has reached the point in *Lumen Gentium* of recognizing a role for the visible Church that orients it toward the less visible and larger reality of the People of God to which all people of good will are somehow related. If we want to go with Robert Bellarmine's vision of the Church as a perfect society, we are not wrong because we see the Church as a visible reality that is somehow complete in itself. Of course it is a visible reality, and to say the Church is a perfect society is never to imply that it is not a Church of sinners. But when we place the reality of the Church more firmly in a historical account of how God's eternal will to the salvation of all has actually developed, and when we rediscover the importance of baptism as entry into priestly people, we see that the Church is so much more than just a perfect society or just

---

[35] *Theological Investigations*, vol. 20 (New York: Crossroad, 1981), 82.

the visible members. Of its nature as a missionary community, it reaches beyond itself to embrace all that God loves, the whole of creation. To the degree that the Church is explicable as a visible reality, it is so only because it is oriented to the invisible, where the grace of God is also efficacious. If you have a lamp, you do not hide it. You put it on a lampstand, not so that others can admire it but so that it can give light to the whole household.

Catholicity, or "Where is the Church?"

If our discussions in the previous section have some merit, then the answer to the present question, "Where is the Church?" ought to be brief. If everyone is somehow or other related to the Church, then the Church—in a certain sense—is everywhere. In all times and all places, the Church exists to draw everyone to Christ. However, the claim to universality or catholicity is one that was made from early in the history of Christianity, long before any credible assertion that in fact it had spread throughout the known world, and we might want to pause therefore and ask ourselves if "universality" primarily refers to geographic extension, or if it has some other meaning. An example comes to mind in a story from an Italian newspaper a few years ago. Under the catchy headline, "The Alien Is My Brother," a short article gave the authoritative opinion of a Vatican spokesperson that, in the event that extraterrestrial life-forms were ever discovered, these beings would be evangelized and, presumably, implied that Christ died for them too. But by no stretch of any imagination can we make the claim that the Church already has a parish or two on Mars. Universality seems not to mean what it first appears to mean.

The question of catholicity as geographical extension, or for that matter of temporal extension—which would bring us right back to our discussion of "when" the Church is—can be clarified by returning again to the tension between visibility and invisibility. The visible Church, whether the classical perfect society or the more contemporary Church as sacrament, communion, herald, servant, and so on, undoubtedly wants to be everywhere throughout the world, since presence is needed in order to be what these images or models exemplify. I cannot serve from a distance in any effective way, and I cannot proclaim the Gospel without "face time." But it is one thing to want and quite another to succeed. While Christ sent the Church to preach the Gospel to all nations, there has been no period of history when Christ's command has been perfectly fulfilled and, indeed, the Church as sign and sacrament of the reign of God is directed more to the eschatological hope that God will one day establish the reign in its fullness than that ecclesial effort will conquer the world. Eschatological hope is not the same thing as utopian longing.

When we examine Vatican II's idea of the Church as the People of God in the light of our question about where-ness, the claim that everyone throughout the world is somehow incorporated in or related to the People of God suggests a more confident response. As we saw in the previous section, the council works with an understanding that the grace of God is universally available, and that through whatever cultural or religious forms it is encountered, it is the grace of God through the saving act of Christ that is received. While this is divine grace—though of course it is the grace of God, not the grace of the Church—a connection exists between the workings of divine grace in the heart of a Buddhist or a Taoist or an atheist and the Church of Christ that is the visible, tangible sacrament and sign of redemption. The Church celebrates the universal availability of God's grace, but it is not aware of most of the occasions on which the grace of God acts upon people. The communion of the members of the Church with God and one another merges into that larger and invisible communion in which the whole human family is united, whether or not it knows it, as the object and providential concern of the love of God.

While it is possible to see the catholicity of the Church as a kind of virtual geographic extension to the whole world (and in principle to our alien siblings around the galaxies), the Church's claim to universality is more about expressing inclusivity than it is a literal commitment to physical presence in the four corners of the earth. That it is concerned to preach the Gospel to all nations is important, but it would not guarantee catholicity. Most religious traditions have some missionary impulse and are open to honest inquirers and admit new members into their communities of faith, just as the Christian Church does. But to be present in the parliament of religions around the world, as one among many, is not catholicity. Indeed, the inclusivity of the Catholic Church can seem sometimes to look very like exclusivity. If divine grace is always through Christ, then the Church of Christ is really the only show in town. It is this kind of reflection that lies behind the consistent claim that the Catholic Church is not a religious denomination but somehow the whole family of God on earth, drawing all human beings to itself. Of course, if this is not to sound like supreme arrogance, it needs to be accompanied by respect for other traditions as genuine conduits of divine grace, without which the Church could not be faithful to its character as the universal sacrament of salvation. For, if Vatican II is right and God's salvation is extended to those of any religion or none, then the Church as the sacrament of that salvation is intimately connected to all religions and embraces all human beings.

With this general statement about catholicity as virtual universality in the background, we can proceed to look at three expressions of the unity and extension of the community. The first is the cherished Catholic doctrine of the communion of saints, the belief that all believers, living and dead, are somehow united in one "cloud of witnesses." The second is very different, namely, the tension between seeing the Church as centered in Rome and spread from there throughout the earth and imagining it as essentially a worldwide family of churches somehow united to one another through an international symbol of unity in the Church of Rome. And the third, which will lead us naturally into the fifth and final section of this chapter of the book, is the issue of missionary activity in the traditional use of the term, that is, the efforts to expand the geographical extension of the Church, to "preach the gospel to all nations."

In most if not all Eastern rite liturgies and in the Anglican Eucharist there is a point before the distribution of communion when the celebrant raises high the consecrated bread and wine and pronounces, "God's holy gifts for God's holy people." This delightful prayer nicely encapsulates the two connected meanings of the *communio sanctorum*, the words from the Creed usually translated as "the communion of saints." While the phrase itself undoubtedly leads us to think first of a body of people, the Mystical Body of Christ, a moment's reflection on it makes evident that it can be read slightly differently as "all that the saints share with one another" or, as the *Catechism of the Catholic Church* expresses it, "communion in spiritual goods" (949–53). Both ideas are easily traced back to the Acts of the Apostles, where we read that "the company of those who believed were of one heart and soul" and that "no one said that any of the things which he possessed was his own, but they had everything in common" (4:32). The doctrine of the communion of saints that slowly developed from this beginning has tended to focus more on the first of the two meanings, leading in later centuries to controversies with Protestants who objected to the Catholic practice of praying to the saints in heaven for their intercessory aid, but it retains both meanings and is certainly distinctive of the Catholic tradition, having eventually found its way into the Apostles' Creed.

The Apostles' Creed is a short statement of basic Christian doctrines that in at least some form predates considerably the Nicene Creed (the creed formulated by the fourth-century Council of Nicea). The later and longer Nicene Creed is more familiar to most Catholics today because it is the one recited at Mass on Sundays, but both creeds follow pretty much the same pattern. Each summarizes the story of God's redemptive action in Jesus Christ, ending with his resurrection from the dead and the coming of the Holy Spirit. There then follows in both a short list of additional doctrines, which differ a little from one another. The biggest difference is that the Nicene Creed omits any reference to the communion of saints, while the Apostles' Creed places it immediately after "the holy Catholic Church." Most scholars understand "the communion of saints" to be a later interpolation into the Creed—which would certainly help to explain why it has no place in the Nicene Creed—and also see it rightly as an expansion or clarification of the preceding phrase, not some separate doctrine from that of belief in the Church itself. So, to say that "I believe in the holy Catholic Church, the communion of saints," is to make one creedal statement, not two, and opens up the way to some very interesting questions about who, exactly, these "saints" are.

The traditional teaching on the communion of saints is that it refers to all believers, those alive at the present time, those suffering for their sins in purgatory, and those enjoying the beatific vision in heaven. Only the souls in hell are excluded from the communion. The use of the word "saint" here, of course, does not refer to canonized saints or those who might be canonizable, but to saints as the Acts of the Apostles uses the term, to refer to all those who believe. These three distinct groups are bound to one another in various ways. The living pray *for* the dead in purgatory, who depend on the prayers of the living, and the living pray *to* the saints in heaven, and depend on their intercession. But the principle bond between them is that all share in the fruits of the redemption. They are the communion of saints because they share the spiritual goods of redemption, a communion in that other sense we mentioned above. The saints on earth celebrate the Eucharist as the foretaste of that final and eternal unity they will one day share with the saints in heaven.

The teaching of Vatican II that all people are somehow related to the People of God raises the question of what a "saint" actually is. Thus, we return to the distinction in thinking about the Church between the visible and invisible, or its body and its soul. *Lumen Gentium*, we can recall, evidently envisaged salvation stretching way beyond the visible confines of the Catholic Church to all Christians or even all those who believe in

God. Historically this question may have begun with concern for the plight of catechumens, those preparing to enter the Church, who die before they are baptized. The Church has traditionally taught that they are the beneficiaries of "baptism of desire" and that they share in eternal life. Similar teaching about "baptism of blood" developed to explain the fate of those who were martyred for Christ without having been baptized. Both these ideas allowed the Church to think of groups of people who were not actually members of the living saints who would yet, after their death and in some sense because of the manner of their deaths, enjoy posthumous membership in the communion of saints. It was not a big step from that to the more general belief that the righteous somehow participate in the soul of the Church even when they do not share the beliefs that would make them members of its body.[36]

Once we admit the unbaptized into the ranks of the saved, then either the communion of saints has to be enormously expanded or we have to imagine heaven with compartments, one for "the saints" who have died in Christ and one for the rest. This latter possibility sounds pretty preposterous, even distasteful. And since it would be quite impossible to make the case that the unbaptized righteous achieve this condition only at the moment of death, sheer continuity and consistency requires us to see them somehow as members of the communion of saints here on earth. These concerns lead us back to seeing the Church as both visible and invisible, and in its turn that entails once again the reduction of the idea of the Church as a perfect society to the status of "partially true." A perfect society image relies entirely on visible and demonstrable membership in a concrete historical community. The idea of the Church as the Mystical Body of Christ has some capacity to expand to incorporate invisible members, but that of People of God or the general notion of a mystical communion accommodates them more easily still. There is, moreover, considerable beauty to the idea that the oneness of the human family under one God, hidden here in history, is made evident in the healing unity of all in the eternal reign of God.

Focusing now on the visible Church for a while, the second question about where-ness has to do with the relationship between the center and the periphery, or between the universal and the local Church. Is the Church's catholicity primarily to be seen as the geographical extension of the Church of Rome, or is it more properly understood as grounded

---

[36] See Charles Journet, *Theology of the Church* (San Francisco: Ignatius Press, 2004), 168–86.

in the full ecclesial life of the local communities of faith? To use an analogy that is definitely oversimplistic but helps to make the extremes clearer, is the Church to be seen as a transnational organization with branch offices in various parts of the world, or is it to be looked at as a federation of local churches with its central administrative unit located in Rome? While neither of these possibilities alone is an accurate picture, the ramifications of leaning in one direction or the other are considerable for an understanding of authority, or religious pluralism, or forms of ministry and liturgy, or many other issues. Indeed, even attempting to hold in balance the priority of the universal and the priority of the local will have implications for all these questions.

When we think about the priority of the universal over the local Church, we understandably couch the discussion in terms of the centrality of the Church of Rome, but at the same time we have to recognize that the historical centrality of Rome is entirely accidental. Even if we are among those who make a close connection between the intentions of Jesus and the founding of the Christian Church, to say that the Roman Catholic Church is the one true Church of Christ is to make a statement about its historical continuity and its doctrinal integrity, not about the city on the Tiber. The Roman Catholic Church could, in other circumstances, just as easily have been the Antiochene Catholic Church or the Corinthian Catholic Church or the Carthaginian Catholic Church. The centrality of Rome to the Western Empire may have accorded a measure of geographical inevitability to the city's becoming the center of the Church, but theologically it is quite irrelevant. Additionally, historians have long known that while Peter and Paul were executed in the city of Rome during the persecutions of Emperor Nero, a vigorous Christian community in Rome with its own bishop was a development of the second-century Church. If there is any historical accuracy at all to the somewhat fanciful list of the early popes that the tradition maintains—Peter, Linus, Cletus, Clement, and so on—their location as leaders of the Church in Rome is not part of it.

While Rome's emergence as the center of the Western Church, however historically inevitable, is theologically irrelevant, the fact that local churches within the Western Empire came relatively quickly to recognize the authority of Rome over at least some matters is of much more consequence. The Church of Rome was accorded priority if not primacy, at least in the West, and was thus a natural adjudicator in disputes between local churches or within one local community. It was also increasingly vocal in addressing heresy. But in neither case should we imagine its status as remotely like the present-day papacy, which all Catholic Christians understand as the supreme teaching authority and the focus of the unity of the world Church. While popes periodically made claims for their authority that seemed at the time outlandish, and may still appear that way, and while for most of its history the papacy was a player in what we would call secular politics, not really before the twentieth century was there a papacy that was understood to be one of purely spiritual authority, nor one whose reach or status was as high.

It is clear that over just a few centuries Rome came to hold a position of primacy within the Church of the Western Empire, but it is also true that there were churches in other places of equal antiquity to that in Rome, and they were not always willing to recognize that primacy. The Churches of the Eastern Empire never bowed entirely to Rome and eventually separated themselves totally, becoming the forerunners of today's Orthodox churches. A similar thing happened to the Church in England during the sixteenth century, and the split between Canterbury and Rome was over much the same issue, that of the nature of Roman primacy. These schismatic (i.e., separatist) churches initially went their own way over the issue of authority, though it had certain doctrinal complications. The churches of the true Protestant Reformation had much more substantial issues of belief and practice to add to the general distaste for the late medieval papacy.[37]

The question of the balance between the local and universal Church is, however, primarily one of how those churches that are in full communion with Rome understand the nature of the relationship. Of course, to put it this way is already to swing the balance toward a priority for the local Church, since if "they" have their own understanding of this relationship they are already asserting a measure of independence. It is testimony to the current and fairly long-standing centralized authority of the Roman Church that the boundaries of the debate over local and universal rights and responsibilities are laid down by Rome itself. Consequently, while there has been a vigorous dialogue of late over how to understand the balance between the two, it is conducted under the explicit assumption of the primacy of Rome.[38] The question in the Catholic

---

[37] The best short survey of these differences is still that offered in just a few pages by Yves Congar in *Divided Christendom* (London: Centenary, 1939), 1–47.

[38] This issue has been most clearly debated in recent years in the exchanges between Cardinal Walter Kasper and the then Cardinal Joseph Ratzinger. Kasper began it in a book chapter, "Zur theologie und Praxis des bischöflichen Amtes," in *Auf neue Art Kirche Sein: Wirklichkeiten—Herausforderungen—Wandlungen* (Munich: Bernward bei Don Bosco, 1999), 32–48. Ratzinger responded in an article in the *Frankfurter Allgemeine*

tradition is never: is "Rome" an administrative convenience for the worldwide Church, or are the local churches emanations of Rome? The question is simply: in the balancing act of knowing what it is to be Church, in the background awareness of Catholicism, do we see the local Church in the context of the universal Church, or do we see the universal relative to the local?

The first answer to this question is a sacramental one. Rome is no more "the church" than is your local parish. Perhaps it is time to recall once more our working description of Church from earlier in this chapter: that community of faith distinguished by the experience that the loving care of God for us is supremely available in our intimacy with the story of Jesus Christ. Or, more scripturally, "where two or three are gathered in my name, there am I in the midst of them" (Matt 18:20). Beside this truth, Rome and all the cathedrals in the world pale into insignificance. The whole Church is present in the local assembly, and all that it takes to be Church is in the gathered assembly. There is faith and sacramental life, baptismal and ordained priesthood, prophetic witness and apostolic mission to the world beyond the community of faith. Ecclesiologically speaking there is nothing more to be had.

The second response is a more sociological observation. While most Catholics look to Rome for at least some kinds of leadership, most if not all Catholics are primarily nourished in their faith life by the local community, not by the diocese or the national or world Church. Most if not all recognize the value of the international family of Catholics, but most do not connect much beyond their own parish, not even at the diocesan level. While Vatican II was at some pains to establish that the fullness of ordained priesthood resides in the bishop, to most Catholics the bishop is simply a distant figure who shows up on an annual basis to do confirmations and is in charge of raising money for the good works of the diocese. It is the local pastor who—sometimes to a fault—is the one around whom Catholic life is centered. All the wonderful flowering of lay ministry notwithstanding, the priest remains central to the life of the faith community, more important to it than the director of religious education, or the bishop, or even the pope. While this would be hard to

---

Zeitung (December 22, 2000), 46. Kasper argued further in "On the Church: A Friendly Response to Cardinal Ratzinger," *America* 184 (April 21–30, 2001) and was answered yet again by Cardinal Ratzinger in *America* 185 (November 19, 2001). The easiest approach to this complicated set of exchanges is provided by an excellent overview from Kilian McDonnell, "The Ratzinger/Kasper Debate: The Universal Church and Local Churches," *Theological Studies* 63 (2002): 227–50.

defend theologically, as a sociological observation it is indisputable. And for this reason, if for no other, the growing shortage of ordained clergy and the consequent relative difficulty of access to regular Eucharist is an enormous and pressing problem.

If the local Church is more important sacramentally and sociologically than is the universal Church, we might be inclined to think that this is the end of the matter. This would be a mistake, since thinking politically about the question allows us to see the other side of the question. The political issue is not that of the role of the Church as an actor on the world stage, though that would be a matter for the universal rather than the local Church, but rather that of the good of the whole People of God. If all that we need to be Church is present in this community or that community, this does not mean that the world Church is simply the aggregate of all the local communities. "Rome" stands for that fullness of ecclesial life that is present in each local Church but that would not be so appreciable without a visible symbol. Rome is the visible symbol of all that these local churches hold in common, the sacrament—we might say—of the *real* presence of God's salvific will made concrete in the local community. Without the ecclesial life of the local community Rome would be irrelevant, since its energy is that of the faith that is only concrete in local communities, including those local communities in Rome itself. Without Rome, the local communities would be shorn of their sense of unity of purpose and devoid of presence to the world beyond the local context.

The missionary activity of the Church is the third component of "where-ness" to which we need to attend. The Church, local and universal, depends upon its outreach or "mission" to keep it focused on and energized for the proclamation of the Gospel. For a number of recent centuries the term "missionary" has been inextricably connected to the imperialist and colonialist project of European Catholicism. In these earlier centuries the geographical understanding of mission made sense, since there were a number of Catholic countries, mostly in Europe, and there were many parts of the world in which Christianity was more or less unknown and the Gospel had not yet been preached. Successful mission meant that the parts of the world where Catholicism was present, its "where-ness," was expanding. Today the Gospel has been preached in pretty much every corner of the world, though not always successfully; but the more significant happening is that the life of faith is diminishing even in the historical centers of Catholicism. Thus mission becomes not only or primarily the geographical extension of the Church to which it was once directed but, rather, the defense, elaboration, or intensification of the life of faith wherever it happens to be. And given that the Catholic Church today is more vibrant in previous mission lands like Latin America, Africa, and Asia, there is even considerable talk about "reverse mission."

Demographic, political, and geopolitical shifts mean that it is no longer helpful to think of missionary activity primarily in geographical terms, and these shifts suggest another way of thinking about catholicity. The cutting edge for evangelism today is not in pushing back the boundaries of heathenism in far-off corners of the world (and that has always meant "far off" from Europe) but in bearing witness to the life of faith in all societies and putting more energy into these efforts where resistance is strongest. The meaning of catholicity takes a turn, then, away from geographical extension toward cultural intensity. Politics, international relations, ethics, social life, the arts, and popular culture become the new frontier for Catholic missionary activity. Catholicity becomes engaged presence in any and every facet of contemporary culture and postmodern society. The challenges to the Catholic community of faith do not come primarily from "other" religions but from religious indifference born of a potent mixture of secular insouciance, rampant materialism, and existential anxieties. The evangelical gauntlet is thrown down not by the Qur'an or the *Analects* of Confucius but by the pervasive ability of large numbers of the citizens of the world apparently to get along fine without any religious sensibility at all.

In this new world of mission, the Church becomes much more lay centered than it was. In the days when the Church thought of itself as existing primarily for the continuing salvation of its own members, the clergy were its focus. When we know as we do now that it exists more for the sake of others than for its own sake, the shift to a lay-centered community is inevitable. The laity, both because of their sheer numbers and their lives in the world, are those primarily charged with mission to the world. This brings us smoothly to the last part of this chapter, the matter of apostolicity.

Apostolicity, or "What is the Church for?"

To say that the Church is apostolic in the first instance connects the community of today with the apostolic Church of the first century. It points to the unbroken continuity of orthodox belief and practice over two thousand years, stretching back to those first followers of Jesus whom the Church—and perhaps Jesus himself—called "apostles." An apostle is literally a messenger, but the word is richer than just someone who is given a message to pass along to someone else. An apostle is a messenger who is somehow marked by the message she or he carries, a true representative of the message. So, the first followers of Jesus and especially the Twelve after Pentecost are messengers in this richer sense, *sent* (the root meaning of "mission") to proclaim the good news that it would be beyond them to represent unless they were filled with faith in its wonder and efficacy. At the same time and equally importantly, they are channels of the good news that comes not from them but from the one who sent them. The true apostle is then both filled with the Gospel and yet transparent.

The basic meaning of the word "apostle" leads the Church in the first instance to think of the twelve men whom Jesus selected to be his particular messengers, with the addition of the apostle Paul, a man who claimed the title of apostle for himself but whose extraordinary importance to the early Church made it a suitable designation. The requirement for being an apostle seems to have been contact with the resurrected Jesus. Whether or not Jesus actually picked out twelve men and specifically called them apostles during his earthly life, their apostolic status is fundamentally dependent on their experience of the risen Jesus and the gift of the Holy Spirit on Pentecost. Without the seal of the Holy Spirit, so the New Testament would suggest, they might never have emerged from hiding and begun their apostolic activity. During Jesus' earthly life, of course, some one or other of the Twelve was sent off to do various errands on his behalf, but only after the resurrection can they make the transition to the proclamation of the good news that Jesus is risen. Selection as one of Jesus' closer followers does not make someone an apostle; if it did, then Judas would have been an apostle in more than name alone. And there are two apostles—Matthias who was chosen by the eleven to replace Judas, and Paul who saw himself designated "the least of apostles" in his vision of Jesus Christ—who were definitely not selected by the earthly Jesus of Nazareth during his public ministry.

The criteria for being an apostle meant that they could not be replaced, though what they represented could continue. As they aged and died or were executed, their number dwindled. Before very long there were no more apostles in this primary sense, and the meaning of "apostolic" came to be a matter of standing in the unbroken tradition of the Church founded on the faith of the apostles. Apostolicity is then primarily a historically verifiable assertion of continuity in faith. It does not mean that everyone has always at all times been utterly faithful to the apostolic tradition but, rather, that the community as a whole over the long haul has remained discernibly in continuity with the apostolic faith. The early heresies that the Church of the first few centuries had to wrestle with were primarily threats to apostolicity; to have succumbed to Arianism, for example, would have been to abandon apostolicity. Consequently, the claim to apostolicity has been used more often than the other marks of the Church in a polemical context. It, more than the other marks, is closely related to the claim to faithfulness.

Although the Church never replaced the apostles, someone had to take up the functions of leadership and preaching that had been their original gift and responsibility, their "office" in the Church. This is a complicated and often confusing story, but when the dust cleared the second-century Church had settled on the office of bishop as a successor to the apostles, though not an apostle himself. The bishop had oversight (Greek *episkopos* or "bishop" literally means "overseer") of the local community of faith. The language to describe the office developed slowly, and sometimes in some places this role was the responsibility of a presbyter. The bishop was typically aided by deacons. Over the first two centuries of Church life the familiar ministerial structure of Roman Catholicism today emerged, with a bishop presiding over a local Church, aided by deacons, and with presbyters perhaps acting in the bishop's stead at outlying communities. Bishop/priest/deacon was not part of the structure of the original Church of the apostles, but it quite quickly came to be the norm, even when the terminology had not necessarily become clarified. Over time, the bishops came to be seen as those in whom the apostolic tradition was handed on, through the laying on of hands that occurs at the consecration of a bishop when his brother bishops from other dioceses confer on him the power of episcopal orders. Hence, we have the term "apostolic succession," which is one important dimension of what apostolicity implies, but is by no means the whole story.

While the note of "apostolicity" in the Catholic Church connects the community of faith throughout history to the original disciples of Jesus and the first Pentecost, the term refers to much more than the simple historical connection, important as that may be. More important, in fact, than the physical connection, though impossible without it, is the continuity in the apostolic faith. Because the Church is born in the events of the first Pentecost, when the apostles received the Holy Spirit and went out to preach Christ crucified, continuity in faith is tied above all to the idea of Spirit-inspired mission to the world, proclaiming the good news that Jesus is risen, sin and death are overcome, and the way to the fullness of the reign of God is open. "The faith," meaning the whole panoply of teachings that have developed over the centuries to elucidate the Christian mystery, is instrumental to the heart of the good news that was preached at Pentecost before there were any councils, definitions, dogmas, or anathemas.

If apostolicity is the characteristic or "mark" of the Church directed toward ensuring continuity in faith, the question of the content of that faith remains. If faith as a set of beliefs or, better, as an ongoing commitment to the message of Jesus Christ is what is being protected, what is the message *for*? The short and correct response is that it is *for* the salvation of the world. Christians are identifiable by their fidelity to Jesus Christ as God's presence in the world, drawing the world into the possibility of a real relationship to God that it did not have before the death and resurrection of Christ. In the life, death, and resurrection of Christ we learn for the first time what God is like when God is human in history and, because God in Christ is human, we also learn for the first time that the gulf between God and human beings is not entirely impassible. While God remains absolute mystery, in Christ God reveals the way toward divinization, to becoming Christ-like and hence God-like. Christians are those who, in baptism, become possessors of the revelation of God in history. The revelation itself is for the sake of the whole world that God wills to save, but as a historically particular revelation in and through the life of one human being, it is offered in the first instance to a particular group of people, the first disciples of Jesus, and then to all those who follow in their footsteps. But while it is given *to* some and not to all, it is given *for* all and not just for some. And so we encounter the intrinsic connection between the possession of faith in Jesus Christ and the requirement to share the revelation that he is.

The content of Christian faith is the revelation of Jesus Christ as the presence of God in history, drawing all human beings to himself, and the responsibility of the Christian believer is to share that good news. Here, however, we need to take a leaf from the book of the great creative writers who follow the maxim, "Show, don't tell," while adapting it with a nod to elementary school children, "Show *and* tell." Sharing the good news is both about showing its transforming power and telling the story of the one in whom this power became effective in the world. Neither of these two components can be omitted, but historically it has to be said that the emphasis has far too often been on telling the story and not on showing its effects. The partial missionary message of the benefits the newly baptized will receive if they accept Christ is the second step in preaching the Gospel. The first is to show the Christian community living in the transforming light of the love of God in Jesus Christ. That and only that makes genuine conversion possible. Only that makes baptism something more than simply initiation into the group; baptism is a sacrament of initiation, of course, but the community of faith that the new member enters is a community with a mission, a "missioned community." That mission is to spread the good news of salvation and, once again, the most effective way to spread the good news is to show its effects upon the community of the Church.

The good news of salvation is a message about the quality and character of human life. It is fundamentally a message of reconciliation with God through overcoming the weight of sin. Too often it has been presented in history as the blood sacrifice of a somewhat sadistic God, in which the death of Jesus ransoms human beings from their sins. There was a time when this particular story was a persuasive metaphor for the Christian community, but today we do not respond to a God who would kill his own son, and the only ransoms that anyone pays are to thugs and terrorists. Fear of God and fear of death have their place in the Christian scheme of things and could have a salutary effect on our world if taken seriously, but they cannot be central to the revelation of how a loving creator God chooses to offer the human race hope and reconciliation. As Christians step out to share God's saving message, they need more persuasively Christian demonstrations of the love of God, that is, of God's love for the world.

God's becoming present in history in Jesus Christ can be explained only in the context of God's creative will. In the first chapters of the book of Genesis we learn of God's creation of a world and of the divine intention to make human beings in the image and likeness of God. What distinguishes human beings from the rest of God's wonderful creation is their being in the image and likeness of God. Evidently, this has nothing to do with their physical constitution, pretty much all of which is identical to the genetic makeup of life-forms in general. Their difference is in their capacity to reason, certainly, but above all in their ability to receive and return the love of God in a truly free act. All of creation aside from human beings gives glory to God through being what it is; its task is easier and it is consequently much more successful. The natural world does not fail in giving glory to God unless human beings pervert it. But human beings choose to give glory to God, not necessarily in knowing and loving God, but in being what God intended them to be. We are in the image and likeness of God when we live loving and generous lives as rational creatures. Then we are most God-like, and we are most fully human. When we fail to love, fail to be generous and fail to use our God-given reason we at one and the same time fail to be God-like and fail to be as fully human as we might be. Sin, surprisingly, is what makes us less human and, because that means less in the image and likeness of the creator God, it separates us from God. Since sin is behavior that is deficient in love, it also puts distance between us and other human beings. Sin is always an offense against humanity as much as it is an offense against God. Indeed, it is an offense against God because it is an offense against our fellow human beings and the world that is our home.

The mission of the Christian community rests in large part in showing and telling the connection between our creation by a loving God, the saving sacrifice of Christ, and the necessity of living lives devoted to fuller and richer humanity. The first step is the showing, both revealing the Church as a community held together in love and fired by the determination to share God's love with the wider world. The moment for telling will return, but the weight of history has overcome much of the world's capacity to hear the story of the Church. The much-heard cry that "I'm spiritual but not religious" is provoked not by secular indifference but by the poor performance of the Church of God in recent centuries. For all the wonder and love that moves it and inspires its members, the Church is seen as riven within by foolish differences, out of touch with the modern world, and lately, corrupted by the sexual abuse of children and the efforts to cover it up. None of these charges is the whole story. The tale of the great social good that Christians of all communities currently work in the world more than balances the folly of those same churches, but the good news is drowned out. What we show the world is not consistent with the story we have to tell.

The mission of the Church to share and spread the love of God for the world requires at the present day that, locally and universally, the Church be in the forefront of the struggles against everything that threatens human flourishing in the world that is our home. The first priority is the defense of human dignity at every level, because everything that threatens human dignity impedes our capacity to live as "made in the image and likeness of God." Love, wonder, creativity, reflection, and joy, these are the things that the human race must choose for all its members if it is to be what God intends in creation. Choosing this way may sound a little bit like a Hallmark card, but the truth is that it requires some hard social and political choices. Acting in defense of the human in our world today is profoundly countercultural. The weak and meek and poor of our world do very little to damage it unless forced to do so by the necessity to survive, but the powerful and strong consistently act in the best interests of their own kind, sometimes simply in their own individual best interests, and we have seen what that does to the world. Greed, terrorism, and fear are the soup out of which we are in danger of fashioning a world in which we will be the enemies of human promise and fulfillment. No wonder if our physical world turns against us at that point.

All the baptized are called to be apostles, baptized into an apostolic community, whose mission to be the hope of human longing has to begin in the local community. All the words of all the popes and bishops are worth nothing if they do not come from a community that is showing what they are telling. Hence, apostolic work starts in the community of faith and in solidarity with all other people of goodwill. Every community of faith in its own locale must be a lamp set on the lampstand, must be the leaven in the mass. Of course it will be centered on its eucharistic worship, bringing the cares of the world before God and drawing sustenance from the sacrament. But God will not value worship if it is not the praise and thanksgiving of a missioned community, up to its neck in the daily struggle for a more human world. The prophet Amos warned as much when God said through him that "feasts and solemn assemblies" are despicable unless they come from a community that seeks to do justice. As Jesus says, "Not everyone who says to me, 'Lord, Lord,' will enter the kingdom of heaven, but only the one who does the will of my Father in heaven" (Matt 7:21, NRSV).

Taking the apostolicity of the Church seriously and asking the question that goes with it, "What is the Church *for*?" requires us to look somewhat differently at the Church than we are accustomed to do. For so many centuries during which Christians thought of the Church as the place of refuge from the world, the gathering of the elect who possessed faith and were moving steadily toward eternal life with God in heaven, the focus was on its internal life and structure. "The Church," indeed, was a term primarily taken to refer to the higher and lower clergy, the rituals and practices and the buildings themselves. The people attended the services conducted by the clergy, received (mostly moral) instruction from them, and were expected to live their lives in the world "giving good example," which primarily meant testifying to the Catholic way of being Christian as it showed itself in pious practices and not eating meat on Fridays. The good works of the institution were primarily directed toward taking care of our own or perhaps somehow reaching out to those who might be moved to enter the Church and so be saved. The Church was a rock and a mighty fortress, proudly isolated in the raging seas of life.

Because the creator God who is love creates as an expression of the excess to which love is given, the Church that bears the name of Christ exists not for its own sake but for the sake of the world to which it is sent. Such a sacramental understanding of the Church is easy to grasp in principle, hard to live out in practice. We rightly say that Christ is the sacrament of God in the world, and that we the Church are the sacrament of Christ. Christ shows the face of God when God is human, and we are called to show the face of Christ when Christ is made flesh again within the community of faith. In the Church, the Eucharist is the sacrament of the continuing incarnation of God, the real presence of Christ. But the Eucharist signifies very little if Christ is not also incarnate in the believing community as the Holy Spirit enlivens them to spread the message of God's love for the world. The Church when it is true to its nature is trinitarian, powered by the Spirit, being Christ in conformity to the Creator's purposes. Like the Trinity, the superabundance of love that is its heart bursts the bounds of its own being and spills over into love of that which it is not. God loves the other of God, namely, the creation that God fashions and preserves. The Church must love not only God but also the human world that is the primary object of God's outpouring of love. The Church is not the center. We need the Church only because the world needs to be saved. If the world had not failed to return the love of its creator, there would be no Savior and no Church.

Focusing on the other-directed or apostolic mission of the Church puts the importance of its structure and its ecclesial ministers, both ordained and lay, in a new light. It is not that they become unimportant or even less important but that their true importance comes into clearer focus. Relative to the internal life of the community the ordained have primary responsibility for preaching and celebrating the Eucharist, and lay ministers foster the internal health of the community. Relative to the other-directed mission of the Church, they are all—in the best possible sense of the phrase—support staff. Their work is vital, but it is not the heart of the Church's mission. Apostolicity, in other words, is a mark of the Church primarily carried by laypeople, since it is the laity who shoulder by far the greater part of the task of being the loving presence of God in the world. If the Church is to work for a fuller humanity and to take sides with all those who fight the forces of the antihuman, it is to the laity that this responsibility primarily pertains. They require the sustenance of the sacramental life celebrated within the community of faith, but the meal is "bread for the journey."

So, through this lengthy discussion of the marks of the Church, we come to today's Church, the Church of Vatican II and beyond, a community increasingly led by the laity, with ordained clergy in much shorter supply than in recent centuries, with a new growth of lay ecclesial ministers whose raison d'être is not simply to be a stopgap for the shortage of traditional vocations. We come to the Church that is far more open to other Christians, to other religions, and to the world around it than before. We see a Church that at its worst is victim to pride, greed, and the rest of the seven deadly sins. But at its best we see a Church that has so much to offer to the world to which it is sent, a message of the signal importance of finding our way to a more truly human community in which the fostering of human dignity can only lead us all to better preparation for the coming of the reign of God. In our next chapter we will turn to consider ten challenges or opportunities facing the Church today as it seeks to be faithful to its calling to be the lamp on the lampstand.

Chapter Two

Ten Challenges for the Church Today

We come to this second chapter armed with some sense of the theological fundamentals that explain the nature of the Catholic community of faith. Perhaps readers may have noticed and been a little surprised to see that much of what was discussed in the previous chapter did not coincide with what most Catholics would pick out as the defining characteristics of the tradition. We have not spent a lot of time on the papacy, Mary and the saints have not been mentioned, and the whole set of issues to do with the moral teaching of the Church have appeared only fleetingly. These omissions are deliberate. All these things, of course, are important to Catholics, but they are not deep structures of the Church. Time, place, identity, and mission are, and they were the focus of the first chapter. What was said there also applied equally to the Church wherever it is around the world and whenever it has been or will be in history. We might answer some of the questions slightly differently in one time or place rather than another, but the elements of who-ness, where-ness, when-ness, what-ness, and what-for-ness are constants.

We now turn in a slightly different direction and look specifically at the Church today and some of the challenges it faces, though these questions are intimately connected to the deeper structural characteristics we have already considered. The Church in every moment in history has had to negotiate ways to continue to be what the Church is in face of the particular challenges of that moment. In our time the challenges may be different from those of a century or a millennium ago, but we address them for just the same reasons that the Church of the past dealt with its challenges, in order to continue to be faithful to what God wants of the community of faith. If some of our challenges lead to strongly expressed differences of opinion and even some polarization among Catholics, this is only testimony to our having gotten the questions right, if not the answers. So the ten questions that follow will lead us into some of the most contested issues in the present-day Catholic Church. Some of the questions themselves may seem bland and innocuous enough, but attempting to point in the direction of answers will take us to the heart of many of the issues that divide Catholics today. It is good to remember that voices do not get raised if something important is not at stake.

This chapter is divided into six internal and four external challenges, though of course such a simple division is only logistical and does not correspond to the reality of a religious tradition whose members simultaneously act in Church and world. We learned in the previous chapter of the need to think of the Church as existing for the sake of the world, not for its own sake. If we hold fast to that truth then every internal concern has external implications, and every external issue rebounds upon the question of the nature of the Church "in itself." Among the internal issues we will be looking at are questions of identity and institutional commitment, authority, the roles of women in the Church, and patterns of ministry. The external questions have more to do with how we think of mission and what sort of public face the Church should present to the world. What unites the two is the Gospel. If we are possessors of good news, our first impulse is surely to share it with others. To share it successfully, however, we have to learn how to say it so that others can hear it. Hence the internal and external blend into one another.

It is also at this point in our story that the inductive or "bottom-up" approach to ecclesiology that we are following here necessitates contextual thinking. The development of a universal ecclesiology in abstraction from any particular concrete ecclesial reality is an impossibility for our way of thinking here. It would be a reversion to the classicist approach that Bernard Lonergan rejected in favor of an empirical method or, in the terminology of Edward Hahnenberg, a one-sided preference for a Platonist over an Aristotelian approach (see chap. 1, n. 33). Accordingly, the discussion of concrete issues that follows here, and indeed the more constructive ecclesiology essayed in the third and final chapter of this book, reflects the context of the Catholic Church in the United States. It is, of course, equally a conviction of empirical or inductive method that multiple contextual reflections interweave to present a more universal reality without allowing it to become an abstraction dominant over the concrete realities that formed it. Empirical method cannot legitimately become idealist.

Internal Challenges

Identity and Commitment

How can the Church remain a cohesive community of faith when patterns of institutional commitment are changing dramatically?

In their 2007 book *American Catholics Today* four distinguished sociologists devote a lot of space to the implications of their surveys for balancing Catholic identity and institutional commitment.[1] Their statistics suggest that among Americans self-identifying as Catholics their sense of identity remains quite strong, but the level of commitment to the institution is declining. So, while often as many as 80% of those asked might declare that being Catholic was something of major importance to them or assent to the proposition that "I could not imagine not being Catholic," regular church attendance actually runs around 30% nationally. Perhaps even more telling, while Mass attendance is so low, when the surveys presented a list of twelve items and asked the respondents to rank them in order of importance, belief in the Eucharist was in the top four (along with devotion to the Virgin Mary, helping the poor, and belief in the bodily resurrection of Jesus). On the one hand, this sense for what is central to the tradition is quite heartening. On the other, it really is quite hard to reconcile devotion to the Eucharist and regular absence from church on Sundays.

Assuming the careful conduct of collecting information and the skilled analysis of the data, we are left wondering about these apparent contradictions. Is it perhaps the case that the respondents lied or misunderstood the questions? Sometimes people don't want to admit to things they are ashamed of, and it might be that they just weren't ready to admit to the interviewer or even to themselves that Catholicism no longer mattered to them anymore. It's hard to cast off your past, and for every ex-Catholic atheist you might encounter there are a hundred who

---

[1] William V. D'Antonio and others (Lanham, MD: Rowman & Littlefield).

would claim to be "still Catholic" but not practice much. On the other hand, why would they lie about this but be apparently completely open about their low level of institutional involvement? And in either case it remains to be explained how their sense of what Catholicism entails remains so healthy. When the claim to continuing identification is coupled with a good feeling for major teachings, talk about "lapsed Catholics" does not do justice to the complexity of the situation.

If we leave aside considerations of poor data collection or less-than-honest responses, we are led toward the conclusion that something is changing in the way in which people born Catholic relate to their religious tradition. Obviously, Catholics do not go to Mass in the way they once did. Even highly committed and somewhat older Catholics are far more likely to miss Mass on some Sunday for reasons that a generation or two ago would have led them straight to the confessional. If it's not the granddaughter's soccer game or the monthly trip to the nearest casino, it might just be that they are particularly angry with the Church this week, or the pastor's homily offended them the week before and they are punishing him by not showing up this time. But once we step beyond the more institutionally committed, Mass attendance is quite sporadic, and among late teens and young adults, regular Mass is the practice of a small minority. There are indeed not a few pastors who have tried to come to terms with this phenomenon by promoting the idea that a sort of commitment or covenant to attend regularly, monthly or every two weeks, might be something for people to consider. Two generations ago that would have been the priest recommending committing only two or three mortal sins a month, which would have been highly questionable pastoral practice. Today, it is the frank recognition that regular if less-frequent attendance is better than drifting from Sunday to Sunday failing to make the weekly Mass. While it is surely still the case that weekly attendance might be the best practice, some self-discipline and intentionality in a regular but less-frequent participation is not a bad second-best. If this is not just to be giving in to the power of contemporary culture, it needs to be accompanied by some kind of sustained reflection on whether there might be positive reasons for this change in behavior.[2]

[2] This more irenic approach is proposed in a new book by Jerome P. Baggett, *Sense of the Faithful: How American Catholics Live Their Faith* (Oxford and New York: Oxford University Press, 2009). Baggett uses an ethnographic method, conducting fewer interviews in more depth than typical surveys, and suggests in his preface that "the

Generalizations can be hazardous to health. And yet it is probably true to say that the human person's need for meaning in life is a zero-sum game. People seem to need and want a measure of order and purpose and pattern in their lives. We can probably do without some of this for periods of time, and most people kick over the traces or use some narcotic—physical or mental—to spend some time in a fantasy world fueled by egoism or hormones. But it is a safe bet that over the course of a lifetime human fulfillment is somehow connected to the sense that my life is more or less in tune with "the way things are." We know that the happiest people are those who build their lives around a set of values, which leads them to particular ways of living in the world. In our best moments we probably know that this is possible for all of us, though the noise around us can surely drown out the message, and we are only too well aware of the ways in which contemporary culture helps us remain deaf to deeper purposes.

Through the Middle Ages and succeeding centuries up to the middle of the twentieth, the Catholic Church provided its members with one of the most complete pictures of the meaning of life and a distinctive method for patterning one's life accordingly. The stages of life, the liturgical year, the practice of repentance, prayer, good works, and the sacraments all came together in a seamless framework of meaning and order. God was in heaven, the members of the Church were heading in that direction, and obeying God in and through the Church would assure a happy death and entry into the presence of God in heaven. For most of those centuries the greater part of the then-developed world was governed by secular authorities who at least paid lip service to Christian values. Expressing dissent by living lives different from the vast majority of those around you was difficult if not impossible; private questioning was no doubt more common but of its nature did not affect the public face of religion. And when the Enlightenment ushered in the respectability of unbelief, the Church simply dismissed it as the work of sin and the devil. At least on the surface, the war between the Church and the world only strengthened the convictions of Christians.

In the end the apparently impregnable fortress of Catholicism was breached by the modern world's discovery of the rights and responsibilities of the human subject.[3] The distinctive communitarian emphasis of

---

ending of one iteration of a religious tradition is often tantamount to the beginning of another" (xi).

[3] Charles Taylor has written eloquently of how much the Church owes to modernity. See *A Catholic Modernity? Charles Taylor's Marianist Award Lecture*, ed. James L. Heft

Catholicism, one of its greatest strengths, leaves it correspondingly weak in its account of the individual. We come to God together in and through the Church, the corporate body. Luther's insistence on the individual standing alone before God in prayer and meeting God in the silence of the heart did not sit well with traditional Catholicism and is frankly today still not always a welcome emphasis. The subordination of the individual to the good of the whole helps explain facets of today's institutional attitudes toward the "rights" of women relative to ministry, the "rights" of gays and lesbians to form civil unions and marry, the "rights" of theologians to speak and write freely in the Church, and so on. There is of course a very healthy recent tradition of rights language in the Church, but it is tellingly focused on so-called economic rights, such as the right to work, to health care, to a secure retirement, to education, and so on. While this stress has been enormously important to the wider culture in countering the classic liberal focus on individual rights so familiar to Americans in their Bill of Rights, within the Church itself it has tended to downplay the significance of genuine individual rights like that of freedom of speech and helps to explain why for so long the Catholic Church refused to recognize the right to freedom of religion.[4]

The twenty-first-century human being's care for subjectivity and the Church's greater concern for the good of the whole were bound to come into conflict at some point. In fact, the critical moment in the emergence of the split between identity and commitment is often located a few decades earlier in 1968 with the popular response to Pope Paul VI's encyclical banning most methods of birth control, *Humanae Vitae*. More liberal Catholics see this as the moment at which laypeople began to become adults and found ways respectfully to disagree with the pope's judgment. More conservative voices view the institution's decision not to act decisively against public dissent as giving away the shop and teaching people, in effect, that dissent would be tolerated.[5] Whichever

---

(New York: Oxford University Press, 1999). Taylor expands the connections between religion and secularity in his masterpiece, *A Secular Age* (Cambridge, MA: Harvard University Press, 2007).

[4] For today's Catholic Church, as for today's Catholics, the most sensitive of all the individual rights is the right of conscience. There is no deeper conviction of modern society than that of freedom of conscience, and nothing brings howls of protest more quickly than any institution's efforts to limit the rights of conscience, even if that institution is the Church. We will have more to say about this issue below.

[5] George Weigel, *The Courage to Be Catholic: Crisis, Reform, and the Future of the Church* (New York: Basic Books, 2004).

group is right, and it could well be both, the Church emerged from the '60s with the beginnings of the divorce between identity and practice that we see so clearly in today's statistical analyses. When Paul VI died in 1978 there began the long pontificate of John Paul II, more than twenty-five years in which this immensely popular figure taught by means of a whole chain of encyclical letters. But the personal popularity never really issued in conformity to his teaching. Whether it was the reiteration of the ban on birth control, the refusal to consider ordained ministry for women, the rejection of secular society's materialism, or the "seamless garment" approach to right-to-life issues, all seemed for the most part to fall on deaf ears. Young people traveled long distances to bask in the presence of the pontiff, but many of them slept with their boyfriends and girlfriends along the way, many of them were pro-choice on abortion, most of those who were sexually active used birth control, and large numbers of them considered same-sex relationships, civil unions, or marriages to be a complete nonissue. They were in Germany or Denver or Australia or wherever to demonstrate their love for John Paul II and their identity as young Catholics, but they were going to make up their own minds about what to believe and how to live.

While on the whole it seems appropriate to celebrate human beings who have determined to live their lives according to what they believe and not by simple obedience to some external authority, secular or religious, the deeper problem that will not go away is the absence of that kind of familiarity with the teachings of the tradition that makes responsible choice possible. If you simply don't know what the Church teaches, how can you make well-informed choices? It's like trying to choose whom to vote for in an election when you are basing it simply on visceral responses to one or the other candidate and not finding out where they stand on the issues. Just as this kind of behavior leads to bad political choices, so the same kind of conduct in relation to religious teachings can only lead to ill-considered choices. Some poor choices can still be right, of course, but right for the wrong reasons. Making the right choice is far better than choosing wrongly, but knowing why you made the right choice is even better. Religious literacy in the Catholic community is in poor shape and needs to be improved. Often discussed, this lack of knowledge is too frequently considered simply to be a failure in rote learning. "Oh," they say, "no one knows what the seven deadly sins are anymore, or the sorrowful mysteries of the rosary," and so on. Certainly, this lack of familiarity with the tradition is a loss that needs to be overcome, but the more important thing is that literacy be an informed literacy, not just the ability to recite the facts without having learned something about how they came to be, and to have been given room to engage the teachings critically.

The correct response to the divorce between claims to continuing Catholic identity and practices that would indicate ongoing institutional commitment is to strengthen the mechanisms of teaching through which the Church hands on its wisdom to the next generation, and the first step in this process is for the institutional Church itself to learn a few lessons about how good teaching takes place. This could begin with the recognition that "student-centered learning" is not just hip jargon but awareness that how we teach must be dictated by the needs and capabilities of who it is that we are teaching. For small children, telling the story of Jesus is mightily appropriate, and adding in a few things about Mary and the saints can only prepare the ground for adult appreciation for the rich tapestry of Catholic devotional life. As adolescence approaches, catechetics needs to shift to a model in which reasons for the whole range of Catholic teachings are presented in a context in which questioning and dissent are welcomed. And adult education, something the Church has signally failed to promote, needs not only to present Church teaching with historical background, celebrating its strengths and, frankly, recognizing its limitations. It also needs to invite adult learners into sharing their own experiences as important components of the formation of teaching itself. The day has simply gone when Church teaching can mean that messages are passed down from on high for the unquestioning assent of the recipients. Unquestioning obedience to any earthly figure, even the pope, is not a value for most Catholics in this moment in history. Every educator also knows that the simple recitation of information to be memorized is not good pedagogy if our objectives are to help the student grow in wisdom and not just get a good grade on the test.

If the teaching Church needs some lessons in pedagogy, the Catholic community needs to value education a whole lot more, and this is far more likely to occur if the institution recognizes its importance. Education does not happen when people ingest information and simply accept it; it happens when they learn the skills of discernment and analysis so that they can make what they are taught their own, when they can even participate in the educational process and sometimes actually teach the teachers something they did not previously know. The teacher brings the tradition into the classroom, and there she or he meets a whole range of experiences. Learning occurs when the tradition collides with, corrects, and is corrected by the experience of the learning community. The fabled passivity of the Catholic laity is a result of poor teaching for many, many centuries. Those who have broken the shackles of passivity are not helped by being considered troublemakers or dissenters. They are the vanguard in the struggle to overcome the gap between identity and commitment, and they need to be cherished, even if sometimes their stated positions are short of nuance.

Ministry, Ordained and Lay

What is the healthiest way for us to balance the responsibilities of mission and ministry among the ordained and the laity?

At the present time "mission," "ministry," ordained and non-ordained, clergy and laity are terms over which the Church is in a hopeless muddle. Mission used to mean going to the two-thirds world to spread the Gospel; now it seems to mean anything we are called to in virtue of our baptism. Ministry is divided up among bishops and priests and deacons and lay ministers, "ecclesial" or otherwise, though sometimes the language seems to suggest that all Christians may be called to some kind of ministry. If preaching is a ministry, is catechetics? If catechetics, what about singing in the choir, or doing the pastor's correspondence, or visiting the sick, or running a food pantry, or making the church grounds look clean and well tended? Then, what is the difference between ordination and other ways of recognizing callings to ministry, and why are some things reserved for the ordained? If certain types of ministries are ecclesial and directed to the community of faith itself, while others are out in the world, why are clergy mostly expected to work within the Church, though some laypeople do too, while the lay work in the world is also occasionally taken up by ordained clergy? And is any of all this changed or needing to be changed because the supply of men for the ordained celibate ministry is apparently drying up, particularly in Europe and North America?[6]

The most important step in addressing this whole collection of problems is to get the question right. The question is not: how can we increase the number of vocations? Every Christian has a "vocation" or divine

---

[6] Excellent current books on ministry in the Catholic Church include: Susan K. Wood, ed., *Ordering the Baptismal Priesthood: Theologies of Ordained and Lay Ministry* (Collegeville, MN: Liturgical, 2003); and Edward P. Hahnenberg, *Ministries: A Relational Approach* (New York: Crossroad, 2003).

calling to a particular place and work in the Church. The much-discussed shortage of ordained clergy and religious that often goes by the name "the vocations crisis" misuses the word "vocation" and consequently impedes more imaginative responses to the situation. The question is rather: what can we do to serve the people of God better and to engage them all in the work of the Church without breaking definitively with some fundamentals of our religious tradition? The first question, the one about vocations, is in principle a form of the second question, but it assumes too much in the word "vocations," essentially imagining no room for development in the Church's conception of what a minister should be or look like.

If the shortage of traditional celibate clergy is the only or primary concern in the vocations crisis, then the commonsense response to it is clearly to consider ordaining married men. Evidently, this is not impossible. We know this to be the case because the Church did it for many centuries, does it today in exceptional cases, and recognizes the validity of the priesthood in the Orthodox Church, many of whose priests are married. It is not even *wrong* to ordain married men, for exactly the same reasons. For just those same reasons again, we cannot argue that married men make poorer priests simply because they are married. No one would argue that the ordination of a non-celibate man is impossible. But this gets us nowhere, because the institutional commitment to a celibate clergy is based solely on unbroken tradition. The official position of the Church is that the linking of priesthood and celibacy in the Roman Catholic Church, while neither absolute nor strictly essential, is so long-standing a tradition that to make a change would be a mistake. It would be inadvisable, so the magisterial teaching concludes, to break with long-standing tradition.

Not to be willing to respond to the need for ordained ministers in any way other than to pray for more of the male celibates who have been the norm for the past thousand years seems to increasing numbers of American Catholics to be an erroneous essentializing of one detail in the rich tradition of Catholicism. Tradition is essential; particular traditions are not. Tradition is a vital theological component of the Catholic Church. The term refers to the great historical stream of fidelity to the message of the Gospel, kept alive by the whole community of faith under the guidance of the Holy Spirit. Without Tradition in this sense the Church would be stuck with the impossible task of trying to read the Gospel the way it was received 1,900 years ago and with a literalist understanding of the decrees of the great ecumenical councils or, at the other extreme, blown around by every contemporary current seeking relevancy. From the time early Church fathers made use of allegorical interpretation of Scripture, Catholicism has never accepted simple literalism or fundamentalism, though it has been tempted at times. It has preferred to believe in the importance of interpretation, whether we are talking about magisterial teaching or about the way the faith of the whole Church, under the power of the same Spirit, manages to perform the tradition truthfully in any age.

If we cling firmly to the belief that Church tradition is the way we remain faithful to the Gospel through the changing fortunes of history, then traditions within the tradition can never be set in stone. They must certainly not be changed lightly, but they must equally certainly be changed when the proclamation of the Gospel—the very mission of the Church—is in danger of being compromised. This is particularly true when the case for any practice in the Church is made primarily if not solely on the grounds of the weight of tradition. True, there are other arguments, having to do with the capacity to give oneself totally to God, or the long-standing claim, now discredited, that celibacy somehow in itself is the high road to holiness. But these kinds of arguments are what theologians call "arguments from fittingness," which really means that they are supplementary arguments that can support a case already made on firmer grounds, but cannot themselves offer conclusive proof. So critical is the shortage of ordained clergy in the Catholic Church in North America and Europe today that it behooves us to examine again the ban on married priests. An argument from Tradition can certainly be strong and is always significant, but it can never be conclusive, not least because Tradition itself is a dynamic principle in Church life. Tradition is the history of how the Church has grown and changed in response to historical currents in order to remain faithful to the Gospel. So what can be said about the Church today that might cause us to look afresh at the Western Church's exclusion of married men from the ranks of ordained priests?

The primary and indispensable role of the ordained clergy is to preside at the Eucharist. It took a while for the early Church to reach this conclusion, since there was a time when the apostles were still alive but the Lord's Supper was celebrated in private homes, presided over by the host. But fairly quickly it became clear that first bishops and later the presbyters, their assistants, cared for the local community and presided at the Eucharist. The leaders of the local Christian community expressed their role liturgically by celebrating Mass in and for the community to which they had been called. The later understanding of bishops as possessing orders and jurisdiction, as though these were distinct responsibilities, was foreign to the early Church. The community called a person to be its bishop, and this individual led the community and because he led the community he was the one to celebrate the Eucharist.

We have now reached the deplorable point in most of the worldwide Church when the Eucharist is not as readily available to the community of faith as it should be, and may before long become even scarcer. Different parts of the world experience this differently. In much of North America the shortage of priests is only beginning to hit a Church that had abundant ministers for at least the last century. In Latin America and Africa, even if in the latter the numbers offering themselves for ordination are increasing, there have never been sufficient priests to provide weekly Eucharist to all Catholics, especially in the rural areas. But the very way in which the problem is explained testifies to how far we have come from the practice of the early Church. The shortage today is a shortage of a commodity called "ordained ministers" or "priests." In the distant past this could not happen because there was no such commodity. Today there is a pool of clergy ordained to serve wherever the bishops choose to send them. In the past a community chose someone to be its leader, usually for life. On the older model it would be impossible to have a "shortage of clergy," because each community had its leader. Each community had its bishop or presbyter because every community had a leader, in many cases chosen solely by the local community, in others through agreement with the other clergy of the region. Wherever a Christian community existed that community called a leader and that leader celebrated the Eucharist. It might be that we have something to recover from that understanding of ministry.

Another and potentially more valuable approach to the question of ministries is to adopt the model of the early Pauline communities in which everyone brought something, a gift or "charism," to the service of the community. As Paul wrote, "there are many gifts but one body," and while there is a hierarchy of these gifts there is no gift that is not from God and that cannot be turned back into service to the community. Because Paul was writing before the Church had any clear structures, these "gifts" do not correspond to any particular offices in the later Church. The gifts of healing or preaching or administration or teaching, all mentioned by Paul, were not assigned to an office but were God-given talents of certain individuals. The idea that the talent gives a hint about the calling or vocation of the individual is something we have lost in the

Church. It could surely only make for a healthier Church if the one who taught was a good teacher, the one who preached was a good preacher, and the one who had some financial skills was in charge of the money. Many fine parish communities work on this basis, though they all make an exception for the role of priest. The office of priest is way too often conferred on people as if the ceremony of ordination itself would supply the grace of all the skills expected of the clergy, making a poor preacher into a good one and someone who cannot balance his checkbook into a competent financial manager of a medium-sized corporation.

When we think of ministries in the Church today as those conferred by ordination, those proper to laypeople in the secular world, and those in-between that laypeople exercise inside the faith community or that some priests engage in outside the confines of the Church, the old clergy/laity split seems to creak quite a bit. If we could just put out of our minds for a moment the clear but irrelevant split between clergy who are male celibates on the one side and the rest of us who are not on the other, we can see that ministry itself and of its nature is on two axes. One is the "axis of leadership," the other the "axis of service." The first would have us place ministries according to the importance of the work to the Church's capacity to be faithful to its mission. The second would place them according to the particular relationship of that ministry to the mission of the Church. So, on the axis of leadership, bishops would always occupy first place because they have overall responsibility for the health of the community of faith. After that, it is not so clear. Leadership of the local community is certainly provided by the ordained minister of the Eucharist, but is that leadership more central to the mission of the Church than, say, a president of a Catholic university or a Catholic hospital, a wise writer of books about the spiritual treasures of the Catholic tradition, or a prophet in the public eye? The axis of service would stretch from one extreme, where ministers worked entirely within the Church, assuring its capacity to engage in mission, to the other at which work was entirely conducted in the world, as a faithful baptized Christian, licensed by baptism and confirmation rather than by some explicit mandate from the institutional Church itself.

Thinking of ministry on two axes, one of leadership for mission and one of service to mission, allows us to move away from the inadequate language of "orders" and "jurisdiction" with which we have been saddled for way too long. "Holy Orders" are one form of ministry of service through which the community of faith is held together and strengthened. "Leadership" pertains to all the influential roles Catholics have within their Church by which its orientation to mission is shaped and focused, and while some of these leaders are ordained others are not. The bishop is certainly someone whose work places him at the intersection of both axes, but his position is unique. Hierarchy is not a helpful metaphor for describing the relationship of all other responsibilities and offices in the Church. The Cardinal who runs a Roman Congregation may have much more administrative responsibility than the rector of the Gregorian University, but he is not possessed of a higher office, and the parish director of religious education with thirty years of experience in the job should not be placed lower on the organizational chart than the freshly minted assistant pastor. Nor, to look at the axis of service, is the pastor's role more central to the mission of the Church than the Catholic Worker member or the Catholic international aid worker. In fact, in many respects the pastor's work is supportive to the mission in which the others are actually more directly involved.

The usual challenge to this effort to overcome the qualitative distinction between ordained ministry and other ministries is the Catholic position that Christ's calling of the apostles was in effect the establishment of the hierarchical priesthood, and hence that ordained ministry in the Church comes directly from the call of Christ and is not a calling from the community, whereas other ministries can be seen as service to and at the behest of the local, regional, national, or international Church. So, in the unlikely event of one of us being summoned to head a papal commission, we would be called by the community to service the community. But if one of us were ordained a deacon to serve the Church, that would be a calling by Christ himself. Ordained priesthood and the baptismal priesthood that is the call to mission have traditionally been understood in the Church as related but independent of one other, qualitatively distinct each from the other.[7] The insistence on this distinction in recent centuries has been prominent in part because of Martin Luther's rejection of ordination as "priesthood" and the ecclesiology that followed in which ministry was licensed by the community's designation, not by Christ himself. But the distinction itself antedates Reformation controversies by some considerable time.

---

[7] LG 10 states that "[t]hough they differ essentially and not only in degree, the common priesthood of the faithful and the ministerial or hierarchical priesthood are none the less ordered one to another; each in its proper way shares in the one priesthood of Christ."

The distinction between calling by Christ and commissioning by the community of faith is an artificial one that does not stand up to any good test. Once we ask the question of *how* Christ calls the minister to serve the community, we can immediately see the problem. The calling is either by some bolt from the blue or somehow by the Church's ratification of the candidate's sense of vocation. In the Church of the present day that validation is entirely in the hands of the institutional Church, represented by seminary rectors, teachers, and spiritual directors, and eventually the bishop. But there is absolutely no reason to see this as calling by Christ *rather than* calling by the community, anymore than for the local community to put a candidate forward would be clearly a calling by the community *rather than* a calling by Christ. Both approaches are simultaneously a calling by Christ and by the community, because there is no other way than the consent of the community to indicate that Christ has genuinely called this person to ministry. We can certainly argue about which methods of ratifying a call are more efficient or more convenient, but we are on shaky ground if we identify the bishop with the call of Christ and the whole people of God with the simple call of the community. This is simply one more area in which we have to recognize that the Holy Spirit is not confined to the work of the hierarchy, and that what the Spirit did in centuries past the Spirit can presumably still continue to do. If bishops in the early Church were legitimately called by the local community acting in the Spirit, this does not of course mean that they must be called in precisely the same way today. But it does seem to mean that this method of ratifying a call cannot simply be excluded as "not the call of Christ." What worked then would work now.

The Roles of Women in the Church

How does the Church need to change in order to allow for the full participation of women?

The Roman Catholic Church is a sexist institution. We need to acknowledge this from the outset because its truth is self-evident to liberals and conservatives alike. In this way we can avoid the rapid descent into polarized debate or the ideological confrontations between left and right that mark consideration of this particular hot-button issue. While women certainly constitute considerably more than half of the churchgoing population and they dominate the entire field of lay ministry, they simply do not have remotely proportional representation in leadership roles at the parochial, diocesan, or international level. The principal reason for this problem—and a problem it is—is not that the Church restricts ordained ministry to men but, rather, that the Church assigns all major leadership roles to the ranks of the ordained, who happen to be men. It is not self-evident that the charism of leadership is intrinsically connected to that of pastoral ministry, but so long as our Church is organized on the assumption that the connection is real, women simply cannot take their appropriate places in Church leadership. There are only two ways in which the present situation can be changed. One is to find the way forward to an ordained ministry that includes women as equal partners with men. The other is to distinguish between leadership and the pastoral ministry of the ordained. Both would involve radical changes in the Church and neither is being seriously considered at the highest levels of Church leadership. Indeed, the first solution has several times been explicitly excluded from consideration by Pope John Paul II, and the second has never even been publicly broached.[8] Nevertheless, we proceed here by examining whether there is room for maneuver on either option.

There are a number of contested issues in present-day Church life where the teaching of the magisterium seems not to have persuaded the faithful as a whole, and the place of women in ordained ministry is high on the list.[9] In such a situation we have to assume the goodwill of all parties involved and their equal concern for the health of the Church. The Vatican is not setting out to put women down, and those many members of the Church, laity and clergy alike, who believe it is time for a change are not trying to destroy the institution but, rather, to save it from itself. It is also incumbent on everyone with a stake in the debate to be neither overly protective of a clericalist status quo nor simply to transpose the rights language of secular feminist debate into the ecclesial arena. Both sides have to place the issue in the context of ecclesial tradition. Those who desire to ordain women cannot simply thumb their

---

[8] The two key documents are *Inter Insigniores*, "Declaration on the Admission of Women to the Ministerial Priesthood" (15 October 1976) of the Sacred Congregation for the Doctrine of the Faith (http://www.ewtn.com/library/curia/cdfinsig.htm); and *Mulieris Dignitatem*, John Paul II's 1988 Apostolic Letter, "On the Dignity and Vocation of Women" (http://www.ewtn.com/library/PAPALDOC/JP2MULIE.HTM). See also *Ordinatio Sacerdotalis*, John Paul II's Apostolic Letter, "*On Reserving Priestly Ordination to Men Alone*" (http://www.ewtn.com/library/PAPALDOC/JP2ORDIN.HTM).

[9] Other similar failures are in teaching on birth control, on capital punishment, and on same-sex relationships, civil unions, and marriages.

noses at the fact that this has never been the practice of the Church. And those who oppose it cannot do so simply in the name of an unchanging tradition. Tradition is important and sometimes normative ecclesial memory; but tradition is a constant process of development, a living stream of change.

The Holy Spirit guides the Church into all truth, and it does so through the teaching authority of the pope and bishops, and in the practice of the whole faithful people, laity *and* clergy. But what are we to make of the activity of the Spirit when there is a serious issue over which the Church is divided? In such a time of controversy it is tempting just to say that the Holy Spirit cannot be at war with itself, and therefore one side is right and the other must back down. It is wiser, however, to consider the possibility that the work of the Spirit may be invested in the discernment process that good debating will produce and out of which the truth the Spirit guarantees might eventually emerge. The Holy Spirit works in just such a long-term way, as the then Cardinal Ratzinger hinted, in the process of the papal conclaves out of which new popes are selected. The cardinal soon-to-be-elected pope commented wryly that if the Holy Spirit was guiding the selection of each new pope, then there were at least a few moments in history where the Spirit seemed to fail the Church and a poor or even a bad pope was chosen. Yet the Church is where it is today because of the popes who have led it, good, bad, and indifferent, and the Spirit has guided it through its own bad choices to a better outcome, onward in faithfulness to its mission and to the reign of God. It seems reasonable to conclude that the Spirit is responsible, not for every particular belief of the Church, but for the Church's fidelity to the process of development that helps it to remain faithful to its mission in changing historical times.

Facing the issue of the institution's unwillingness to consider the ordination of women and the convictions of many theologians and faithful Catholics that there is no good reason why they should not, three and only three possible conclusions can be drawn. The first is that the arguments presented against the ordination of women are bad arguments and should be abandoned. The consequence of this step would be either to proceed to ordain women or to find some more persuasive arguments why the ordination of women is impossible or undesirable. The second possible conclusion would be that while the arguments offered against the ordination of women are sound arguments, they are obviously not persuasive. The consequence of considering this conclusion to be true would presumably be either to find a way to present the arguments more effectively or to abandon these arguments as true but unhelpful and find better arguments with which to persuade the Church that women cannot or should not be admitted to ordained ministry. The third possible conclusion is that human sinfulness is at work either blinding sectors of the Church to the clarity of the arguments or causing the teachers to make a case based more on self-protection or the avoidance of change than on any genuine merit to the argument. It is a rare argument in which the concern for truth is not at least a little adulterated by less-laudable motivations. However, the surer we are that the parties to the dispute are arguing in good faith and believe they have the good of the Church at heart, then the longer the debate continues, the less likely it is that human sinfulness affects it in any serious way. We must, though, consider the first two possible conclusions in a little more detail.

It is quite possible that the problem the magisterium has in quieting discussion over the admission of women to ordained ministry is caused by poor argumentation or poor arguments. To some degree the magisterium has admitted the truth of this claim by downgrading certain arguments that had previously been given greater prominence. For example, the claim that the priest represents Christ at the altar and that maleness is a requirement for being representative was a major pillar of the case against women but has been distinctly relegated to second place behind the argument from tradition. At best today it would be considered an "argument from fittingness," brought in after the case had been made on stronger grounds to fill out and strengthen the conclusions. And even this status is often plausibly countered by pointing out that it is Christ's humanity, not his masculinity, that is instrumental in salvation.[10] Just as we saw earlier in our discussion of clerical celibacy, the case against ordaining women is made today almost entirely on the argument of unbroken tradition. Priesthood, so it goes, can be traced somehow back to Jesus Christ, and despite his well-attested and even notorious openness to women he chose only men to be apostles. Faithful to this pattern, the Church throughout history has only ordained men as bishops, priests, and deacons. So unbroken is the tradition, it constitutes a fundamental of the Church that could not be changed, even if the Church thought it was a good idea. It is beyond debate.

---

[10] See here the classic article by Rosemary Radford Ruether, "Can a Male Savior Save Women?" in *To Change the World: Christology and Cultural Criticism* (New York: Crossroad, 1981), 45–56. The text is also available at http://www.womenpriests.org/theology/ruether1.asp.

The problem for the institution's position on the ordination of women is that it is making its case with an argument that carries very little weight with people of faith today, especially those at the younger end. No statement is more inimical to the contemporary consciousness than the claim that "it's never been done and so it can't be done," and that is often all there is to some "arguments from tradition." The sheer fact of longevity does not cut it. Nor, need it be said, is the declaration that no further discussion should take place likely to be well received. Of course, this particular form of the argument from Tradition is stronger because the tradition is linked to the practice of Jesus. But the problem with that is that the more you know about the emergence of the early Church, the trickier it is to associate this or that element in it with the will of Jesus himself. And if one adds to these suspicions the recognition that so much of what happened in the early formation of the Christian Church was a product of historical happenstance, the net result is a reluctance to accept any argument for unbroken tradition, even one that rests upon the claim that it represents the mind of Jesus.

A better way of understanding tradition might be constructed, but it is not so certain that a whole argument against the ordination of women could rest upon it. Just as we saw in our discussions of the celibacy law for diocesan clergy, so here it is important to distinguish between Tradition and traditions. Even "traditions" can be subdivided, as the Council of Trent did, into those that "pertain to faith" and those that do not. But while traditions are individual practices or beliefs, Tradition is the whole historical memory of the Church throughout history. As we said earlier, traditions can wax and wane in importance, but Tradition we always have with us. Tradition is the dynamic element in the Church, linked directly to the promise of the Holy Spirit to be present in the Church throughout the ages. Of its nature an argument from Tradition is not dogma. Things *could* change.

A secondary problem with making an argument about women and ministry on the basis of Tradition is that it is an argument from absence. It is one thing to say that there is something we have always done, and then give it at least a place of considerable honor in the Church's self-understanding. It is quite another to say that we have an unbroken tradition of not doing something. The only way to give authority to the absence of a practice is to link it to the will of the founder. Analogously, the fact that the presidents of the United States have all been men is not an argument for the rejection of any women candidate unless we can show that the founding fathers (and mothers?) intended to exclude women. Of course it probably never crossed their minds because women didn't even have a vote and were just a different kind of creature, or so they thought. But if it had, and if they had been excluded explicitly, would we today honor that exclusion? Barring a few strict constructionist ideologues, we would probably at least want to know why they excluded women and would subject their reasoning to considerable scrutiny. So, if Jesus really did consciously intend to exclude women, and was not simply reflecting or bowing to the consciousness of his times, the force of the tradition must surely depend on the reasoning behind it, and not on the authority itself. Jesus Christ did not act on whims, so what were the reasons for choosing only men?

When we pursue the argument from Tradition and find that we want to know the reasoning behind the origin of the practice of ordaining only men, the force of the Tradition argument obviously unravels and becomes dependent on some other set of criteria that justified the exclusion of women in the first place. Since the argument from Tradition is linked directly to Jesus' actions it will not do to bring forward once more the claim for the symbolic parallel between the priest and Jesus in the sacrifice of the Mass. Jesus was choosing apostles at most, not laying down sacramental theology for a non-Jewish set of liturgical practices. And if Jesus thought women were inferior in some ways, which would be entirely appropriate to his time though somewhat contradicted by his practice of talking to them as equals, the utterly changed understanding of women in the Catholic Church's public proclamations today is evidence enough that this kind of historically conditioned prejudice has no argumentative force, even if one could tie it to the mind of Jesus himself.

This set of considerations seems to lead to the conclusion that the problem with the Church's position on the ordination of women lies in the first instance in a poor choice of arguments that simply do not convince a faithful people as a whole. In such a situation a good teacher will look around for better ways of explaining why something is the case. But where can the Church look for the kind of argument that would be the clincher it so obviously needs if discussion of the matter is to end, as the Vatican apparently wishes it would? The approach taken by John Paul II in particular has been to somehow link the origins of the tradition to the will of God.[11] In an address in 1977 Pope Paul VI had said about

---

[11] See the helpful discussion in Sara Butler's online article, "Ordination: Reviewing the Fundamental Reasons," http://www.wf-f.org/04-3-Ordination.html.

the teaching on women's ordination that "[t]he real reason is that, in giving the Church her fundamental constitution, her theological anthropology—thereafter always followed by the Church's tradition—Christ established things in this way."[12] Quoting Paul VI in his 1994 letter, *Ordinatio Sacerdotalis*, reaffirming the exclusion of women from ordination, John Paul II explains how a tradition can be normative in similar terms. In making his choice of men as apostles, thinks the pope, Jesus is establishing "a perennial norm." The solemnity of his action is based on his having "spent the night in prayer."[13]

But we need to turn back to the earlier and lengthier discussion in *Mulieris Dignitatem* to see the deeper reasons for the normativity of what might look to many of us like one more set of political choices in a male-dominated world. There we find a discussion of the role of the priest in the Eucharist, in which his maleness is somehow essential. For John Paul II, "It is *the Eucharist* above all that expresses *the redemptive act of Christ the Bridegroom towards the Church the Bride*," and "[t]his is clear and unambiguous when the sacramental ministry of the Eucharist, in which the priest acts 'in *persona Christi*,' is performed by a man."[14] Since Christ, continues the pope, "in instituting the Eucharist, linked it in such an explicit way to the priestly service of the Apostles, it is legitimate to conclude that he thereby wished to express the relationship between man and woman, between what is 'feminine' and what is 'masculine.'" It seems that we are now back with an argument that the representative status of the priest is not simply "fitting" but somehow located in Christ's own will, and that it is this fact that makes the unbroken tradition important. This is a wholly more difficult argument to counter, since it requires us to get into the murky christological waters of what Jesus might or might not have intended.

To conclude this discussion of the role of women in the ministry we need to consider the second possibility we suggested, namely, that the arguments against the ordination of women are sound, but since they are evidently unpersuasive some other approach must replace or augment the present one of simply reiterating the arguments and declaring the discussion to be over. What needs to be done here is easy to see and is in any case a desirable step whatever one thinks of the particular ques-

[12] *Angelus* address of January 30, 1977, "Women in the Plan of God," *The Pope Speaks* 22 (1977): 124–25.

[13] *Ordinatio Sacerdotalis* 2.

[14] *Mulieris Dignitatem* 26.

tion. For the Church's official position on the ordination of women to be accepted, the same official Church needs to show by deeds and not just words that it accepts women as fully equal members of the faith community. This will be convincing only if women are increasingly found in all the places in the Church, especially leadership positions, in which ordination is not an issue. Lay ecclesial ministry in parishes is not sufficient. Even chancellors of dioceses, a few of whom in the United States are women, do not possess the genuine authority that Vicars General hold, and *they* are all men.

The promotion of women in large numbers to roles of leadership could occur in all kinds of ways. Three that could show the scope and consequences of taking this step seriously are: (1) gender-blind hiring practices for staffing diocesan seminaries, (2) opening the ranks of the Vatican's diplomatic corps to Catholic women diplomats from around the world, and (3) gender-blind staffing of all levels of the Roman Curia. Taking these steps seriously would mean that within twenty years or so as many as 25% if not more of the positions teaching in and presiding over seminaries, representing the Vatican to nations around the world, and running departments like the Congregation for the Doctrine of the Faith and the Congregation for Clergy would be held by women. If this did not happen then it would mean only one of two things: either not enough suitably qualified women came forward for the selection process, which would be easy to determine, or the commitment to equal treatment of women was not being taken seriously. But if it were to happen, what a remarkable testimony it would be to the seriousness with which the talents of women were being employed in Church leadership!

One further important consequence of opening leadership to women in roles not requiring ordination would be the pressure it would put upon the long-standing association of orders and jurisdiction. While it is entirely understandable that for historical reasons bishops and even sometimes priests exercise a kind of jurisdiction over the communities they serve, there is no reason other than clericalism why it should lead to assumptions that only bishops can lead Vatican departments or you have to be a priest to run a seminary. Above all, there is no good reason why laypeople, both women and men, should not hold positions in the Church that sometimes result in them exercising authority over priests and even bishops in some situations. Why in departments of the Vatican bureaucracy or in a diplomatic team in Paris or Washington could a laywoman not be senior to an ordained minister? The only reason for rejecting that possibility would be the assumption that in all official leadership positions the ordained lead and the laity follow. But if it is to remain the case that women cannot be ordained, then the consequence is to make a mockery of any claim that women have an equal place in the community of faith. Only a second-class citizen is excluded as a matter of course from leadership positions.

Church Teaching and the Individual Conscience

What is the appropriate balance between individual conscience formation and the teaching authority of the Church?

The short, cute answer to this question is that a properly formed conscience will always lead a Catholic into conformity with the Church's teaching. Certainly on any single given issue of sufficient gravity, if the Church is teaching with its full authority, then a member of that Church who is unable in conscience to give full assent to the teaching has to wonder if she or he really belongs. Let us examine an example about which there would be little disagreement. From earliest times the Church has taught the humanity and divinity of Jesus Christ. This doctrine is not easy to understand but it is absolutely central to the message of the Gospel. Most Catholic Christians "take it on faith," as they say, which amounts to trust in the longevity and centrality of the tradition coupled with the recognition that without this belief the individual's faith life would fall apart. Yet it is quite possible to imagine someone making a thorough study of Christology and coming to the conclusion that Jesus Christ is possessed of divinity in some lesser way than the Father. Lots of people did that in the early Church; they were called Arians and it looked at times as if their point of view would win the day. But once orthodox Christianity was clarified and the Arians condemned as heretics, the choice for someone who could not accept orthodox teaching was clear. They belonged somewhere else, in an Arian church. The right of individual conscience is always paramount, even in error, but in certain circumstances it can lead someone away from the Church. Given the Church's teaching based on Scripture that the Holy Spirit guarantees the Church's remaining in truth, to decide to leave the Church cannot be a decision taken lightly.

While few would disagree that someone who cannot in conscience follow a fundamental teaching of the Church does not belong within it, the issue of conscience versus authority has far greater relevance at the level of much less basic doctrines. The balance of the right of conscience versus the authority of Church teaching is easily settled when the divinity of Christ or the Trinity or the necessity of grace for salvation is at issue, but the real crunch comes with that whole host of much less important issues about which it seems possible to disagree with teaching authority and yet remain a fully active member of the community. Surveys of opinion among Catholics at the present day show wide variations among them over many of these secondary but still important doctrinal and ethical teachings. Catholics in most so-called developed countries mostly just ignore papal teaching against contraceptives, and there are many Catholics who do not accept the current teachings on the death penalty, on same-sex relations and marriages, on divorce, and even on abortion. In the area of more narrowly doctrinal issues, many disagree profoundly with claims made by the Church for the superiority of Catholicism over both non-Catholic Christian traditions and non-Christian religions. Lots of people fail to find the Church's teaching about the necessity of celibacy for the clergy to be persuasive, while others consider the exclusion of women from ordained ministry to be frankly sinful. People who disagree with Church authority on some or all of these issues attend Church regularly, pray and receive the sacraments, sometimes teach catechism, and almost always contribute financially to the Church.

The bigger challenge to the institutional Church is not that a person has difficulty with a particular item of moral or doctrinal teaching but, instead, the general and evidently growing sense that disagreement on a whole host of issues is frankly irrelevant to my standing as a member of the Church. I can pick and choose, illustrating the contemporary phenomenon that is often called "cafeteria Catholicism." The splendors of doctrinal and moral teachings are seen as laid out upon a kind of giant buffet table, along which Catholics pass, picking up those things that they find nourishing or attractive and leaving untouched the things they think harmful to them or that they simply do not like. The result, of course, is that the plate each of us ends up with, while it has many items in common with the next person in line, is never quite the same as that which others have selected, and the whole idea of a common tradition is threatened, or so it seems to some. But what one person might see as disastrous someone else could celebrate as healthy pluralism.

Traditional Church teaching leaves some room for maneuver in its recognition of the primacy of conscience, however heavily qualified. The *Catechism of the Catholic Church* addresses this matter when it says that "a human being must always obey the certain judgment of his conscience," and if someone were "deliberately to act against it, he would condemn himself." It goes on immediately to point out that the conscience can be wrong, and that sometimes the error is one of personal responsibility— and so it is culpable—while at other times it is not the person's fault. But even in this case there is evil, though not evil for which the individual can be held accountable. In such cases it is necessary to "work to correct the errors of moral conscience" because "a good and pure conscience is enlightened by true faith" (1790–94). It is hard for anyone to disagree with this generous recognition that error has at least some rights and that even an erroneous conscience is something the individual must follow. No one can expect you to do what is against your conscience, though your judgment may be mistaken. The passage that requires more attention, however, is the claim that "a good and pure conscience is enlightened by true faith." It would certainly seem to suggest that anyone abandoning the tradition might be acting in good conscience but inevitably erroneously. On the lesser issues over which dissent would not lead a person to leave the Church, though, it really is all going to depend on what we mean by "true faith."

The claims of conscience connect closely with the right to dissent from Church teaching, though "dissenters" are rarely considered anything but mistaken at best. The "true faith" that the *Catechism* says enlightens a "good and pure conscience" cannot be defined simply as "what the Church teaches," because that would be difficult to square with the incontestable historical judgment that sometimes the teaching Church has been in error. Open dissent from some aspect of Church teaching cannot simply be dismissed as wrong, since it is possible that conscientious dissent may be over a teaching that turns out at some future point to have been mistaken. And, given that doctrine develops and that our understandings of at least some teachings grow with time, it may well be that the dissenter, the one whose conscience precludes simple acceptance of this or that teaching, is in fact closer to the truth than the magisterium has yet arrived at. It would then be enormously unwise to dismiss all claims to conscientious dissent with the tag of "sinful" or even simply "erroneous." They could certainly be labeled disobedient, but this would be disobedience to teaching authority, not to the truth itself.

If we cannot dismiss all conscientious dissent as wrong, we also cannot canonize the individual conscience as an infallible guide. Surely all of us have at times found that a position we maintained or a truth we upheld turned out not to be accurate or perhaps even not honorable. We were not wrong to hold it, but what we held was wrong. If this is true, then it most probably means that some positions held today by some Catholics as true are in fact not so. Perhaps it is those who want to ordain women, perhaps those who do not. Perhaps it is those who believe we should give foreign aid generously with no strings attached, perhaps those who disagree. It is also a little puzzling to contemplate that Catholics on different sides of the same issue, if they speak honestly and with integrity, will presumably all claim the guidance of the Holy Spirit whose other name is "the Spirit of truth." Since the Spirit cannot be at war with itself, either one side is wrong that the Spirit is with them, or the Spirit is somehow present differently.

If the individual claiming guidance of the Spirit for his or her opinion may be in error, can this also be true for the Church's teaching authority itself? If we accept that there have been times when the Church has been wrong, then it would seem we have to say yes, and the consequence of this is that conscientious dissent from Church teaching cannot simply be dismissed on the grounds that the Spirit guides the teachers in a way that means they are never wrong, while students are always wrong if they do not accept Church teaching. This, indeed, is what the *Catechism* seems to be claiming with its remark that "a good and pure conscience is enlightened by true faith." Once again, a hint about how to resolve this problem is offered by that remark of Cardinal Ratzinger in advance of the conclave that would elect him pope. Since the Church has sometimes chosen bad popes, it is probably wrong to imagine the protection of the Holy Spirit covering each and every decision of the Church, and better to think of the Spirit guiding us through good and bad decisions and good and bad popes toward the reign of God. And this in its turn would suggest that the process by which the Church discerns how best to express the truth it possesses may require debate and even dissension between individuals and magisterium in which the magisterium is not necessarily always in the right. The requirement for the individual is to listen and learn, to inform one's conscience before proceeding. By the same token, the requirement for the magisterium is to be similarly humble before the possibility that it might just have gotten something wrong. It has happened before; it could happen again.

Writing of the relationship between the Holy Spirit and personal freedom, Yves Congar stressed the personhood in the Church that comes with baptism. Among the rights and duties of a person, he wrote, "the rights and duties of freedom are certainly not the least." The essential point for laypeople is *"to become adult Christians, free men."* This kind of internalized spirituality focuses not on rules and regulations but on personal conviction. Too many Catholics, Congar thought, do not have a skeleton so they go looking for a shell. They want "to shelter behind some authority, some law or decision or extract from an encyclical letter or papal address."[15] So the formation of Christians should take precedence over forming Christian organizations. This entails risks:

> Freedom calls for open discussion and frank give-and-take: it is therefore a threat to dogmatism (I do not say "to dogma"!). Freedom involves the acceptance sometimes of uncertainties and hazards; these are things that alarm a short-sighted authority, or one that is too self-conscious, an authority that is inclined to "paternalism." And, even when it works within the limits that it must not over-step, the spirit of freedom cannot fail to express itself outwardly in certain dissentient attitudes that insist on asking questions.[16]

When the Church becomes too legalistic, it tends "to capture and monopolize *spiritual* matters," and "this can in practice lead to regarding orthodoxy as essentially a defence of the clergy's authority, and to exalting obedience as *the* virtue of the good Catholic."[17] But we should not settle for "concealed conflict" between leaders and rank and file. The Spirit breathes in each of us and "to be God's servant, that is the only Christian freedom."[18]

Following Congar, we can say that so long as we all keep our eyes on the prize, conflict is neither necessary nor inevitable. The challenge to the members of the Church is to practice responsibility, to be aware of the Spirit at work in each of us, and to see our lives in terms of the mission of the Church to bring the world closer to God. The problem for the leaders of the Church is not to become so fixated on the rules and regulations that exist to serve the mission of free adult Christians, not to impede or regiment them. The voice of conscience is a corrective to each of us, bishop and layperson alike; it is the Holy Spirit working on us from within, urging us toward God's truth wherever it may lead, beyond self and beyond the self-protection of the institution. A healthy Church will be one in which the leadership does not imagine that obedi-

---

[15] *Laity, Church, and World: Three Addresses by Yves Congar*, trans. Donald Attwater (Baltimore, MD: Helicon, 1960), 26.

[16] Ibid., 27–28.

[17] Ibid., 32.

[18] Ibid., 34.

ence is the prime or even the only virtue, and the members of the community of faith can explore their concerns and their dissent in a context of understanding, in a place where we can all learn together, in a community where humility belongs to leaders and laity alike.

The Religious Formation of the Young

How can the Church ensure the sound religious formation of its youth?

How the Church incorporates the children and young adults of its community of faith is not simply or primarily about filling the pews or ensuring the future of the tradition. Granted, some of the concerns that Catholics generally have are connected to the disinclination of the young to attend Church and what consequently appears to be a graying community, but the real issues lie deeper. Young people are typically more enthusiastic, more energetic and more idealistic than their elders. If they are not participants, then somehow the community is falling down on its responsibilities. The Gospel has inspired energy, enthusiasm, and idealism throughout the ages. If it's not working the old magic anymore, it's probably our fault. What have we done to take an extraordinary message about Jesus Christ and turn it into something that leaves cold the very people it should inspire the most? If it were the aging who were jaded it would make more sense, but that the young are bored with the Gospel, that is a mighty condemnation of those who bring it to them.

The first problem we have to face is the near bankruptcy of the way in which children are taught about and initiated into sacramental life. They are baptized before they know anything about what is going on. They are introduced to first penance before they have anything much to be penitent about and in a way that almost assures that their first confession will be their last. They approach first communion in a somewhat better spirit, but often not in a family context in which Mass attendance will be anything more than sporadic. And, worst of all, they receive the sacrament of confirmation as a kind of license to conclude their religious education just when it should really be becoming significant, and as a rite of initiation into nonparticipation in the community of faith. So confirmation comes to be known as the sacrament after which you no longer need go to church if you don't want to. All of this may have made a little sense when most of them attended Catholic schools where the habits of participation were inculcated into them, with the assistance of families who for whatever reasons supported religious practice. But today far fewer parents prize the sacraments themselves, and most children do not go to school where a more confident appropriation of the message of the Gospel might be possible.

There is no way a sacramental catechesis that will attract the young can be possible until adult Catholics freely engage in a much less passive way in a life of faith that evidently makes a difference in our society and in our world. Worship and mission belong together; either without the other is hollow. The best of our parishes put a lot of effort into preparing liturgy with great care, and they have support groups for everything. The community is well provided for. Many of them also reach out to the local community around them, engaging in feeding the hungry, clothing the naked, visiting the sick and the imprisoned, and so on. All this is wonderful. But relatively few faith communities pursue the path of promoting structural change in their societies. To a large extent small units like parishes cannot do this well on their own; they need the support of the diocese or, better even, the regional or national Church. Unfortunately this is not usually forthcoming. Our Church is pretty good at promoting Church teaching on particular issues but far less effective at promoting the overall vision of society, which makes the single-issue stands that much more comprehensible.

Toward the end of the first chapter of this book we considered the purpose of the Church, what its mission might be, and identified the way of the Gospel today to be the promotion of everything that is in defense of human dignity and that combats the antihuman forces at work in the world. The promotion of human dignity, the furtherance of the common good, and the commitment to a "consistent ethic of life" are the pillars of a distinctly Catholic way of imagining and working for a better world. Together they constitute the foundations of what has come to be called Catholic Social Teaching. The problem with naming them that way is that they come to be seen as a subsection of Catholic teaching, sometimes even as a kind of optional extra. They are not well known to the faith community at large and are often referred to as "the Church's best-kept secret." When they are promoted and debated publicly they are rarely if ever treated with the same solemnity accorded more narrowly doctrinal issues, and the result is that they are not taken as seriously as they should be.

The vision of Christian praxis outlined in Catholic Social Teaching *is* the mission of the Church at the present day. It is not an optional extra; it is the responsibility for mission that we acquire at our baptism and shoulder as adults in our confirmation. The promotion of human dignity, work for the common good, and the espousal of a consistent ethic of life *are the ways in which we demonstrate the Church's love for God and love for our fellow human beings.* They are not a pious optional extra. They are not secondary to assent to Catholic doctrines like the Trinity or the divinity of Jesus or the Virgin Birth or whatever. They are principles we must proclaim loudly but, more important, put into practice fearlessly. As the great Hebrew prophets made clear over and over again, God is not impressed by claims to belief or acts of worship that are not a reflection of a community that does justice. The single most important measure of the faithfulness of the Hebrew people to the covenant with God is how they treat the weakest and most defenseless members of their own society.[19] The Church that possesses the wisdom of Catholic Social Teaching will be the more culpable for failing to put its own principles into practice, and will of course fail to persuade anyone else, however sublime its vision.

While small children should primarily be taught the stories of the Hebrew and Christian traditions as they are found in Scripture, adolescents and young adults need to be introduced to a working Church making a difference in the world by promoting a social vision that it is itself attempting to live out. They will not on the whole be impressed by being told to love the Church or to follow the teaching of the pope and the bishops. Taken in isolation they will not see the point of going to church, finding it frequently to be boring (which it often is) and being unimpressed by sermons that do not inspire (and many sermons sadly do not communicate the excitement of being Christian). They will be turned off by what they see as uncaring or unjust attitudes toward same-sex relationships, blanket condemnations of extramarital sex, or unfeeling rejection of divorced people. But if they can see the Church striving to make a positive difference in the world, with leaders who are in touch with the cares and concerns of real people, the spirituality they undoubtedly possess will encourage many more of them to make the connection between a Church of integrity and worshiping within the community.

The core meaning of the well-examined phrase, "I'm spiritual but I'm not religious," helps to clarify the nature of the problem that youth seem to have with religious belonging.[20] The phrase itself is more or less a plea to be considered a good person, even if not a churchgoer. There

---

[19] On this topic see the seminal article by John R. Donahue, "Biblical Perspectives on Justice," in *The Faith That Does Justice: Examining the Christian Sources for Social Change*, ed. John C. Haughey (New York: Paulist Press, 1977), 68–112.

[20] See Reid B. Locklin, *Spiritual but Not Religious? An Oar Stroke Closer to the Farther Shore* (Collegeville, MN: Liturgical Press, 2005).

is nothing in itself wrong with this; many a good person does not go to church regularly or even at all. There is absolutely no reason not to believe the claim to be spiritual while not religious, and there is lots of evidence that young people have just as deep an inner life as anyone else. However, the question that needs to be raised and that they ought to be ready to consider is whether the spirituality they claim might not be better with a more developed communal dimension to add to personal conviction. There is a deep wisdom to the Catholic Church's conviction that salvation is through the Church. While this sounds at times too regimented and it has sometimes worked that way, at bottom it rests upon a belief in the unity of the entire human race. The Church is, in a sense, the whole human race, and the claim for the centrality of the Church is more a statement about the universality of God's will to save all human beings than it is a stick with which to beat the lazy or the recalcitrant.[21]

Young people not only demonstrate higher energy levels than older ones, they also typically are "joiners," and the Church needs to evangelize the young by making the faith community into something people might actually want to join. Older people with a developed sense of themselves and their faith may be drawn to the Church for all kinds of reasons: loving the liturgy, appreciating the theological and cultural tradition, knowing and liking other Catholics, and so on. For the most part, young people are not there yet. If they are to commit themselves to the Church they have to see it as welcoming and relevant. It has to "get up to date," as they often say, which does not so much mean that it has to abandon less popular ethical teachings—though it might try to explain them better—but that it has to show how it is a player in the challenges our world faces today and in building a better society. Worship and belonging to a faith community make sense when this is where we make intentional our commitments, and where we see the close connection between love of God and love of our neighbor. Worship that is disconnected from our daily lives and the struggle for a better world will not only not appeal to the young; it will not appeal to God either.

The best approach for the Church in attracting and retaining young people lies in internal reform in two directions. We must find ways to speak more clearly about the vision of good life in society that is ex-

---

[21] This theme is discussed sublimely in Henri de Lubac's classic, *Catholicism: A Study of Dogma in Relation to the Corporate Destiny of Mankind* (London: Burns, Oates & Washbourne, 1949), esp. 4–33.

pressed in the body of Catholic social teachings, and we have to show in our practice that we abide by those principles ourselves. The worst turn-off is to be guilty of hypocrisy. And if we think about those two ways forward for even a moment, it is obvious enough that by fulfilling the second of the two we take a big step toward the first, while concentration on the first without the second will be an utter waste of time. On the whole the Church has tended not to see the connection between Catholic Social Teaching, which is understood as a program for social reform, and the inner life of the Church itself, far too many of the details of which are asserted to be of divine origin and thus, presumably, beyond reform. But if universal human dignity, the common good, and a consistent ethic of life are important in secular society, they surely ought to be as important in the community of faith. You cannot preach a special concern for the poor and weak members of world society if you ignore your own, and you cannot effectively insist on political leaders attending to the common good if ecclesial life seems to have its own class structure, differentiation of power, and serving of special interests. At that point, you do not even deserve to attract the young.

In order to bring about more consistency between social teaching and the life of the Church we need to see a number of reforms, in the first place in ecclesiastical administration. Rome itself has to change so that it is clear that the various Vatican departments serve the local churches around the world and do not dictate to them. This will be assisted by returning to a respect for national and regional bishops' conferences, which will make it easier for the Church to respond to more local concerns. But the single most significant step might be to elevate the periodic Synod of Bishops in Rome to the status of a deliberative body that debates openly the issues of the day. Currently the synods are mere talking shops, ostensibly to help the pope think something through, and so many of the really significant concerns are "off the table" before the debating begins. By the way, this is one of the few spots in inner-Church politics where the bishops could legitimately stage something of a palace revolution. Not to want to attend an event that is mere window dressing is entirely understandable. When you are as busy as most bishops are, staying away in large numbers would be a wonderful way to signal the synod's failure as an exercise of effective collegiality.

The way in which people are attracted into ordained ministry must change, even now before there is any loosening of the requirement of celibacy, so that all the "cultic" aspects that stress difference from the rest of God's people are eliminated. Most important of all is to break down a clerical structure that rewards ambition more than it does genuine pastoral leadership.[22] No one would want to deny that many of the parochial clergy and the bishops are wonderful men who give their lives generously in service to the Church. But at the same time we have to recognize that by and large those promoted to senior leadership in the Church come from the ranks of those who fashion their ecclesial careers to be noticed in this way. The ancient Church had a firm belief that a pastor or bishop was married to his local Church, so much so that moving to another community was considered to be a form of adultery. While it may be hard today to imagine that level of stability, there is no question that to understand pastoral ministry in such a way drives a stake into the heart of ecclesiastical careerism, and it would do wonders for the Church today. Ecclesiastical preferment for the talented, for sure, but only for the talented from among the ranks of the truly reluctant would be a great step forward.

Education for ministry must change too; any effort to train future priests in isolation from the people they will serve needs to come to an end. Yves Congar made this point very well some fifty years ago when he wrote of the need for Christians to become adults and added that "the laity cannot become more adult if the clergy do not become more adult too." For us today this means narrowing the gap between the worldview and lifestyle of laity and clergy. One important way forward that would benefit both would be to dismantle the current seminary system of education in favor of future clerics and laypeople studying alongside one another in properly accredited institutions of higher education. Future priests must be expected to study more theology and study it more seriously than they do today, but they also need to be grounded in the way people live and the problems they face. They need to know the tradition well and learn to apply it here and now, but they need also to know firsthand the trials and tribulations of ordinary living. Clearly many do, but many do not, or they did but they abandon it when they enter that strange clerical subculture that begins not so much at ordination as at the moment their seminary training begins.[23]

---

[22] See the powerful words of Cardinal Carlo Maria Martini, retired archbishop of Milan, as reported in the "Rome Diary" of Robert Mickens in *The Tablet*, June 14, 2008 (p. 34).

[23] Several works by Donald Cozzens, Catholic priest and former seminary rector, address various aspects of the crisis in the priesthood. See *The Changing Face of the Priesthood: A Reflection on the Priest's Crisis of Soul* (Collegeville, MN: Liturgical Press, 2000); and *Sacred Silence: Denial and the Crisis in the Church* (Collegeville, MN: Liturgical Press, 2002).

The conclusion of all this is that only when the Church shows a consistent face to the world as a community that practices what it preaches and is well adapted to the task of bringing the love of God to the world does it have a hope of bringing young people back into active participation. What we might call the devotional discipline of previous times is a thing of the past. It was tied to an understanding of the Church as a self-enclosed community of people, a true subculture within world society, for the most part turned in upon itself and functioning extraordinarily efficiently. Young adults have always been less participatory in the Church than children or older people, but it used to be said truly that once they married and especially when they had children, they returned to the Church in large numbers. They wanted their own children to be a part of this living tradition. Today it is not the same, because the Church exists in a pluralistic society as a faith community whose task is outwardly directed for the sake of the world. While the rich sacramental life of Catholicism is deeply important to the capacity of the Church to be what God wants of it, the point of reentry into the Church must be through its face of mission. This will lead to the face of devotion too, but without active mission to the world it will not command assent.

To bring this section to an end we need frankly to face the fact that the lifestyles of adolescents and young adults today are not comfortably accommodated within traditional Church teaching, especially on sexuality. Young people are simply uncomprehending in face of teachings about birth control, the use of condoms to reduce the spread of AIDS, homosexuality, and premarital sex. They are far less likely than their elders to accept the Church's teachings on abortion and on divorce. While we cannot lump together all these teachings as equally outdated or just plain wrong, we can ask the same question of all of them that we raised earlier in our consideration of women's roles in the Church: "Are we teaching the wrong things, or are we just teaching the right thing very badly, because people of goodwill just don't find it convincing?" Or, of course, is all this failure to comprehend and obey just one more example of human sinfulness?

Evidently when sex is the issue there can be a whole lot of self-deceit in order to follow our desires, but the problem here is that even if we could eliminate all sexual activity that is driven solely by lust and self-gratification, objectifying and exploiting a sexual partner, Church teaching would still oppose however much premarital sexual activity remained. If we could reduce all abortions in our society to those where the physical or psychological trauma of the pregnancy is overwhelming, Church teaching would still oppose those that remained. If everyone remained a virgin until after marriage and stayed faithful to their spouse, the use of the condom or the pill to regulate pregnancy and plan a family would remain suspect in the eyes of Church teaching. And when we turn to the other issues on our list, like treatment of divorced and remarried Catholics or GLBT Catholics or dealing with AIDS or overpopulation, disagreement with Church teaching is mostly motivated not by self-interest but by concern for the human family, and often for its most vulnerable members.

To help us to distinguish between our erroneous teaching and teaching that we are just not communicating effectively, we need to remind ourselves one more time of what exactly the Church *is*. One of the things that Yves Congar and Henri de Lubac, those two theological giants of the twentieth century, stressed when they wrote about the Church was that *we* are the Church. We should never say "Church" when we simply mean the institution, still less when we are talking about the hierarchy or the teaching authority. These are facets of the Church that at bottom is *us*. Vatican II said as much when it wrote so eloquently of the Church as the People of God and of the baptismal rights and responsibilities of all the faithful (and, by the way, the pope and the bishops are included within "the faithful"). What this is going to mean is that we the Church need to determine for ourselves what ethical teaching does or does not makes us more effectively the kind of loving and faithful community we need to be. One way to look at this might be to turn to see which ethical teachings further the consistent ethic of life that is central to Catholic Social Teaching. It is pretty obvious why teaching on the ethics of abortion or euthanasia or world hunger or just war or the death penalty relate directly to an ethic of life. These are the teachings we cannot abandon, though we certainly need to scrutinize them to determine which need to be clarified or nuanced. It is frankly a whole lot more difficult to see questions of birth control or other issues of personal sexuality as so central to the ethic of life. And when it comes to how we address the spread of AIDS or how we treat gays and lesbians or the divorced and remarried we can be forgiven for thinking that sometimes the way these teachings are presented seems to run counter to that concern for human life and its dignity that we proclaim.

Ethical teaching, especially personal and sexual ethics, is always a difficult area to deal with, because people want to do with their bodies what they want to do with them, and they do not always see that what we do with our bodies we are also doing with our souls. However, effective ethical teaching, precisely because of its sensitivity, is the prerogative of a teaching office that can be trusted in a Church that is aware of sexual sin, certainly, but not obsessed by it, and that can mitigate cold reasoning with the warmth of human compassion. The entrée into a life of self-discipline is going to be so much more likely if it is all placed in the context of a Church at work on its mission to the world and not so focused upon its own internal order that it becomes a barrier to the involvement of the young that the future of the Church depends upon.

The Scandal of Sexual Abuse

How can the Church ensure that the scandal of sexual abuse will become a thing of the past?

In the years since 2002 when the scandal of clerical sexual abuse of children and young people became public knowledge, the Church has been challenged to address its dysfunctions and own its shame. Sexual abuse accusations continue in the Church today and there is probably no reason to believe that abuse will ever entirely disappear, but as far as we can tell the seeds of this problem lie in the 1950s. In that decade, if not before, the American Catholic Church and others suffered from its own success, and institutional complacency set in. Large numbers of priests, seminarians, and religious men and women served the needs of a burgeoning Church of mostly passive lay Catholics. The social hierarchy of a clerical/lay Church was taken for granted, and the career structure of the clerical state itself was firmly in place. At its best and its pettiest this is visible to those who do not remember it in the pages of J. F. Powers's remarkable short stories and novels,[24] a salutary corrective to Bing Crosby's Fr. Chuck in *Going My Way* and *The Bells of St. Mary's*. These movies may themselves have been responsible for large numbers of "vocations" to the diocesan priesthood, but many of the candidates could no more match the muscular Christianity of Fr. Chuck than they could Crosby's crooning.

Self-deception seems to have played an enormous part in the sexual abuse scandal.[25] In the first place most of those who became abusers

---

[24] There are two novels, *Morte d'Urban* and *Wheat that Springeth Green*, and his *Collected Stories*, all recently republished by New York Review Books Classics (New York, 2000).

[25] The literature on the sexual abuse scandal is enormous. Among the best treatments are *Confronting Power and Sex in the Catholic Church: Reclaiming the Spirit of Jesus*, by Bishop Geoffrey Robinson (Collegeville, MN: Liturgical Press, 2008); and *Sin against the Innocents: Sexual Abuse by Priests and the Role of the Catholic Church*, ed. Thomas G. Plante (Westport, CT: Praeger, 2004).

surely did not set out to find a career in which they could be predators. Indeed, most of the abusers seem not to have lived lives as serial predators at all but to have been guilty of one or two instances of abuse, often early in their careers, and sometimes to have gone on to fairly positive lives as pastors. Far too many, of course, have preyed upon young people over a lifetime, often with what looks like collusion on the part of clerical authority. But even of these people it cannot be said with any conviction that they chose priesthood in order to be abusers. Indeed, it seems likely that the opposite is true; they became abusers because they chose priesthood.[26] They may have chosen it consciously for generous and worthy motives of service, but perhaps not with the self-knowledge or maturity to make that choice. Fifty years ago many young men entered seminary at the age of fourteen, and most were ordained before they were twenty-five years old, having never lived as adults in contact with laity of either sex, not even their siblings or parents. While it would be hard to argue convincingly that such seclusion *creates* abusers, it is equally hard to deny that it is not the best possible context in which to grow into personal spiritual and sexual maturity. Celibacy, for far too many of these men, was a refuge from their own sexuality and not—as it should be—a way of expressing it. Emerging from the seminary in their early twenties, the newly minted priests were thrown into parish life and often, because of their youth, assigned to responsibilities with the young people of the parish. Suddenly their selfhood as sexual beings was something they had to come to terms with in ways they had mostly not encountered before, and the wonder is that most of them negotiated this difficult transition successfully. Sadly, as we now know, many did not, and the tensions and fears and frustrations of the life of a young priest led them into inappropriate and sometimes frankly criminal behavior. The people they victimized will always remain the Church's primary responsibility, if only because for decades they were ignored or treated as if they were the problem. But, the classic pedophiles and the serial predators aside, abusing priests should also be seen as victims, this time as victims of a clerical system that signally failed to select and prepare its seminarians

---

[26] Many will dispute this interpretation of the cause of abuse, and it is by no means the only one. See George Weigel's *The Courage to Be Catholic: Crisis, Reform, and the Future of the Church* (New York: Basic Books, 2004), 68–72, where he enunciates the more conservative theory that a general decline in national mores and clerical discipline is to blame. But if this were so, why would abuse not be increasing in our progressively more sexualized culture, rather than (apparently and thankfully) declining?

appropriately, or to provide young clergy with an adequate affective support system for a lifetime of celibate commitment.

The self-deception of abusing priests seems not to have excited the anger of the laity, particularly those not directly affected by abuse, so much as the self-deception of generations of complacent clerical leadership. While some of the anger is directed toward a system in which fellow priests turned their backs on what they knew was going on in the bedrooms or weekend retreats of the abusers, the ire of the Church has mostly been vented upon the bishops. There are a number of reasons for this, not least that while the bishops obviously take a large share of the blame for failing to recognize and act on the problem, very few of them have been called to account. With the exception of Cardinal Law of Boston who resigned at the end of 2002, no U.S. bishop has lost his position because of failures in addressing the scandal of abuse, though a few have been removed because they themselves were abusers. Of course, many of the most egregious examples of neglectful behavior are no longer alive, and the current U.S. hierarchy is on the whole guiltier of ineffective handling of the problem rather than actually exacerbating it by moving predator priests around. But it seems safe to say that the Catholic laity expect more of their bishops than they have done in the past or than they seem to be doing in the present to lead the Church beyond the scandal. Looking forward to a day when sexual abuse in the Church will be a thing of the past, not a few Catholics think that the fundamental problem is systemic rather than psychological. In other words, the issue with bishops, as with abusers, is not their individual human weaknesses but a system that ignores and even encourages them.

The problem for bishops and clergy that contributes to a climate of lack of self-knowledge is, in a word, clericalism. "Clericalism" is not a way of denoting "the clergy," so that to say clericalism is a bad thing is to say that the clergy are bad people. On the contrary. Clericalism refers to the social system or subculture that has grown up around the clergy, which has over the years separated them from many of the normal dynamics of ordinary human life and kept the weaker among them from ever growing up. When things go wrong in any closed system, be it the clergy or the police or the legal system or Wall Street or Washington, the reform of the system cannot safely be left in the hands of those who have caused the problems. Most often in secular society we find a way to conduct independent inquiry and to try to fix the problems. In the Church as presently constituted, this is quite impossible. As we have seen earlier, all jurisdiction in the Church is held in the hands of those in Holy Orders, who collectively form the caste who populate clericalism. If criminal behavior is identified, the legal system has a role, but while the law can and should address sexual abuse on the part of the clergy, it cannot and will not attempt to redefine the lifestyle of the clergy in order to address the problem at its roots. And when, to their credit, the American bishops at their crisis meeting in Dallas in the summer of 2002 attempted to create boards in which some oversight of clerical behavior was assigned to responsible lay leadership, Rome said a firm no to the idea. Bishops, they implied, cannot be overseen by laypeople. But then, short of criminal behavior, who polices the police?

Within the ranks of episcopal leadership today some have identified a kind of collective failure of attention to the problems within the clerical life. Sometimes it seems as if the bishops do not or cannot recognize that the priesthood as we have known it is in crisis. The ranks of the clergy are declining in numbers and those reaching retirement each year vastly outnumber those being ordained. Both secular and religious order clergy are affected in similar fashion. The two most common responses to the problem, when it is addressed at all, are to pray for vocations and to import priests from other countries. The latter practice has not been a happy solution, either for many congregations or for many of the priests.[27] Praying for vocations in the Church is something that the faith community should always have time for. However, we need to recognize that vocations in general in the Church are as healthy as they always were, with large numbers of lay ecclesial ministers filling the gaps left by priests and religious sisters. We also need to couple our prayer for vocations with a nod to the imagination of the Holy Spirit. It may be that the priestly vocations of the future will not look like those of the past, though nothing the bishops say or do seems to envisage this possibility. Furthermore, those priests who are in ministry are stretched more thinly and are disproportionately older rather than younger. Add to this the fact that the mostly positive development of ordaining men a decade or so older than had been typical in the past means that the working life of a priest is correspondingly shorter. Even without a sexual abuse scandal much needs to be done to imagine and plan for the future shape of the ordained ministry, but it does not seem to be happening. Addressing the root causes of the scandal is also going to shine the searchlight on the way we select and prepare our future priests.

---

[27] See Laurie Goodstein's three-part article, "Divine Recruits," in *The New York Times*, December 28, 29, and 30, 2008.

If the bulk of the responsibility for the sexual abuse scandal lies with the bishops and the phenomenon of clericalism, it also has to be said that a mostly passive laity over the last century has contributed to the climate in which the problem could grow and flourish. This criticism of the laity has to be moderated by the fact that the laity in the Church until recent times were pretty much the creatures of clerical fashioning. The laity were who the priests said they were, and their responsibilities were those the priests allowed them. Even today Vatican II's clear declaration that it is the right and sometimes the responsibility of laypeople to speak out for the good of the Church (LG 37) is "more honored in the breach than in the observance." But in earlier days it was almost unimaginable that public lay critique of the clergy could have taken place. Until fifty years ago most Catholic laity were not well educated and had a habit of almost automatic deference to the priesthood that to a degree continues today. So both the victim of the abuse and the parents who learned of their child's ordeal were for a long time unlikely to bring it to the attention of pastor or bishop, and when they did were easily fobbed off with a "leave it to me" or a small check.[28]

Today laypeople in the Church are neither poorly educated nor likely not to speak up for their rights and responsibilities in secular society. In consequence, their responsibilities to speak in the Church are clear, and the failure to do so is a contributing factor, if not to the abuse itself, then at least to the conditions that made it possible and to the continuation of a system in which it will be hard to eradicate it entirely. Every instance of clerical abuse from now on will be on the conscience of those members of the Catholic laity who are not ready and willing to insist on full disclosure of the past and a wholehearted effort to make the structural changes that are needed to prevent its continuation into the future. We are either active and vocal in our determination to address all dimensions of the problem, or we are enablers. There is no other place to be. This is the simple consequence of the truth at the heart of all thinking about the nature of the Church over the last century: *We* are the Church. The problems of the Church are our problems, and the solutions lie in our hands. Not the clergy or the laity alone, but all of us, the whole Church, together.

While there are many structural changes that the Church must consider if the sexual abuse scandal is to be a thing of the past—and if it is

---

[28] An even-handed discussion of the respective responsibilities of laity and clergy for the dysfunctions of clericalism can be found in George Wilson, *Clericalism: The Death of Priesthood* (Collegeville, MN: Liturgical Press, 2008).

not to be replaced by a financial mismanagement scandal—the single most important move that we can make is to do whatever it takes to permeate the Church with the virtue of accountability. Accountability is such a simple idea, one with which every member of a family or worker in a company of whatever size is familiar. The health of the family or company requires that all its members recognize their responsibility to and for one another, that they act with honor and self-discipline in the best interests of the group, and that they own their failures. If this does not happen the family falls apart or at best limps along, the company fires you or closes down. In an institution like the Church, the accountability we need must work a little like the way it does in the family and must also have some characteristics of institutional accountability. As in a family, it must transcend structures, but like the institution, it must have them. It requires a sense of ownership and pride that comes from knowing you count. But it also needs open two-way structures through which the sense of ownership is realized and supported. The changes that this will require are matters we will turn to in chapter 3 of the book.

External Challenges

Ecumenism

How can the Catholic Church best fulfill its responsibilities to other Christian communities?

As we turn outward to consider some of the challenges the Church faces in its mission, the notion that we have responsibilities to other Christian bodies may seem an odd one. It is certainly not the way that the Church has typically thought of the issue. On the contrary, *they* have usually been considered the ones with the responsibility, namely, to recognize the errors of their ways and to heal history and Christianity by returning to the welcoming arms of the Roman Catholic Church. Indeed, the first genuine ecumenical breakthrough in Catholic theology came in 1937 with Yves Congar's first book, *Divided Christendom*,[29] a text that still reads today with extraordinary freshness. In some ways the liturgical movement that began in Europe in the middle of the nineteenth

---

[29] Yves Congar, *Divided Christendom: A Catholic Study of the Problem of Reunion* (London: Centenary, 1939).

century had laid some groundwork, for it crossed denominational lines and Congar recognized his debt to it. But it was with Congar's substantial discussion of the issues and, above all, because of the gentle tone in which his book was written that ecumenism began to emerge in Catholic circles. Ironically, Rome continued for some time to forbid Congar to participate in the very ecumenical conferences that had been enlivened by his work.

Over the years since Congar wrote and particularly in the decades since the council there have been many formal ecumenical exchanges between the Catholic Church and other Christian bodies, and conversations continue. Relations have certainly improved with three conversation partners in particular, the Orthodox, Anglican, and Lutheran churches. In the case of Orthodoxy, most theological differences are minor and the biggest obstacle to overcome in any rapprochement—beyond the hurts of history—is the fear that the great theological and liturgical traditions of the Orthodox churches would disappear in any future union with the much larger Roman Catholic Church. The Catholic Church distinguishes between the challenges of its relationship with Orthodoxy and with Protestantism, making clear that the former is a genuine Church while resisting referring to Protestant denominations in quite the same way. But the Catholic/Anglican dialogues made considerable headway, especially on the question of the validity of orders and the understanding of Eucharist, and the Catholic/Lutheran dialogues produced a major joint statement on justification, the principal bone of contention between the two churches over the centuries. Church judgments about the possibility of further convergence, as we shall see in a little more detail below, are based on the presence or absence of a true sacramental tradition, on a determination of the validity of orders, and on some major theological disagreements.[30]

The formal dialogues between church bodies are complemented, informed, and at times challenged by the less formal exchanges of theologians of all confessions, though of course theologians have always played a part alongside church leaders in the various official dialogues. But the work of theology, proceeding as an academic discipline, is often ahead of the deliberations of formal conversations. In fact, this is generally true of the relationship between public opinion and official pronouncements in many areas of human society, and it is in the nature of

---

[30] For a primer on the current state of ecumenical dialogue, consult *Receptive Ecumenism and the Call to Catholic Learning: Exploring a Way for Contemporary Ecumenism*, ed. Paul D. Murray (Oxford: Oxford University Press, 2008).

ecclesial life too. The body of believers may demonstrate a wide range of opinions and beliefs on issues great and small, but Church pronouncements are far more often the authentication of matters that have become the actual belief of the Church than they are initiatives to change or curtail those beliefs. Authority in the Church is not itself the process by which belief develops but the process by which beliefs are recognized as authentic. Of its nature, therefore, the papal exercise of authority, even infallible authority, is intended as a clarification of the *sensus fidelium*, not a correction of it. Since, as Vatican II points out, both are exercises of the Holy Spirit, the idea that the Spirit could be divided within itself should make us theologically uneasy.

The work of theologians is an investigation of truth, conducted in dialogue with others in the academic community and bound neither by institutional caution nor by the pragmatic implications of the directions in which their research may be leading them. It seems safe to say that the nature of this process is neither particularly well understood nor much valued in today's Catholic Church, especially when these theological opinions—for this is all that theologians produce—are disseminated among the faith community as a whole and seem to run counter to some official positions. In the ambit of ecumenical relations, one of the most obvious of these differences is over the nature of apostolic tradition, to which is connected the question of the validity of ordination in ecclesial communities other than the Catholic Church. While many theologians want to stress continuity with the apostolic *faith* as what is crucial for the "mark" of apostolicity, the teaching Church seems to give pride of place to the physical, historical continuity of ordination itself.[31] Many theologians too would read contemporary Christian pluralism as a reflection of the variety of ecclesiologies at work in the early Church, while the official Catholic position interprets it as a failure to recognize the emergence of "early Catholicism" in the second century as the resolution of the debates over the nature of the Church. All of this leads to disagreement over the ways in which we should understand the relationships between the various Christian churches and the Catholic tradition.

All these differences between the official positions of the various churches and the unofficial theological convictions of theologians from all the churches came to a head in the response to *Dominus Iesus,* a document issued by the Vatican's Sacred Congregation for the Doctrine of

---

[31] See John J. Burkhard, *Apostolicity Then and Now: An Ecumenical Church in a Postmodern World* (Collegeville, MN: Liturgical Press, 2004).

the Faith in the year 2000 and signed by the then Cardinal Joseph Ratzinger, Prefect of the Congregation.[32] Chapter 4 of the document considers the situation within and among Christian ecclesial communities. It first argues for the unity of the Church as an intention of Christ and a guarantee of the Spirit and then goes on to say that "the Catholic faithful *are required to profess* that there is an historical continuity—rooted in the apostolic succession—between the Church founded by Christ and the Catholic Church." Using the language of *Lumen Gentium*, the Sacred Congregation adds that "this Church, constituted and organized as a society in the present world, subsists in [*subsistit in*] the Catholic Church, governed by the Successor of Peter and by the Bishops in communion with him." The phrase "subsists in" was preferred by the council fathers over the simple "is." *Dominus Iesus* explains that the phrase serves two purposes. It makes the point that this one Church of Christ "continues to exist fully only in the Catholic Church," while at the same time it recognizes that "many elements . . . of sanctification and truth" can be found in "those Churches and ecclesial communities which are not yet in full communion with the Catholic Church." However, these other Christian bodies "derive their efficacy from the very fullness of grace and truth entrusted to the Catholic Church." Finally, in the context of praising these churches and ecclesial communities for their "significance and importance in the mystery of salvation," the document adds that "we believe they suffer from defects."[33]

Dominus Iesus was met with howls of protest from ecumenical partners offended by the language of "defect" and by Catholic theologians who challenged the interpretation of the phrase "subsists in." The word "defect" is an unfortunate choice, if only for diplomatic reasons. The point that the document seeks to make is that the Catholic Church contains all the elements of what it is to be Church (though it does so imperfectly), while all other Christian traditions, simply because they do not share full communion with the Catholic Church, are lacking that comprehensiveness. But "defect," still more "defective," inescapably suggests in English some kind of moral deficiency, which the document presumably does not mean to impute to Orthodox or Protestant churches. As for "subsists in," the question is the significance of the change of wording from "the one Church of Christ *is* the Catholic Church" to "subsists in" the Catholic Church. *Dominus Iesus* takes this to mean that

---

[32] *Dominus Iesus* is available at http://www.usccb.org/pope/doctrineoffaith.htm.
[33] Ibid., 16–17.

only the Catholic Church has the fullness of what it is to be a Church; others wondered if it could mean that the fullness of what it is to be Church is not exclusive to the Catholic Church.[34]

Ultimately, more important than either Church statement or theological opinion has been the impact of all kinds of cultural factors upon the Catholic population, changing their perception of "non-Catholic" Christians and, indeed, of non-Christian religions. Surveys like those of D'Antonio, Davidson, and others that we have previously mentioned indicate that Catholics continue to think there is something special about their own tradition while roundly rejecting any suggestion that other religions or other Christian traditions are somehow lesser. Large majorities of those questioned agreed that "so long as you believe in God it doesn't matter which tradition you belong to,"[35] a statement that seems as generous to theists as it is apparently ignorant of the nontheistic dimensions of Eastern religions. However, when we take these apparently conflicting points of view together the position of the *sensus fidelium* may not be all that far from official Church theology. Before and behind the inadequacies of *Dominus Iesus* is the belief that the Church of Christ is bigger than the Catholic Church and that other Christian traditions also share in it. Yes, the Church of Christ subsists in the Catholic Church, but there is a certain healthy agnosticism about the extent to which it is present in other churches. Moreover, there are good reasons to believe that both Vatican II and John Paul II did not intend the term "ecclesial community" as a kind of relegation of Protestant traditions to a second class status.[36] So when lay Catholics claim a special status for their own tradition but do not proceed to assign lesser status to other Christian communities, their beliefs express a solidly ecumenical theology.

The truth of the matter of ecumenical relations is that a posture of humility and service works, while arrogance does not. Theologically speaking this means that the Church has to banish everything from its proclamations on ecumenical relations in which it appears that unity is a matter of other traditions recognizing their need to come closer to the

---

[34] There is an excellent discussion of *Dominus Iesus* in a lecture given at the Centro Pro Unione in Rome in 2001 by the distinguished Notre Dame theologian, Richard P. McBrien, available at http://www.sedos.org/english/McBrien.htm. McBrien argues cogently that the document both misinterprets Vatican II and is at some variance with the views of John Paul II in his encyclical on ecumenism, *Ut Unum Sint*.

[35] William V. D'Antonio and others, *American Catholics Today: New Realities of Their Faith and Their Church* (Lanham, Md.: Rowman & Littlefield, 2007), 30–35.

[36] See the McBrien article referenced in n. 34 above.

Catholic Church, in which the Church of Christ "subsists." As Yves Congar tried to explain some seventy years ago, all the Churches are in process of change, the Catholic Church no less than the others.[37] If Christian unity is to be real in the future it will come about when changed Protestant churches and a changed Catholic Church find their way together into a unity within the one Church of Christ. We can certainly make claims for the way in which our own tradition is an instantiation of the Church of Christ, but we would do well not to be quite so sure about how other traditions stand. We simply do not know whether their differences from the Catholic Church have any bearing on how they stand vis-à-vis the one Church of Christ. And we would do well to meditate frequently on those things they do so much better than we.

The responsibility of the Catholic Church to other Christians can best be carried out, it would seem, by recognizing how the Spirit is guiding the whole of the Catholic faithful toward a healthy estimation of our own tradition that does not need to be negative about others. This can of course require the teaching authority to tweak the *sensus fidelium* at times, but the constant emphasis in *Dominus Iesus* on the need for obedience is quite out of place. Following Congar again, the virtue of obedience is not the only or indeed the most important virtue of Catholics. A prayerful people are guided by the Holy Spirit toward truth in a climate of gospel freedom. When this is working right, obedience is unnecessary. In a faithful people the default mode cannot be correction; while the celebration of God's presence among all Christians cannot be without at least a little oversight, caution and reserve should be distinctly secondary to joy and hope in the coming of the reign of God. And *all* Christians live in and celebrate that hope.

Religious Pluralism

How can the Church grow into a healthier grasp of its relationship to the other great religious traditions of the world?

The biggest difference between religious pluralism and ecumenism is that while all Christian traditions see Christ as their unique Savior and thus have far more in common than they have that separates them, only Christianity among the world's great religions accepts Jesus Christ as Savior. Though this is obvious enough, it has major implications for how

---

[37] Congar, *Divided Christendom*, 249–75.

the Christian churches proceed to enter into dialogue with Buddhism or Hinduism or Islam. To suggest to a Methodist that he or she is saved through membership in the one Church of Christ is hardly controversial. To tell a Jew that her salvation, whether she knows it or not, is through Christ would be a very difficult message to communicate, one almost impossible for the Jew to hear at all. And while the Church's claim to being somehow a fuller expression of Christianity than other churches might occasion only humor, frustration, or mild disbelief, to say that other religions are saved through Christ, whether they like it or not, is potentially much more scandalous.

Dominus Iesus is central to considering how the teaching Church sees the place of non-Christian religions in the plan of salvation. But while it received similarly negative reactions from world religious leaders as it did from the Christian churches, the insistence on Christ as the one universal Savior is addressed more to Catholic theologians whom Rome deemed to be in error than it is to Buddhists or Muslims. The great world religions, like Christianity itself, proceed on their own paths in their own ways without giving a whole lot of attention to what the Catholic Church has to say about them. Of course, they do not respond well to what they perceived to be gratuitous insults—who would?—but in a certain way they would not expect anything other than that Catholicism would be as convinced of the special character of its own revelation as they are of the wisdom of theirs. Indeed, the Catholic Church today is almost invariably courteous and respectful in its comments on other religions and in its treatment of their leaders. Vatican II recognizes that all religions convey saving truth to their adherents, and the Church does not commonly try to instruct Buddhists and Hindus that their salvation is through Christ. However, Rome is much exercised when Catholic theologians seem to them to be in the process of reinterpreting Jesus Christ as one savior among others. In recent years Rome has been suspicious of a number of theologians who, while they are not mentioned by name in *Dominus Iesus*—encyclicals and Vatican documents in general rarely name names—are evidently the targets of criticism.[38]

While *Dominus Iesus* is directed more at Catholic theologians' "errors" than it is at those of world religions, its argument helps us understand

---

[38] See as examples of those targeted but not always named: Jacques Dupuis, *Who Do You Say I Am? Introduction to Christology* (Maryknoll, NY: Orbis, 1994); Paul F. Knitter, *One Earth Many Religions: Multifaith Dialogue and Global Responsibility* (Maryknoll, NY: Orbis, 1995); Roger Haight, *Jesus: Symbol of God* (Maryknoll, NY: Orbis, 2000).

how the Church has traditionally seen its relationship to the latter. Quoting Vatican II, the Congregation writes that "the deepest truth about God and the salvation of man shines forth in Christ, who is at the same time the mediator and the fullness of all revelation." In consequence, "[t]he Christian dispensation" as "the new and definitive covenant, will never pass away, and we now await no further new public revelation before the glorious manifestation of our Lord Jesus Christ."[39] "Only the revelation of Jesus Christ, therefore," the document adds, quoting John Paul II's encyclical *Fides et Ratio*, "introduces into our history a universal and ultimate truth which stirs the human mind to ceaseless effort."[40] What theologians do not seem to understand, the document argues, is the difference between revelation and mere wisdom. "Faith, therefore, as *'a gift of God'* and as *'a supernatural virtue infused by him,'*" is a "dual adherence" both to God and to the truth God reveals. For this reason:

> [T]he distinction between *theological faith* and *belief* in the other religions, must be *firmly held*. If faith is the acceptance in grace of revealed truth, which "makes it possible to penetrate the mystery in a way that allows us to understand it coherently,"[41] then belief, in the other religions, is that sum of experience and thought that constitutes the human treasury of wisdom and religious aspiration, which man in his search for truth has conceived and acted upon in his relationship to God and the Absolute.[42]

In other words, Christianity is the wisdom of God; the other religions are human wisdom. To be respected for sure, but just not on the same level. Ultimately, their explanation—the answer to the human yearning for religious truth—is to be found only in Christ, if *Dominus Iesus* is to be believed.

The Vatican critique of these unnamed theologians is occasioned by a fear of relativism which, at its starkest, would simply say that while Christianity is true for Christians, the teaching of the Buddha performs exactly same role for Buddhists, and the Buddha's teaching cannot and need not be seen as a kind of stealth Christian revelation. The arguments over whether one theologian or another really maintains such a

---

[39] *Dominus Iesus* 5, quoting *Dei Verbum* 2.

[40] *Dominus Iesus* 6, quoting *Fides et Ratio* 14. *Fides et Ratio* is John Paul II's encyclical letter on the relationship of faith and reason, available at http://www.vatican.va/holy_father/john_paul_ii/encyclicals/documents/hf_jp-ii_enc_15101998_fides-et-ratio_en.html.

[41] *Fides et Ratio* 13.

[42] *Dominus Iesus* 7, quoting *Fides et Ratio* 31–32.

position are complex and need not detain us here. But a way beyond the arguments themselves that might aid not only in reconciling Rome and its theologians but also in stimulating interreligious dialogue is to be found in the text of *Dominus Iesus* itself. In the act of proclaiming traditional Catholic teaching that "the words, deeds, and entire historical event of Jesus . . . have nevertheless the divine Person of the Incarnate Word, 'true God and true man' as their subject," they add parenthetically that they are "limited as human realities." And when they draw the conclusion that "they possess in themselves the definitiveness and completeness of the revelation of God's salvific ways," they add the disclaimer, "even if the depth of the divine mystery in itself remains transcendent and inexhaustible."[43]

There is no way for Christians in general and Catholics in particular to see Christ as anything other than the perfect revelation of God in history and to understand Scripture and Sacred Tradition as anything other than divinely inspired testimony to this revelation. The mystery of salvation is located in the person of Jesus Christ revealed in his death and resurrection as God's saving presence in history. Scripture and Tradition are witnesses to and avenues of the revelation that is Christ to believers and, through them, to the whole human race. It would be a strange Christianity that did not adhere to this belief, and it would be looked on askance by members of other world religions, who would surely wonder what kind of faith it was that could harbor a profound relativism about the boundaries of its saving message. The teaching of the Buddha and the Holy Qur'an are understood by Buddhists and Muslims respectively to be universally applicable religious truth, and Christians would surely laugh aloud if a Buddhist or a Muslim said these were true only for the adherents of their religious traditions. When the Buddha teaches that the soul or ego understood as a transhistorical reality is an illusion, he is not speaking just about Buddhist souls. When the Muslim creed proclaims that "there is no God but God and Mohammed is his prophet," they are not silently adding (but only for Muslims). All religions, of their nature, intend their truths as universally applicable.

The mistake the teaching Church can sometimes be guilty of is not the claim to universally applicable saving truth but, rather, an overconfident judgment of the degree to which we comprehend the divine mystery itself. God's revelation to Christians is not a book or a tradition but a person who is accessible to us in a number of ways, none of them

---

[43] *Dominus Iesus* 6.

entirely free of the ambiguity that surrounds any mystery. We find Jesus Christ in the Scriptures in the form of parable and miracle, and we find him again in the historical memory of the whole faithful people throughout history, which we name Tradition, and which is guided by Church teachers from the early fathers to the present-day pope and bishops. And we meet him a third time in the silence of our hearts at prayer, and a fourth time in our human brothers and sisters in the world we share. In all these ways, Jesus Christ the revelation of God is present to us. But not one of them is obvious and unambiguous; were it so, the virtue of faith—fidelity to hope—would not be required of us. And because this is the way it is, we have to be very careful not to think we know all there is to know about how God's gracious revelation in Christ is present in the world.

The gift of the Holy Spirit to the Church to guide us into all truth means that in various ways the Church teaches and believes with a certain "infallibility," but this charism or gift of the Spirit most certainly does not mean that we now know—infallibly or otherwise—everything there is to know about the workings of God in history. Pope and bishops teach infallibly in particular circumstances. The body of the faithful live their faith in the same infallibility. But the gift of the Spirit to the Church means that portions of divine mystery are illuminated for us, not that we have the whole mystery of God under floodlights, where every nook and cranny is clearly visible. Saint Paul's words in 1 Corinthians make this point very well: "For now we see through a glass, darkly; but then face to face: now I know in part; but then shall I know even as also I am known" (1 Cor 13:12, KJV). The fullness of revelation is reserved to the reign of God, where one day we shall know perfectly what here and now we know only in part, and "darkly" at that. Were this not so, the great adventure of a life of faith, of fidelity to hope, would become a flat and boring awaiting of the inevitable. Purgatory would be here and now.

The way in which God's salvation in Christ is present in other religions is one of the more mysterious dimensions of revelation. Christians are committed to the belief that salvation is through Christ. At least since Vatican II, Catholicism has insisted that other world religions are the context for the salvation of their adherents and that nonbelievers come to God (presumably through Christ) by way of living authentically according to their deepest values and convictions. Catholics then are entirely consistent when they proclaim Christ as the universal sacrament of salvation but respect and revere as "saving" those religious traditions in which Christ is invisible. The practice of the Church evidently substantiates this; why else would we treat Buddhists and Muslims and all the others with reverence as people of faith? Moreover, the reverence they deserve means that while we would be inauthentic if we backed away from belief in Christ as universal Savior, we would be disrespectful to the mystery of God's revelation to treat world religions as if they were some poor substitute for Christianity, destined to disappear. One day, in the reign of God beyond history, Christianity will disappear too. Christianity is a means to an end, the reign of God, and world religions are means to that same precise end.

The problem for the teaching Church is that while it wants to treat world religions exactly as we have just described them, and most of the time these days it succeeds, it has to deal with its own and does a poor job of understanding the ecclesial role of the theologian. The Church cherishes, proclaims, and lives by divine revelation. The theologian tries to understand. A theologian works *liminally*, that is, as a kind of frontier person, on the boundaries between what we know and what we do not know. No theologian, anymore than any Church leader, can produce new revelation, but it is the theologian's role in the Church to explore the boundaries of what can be said. It is the role of the teaching authority in the Church to determine, eventually, which of these liminal explorations are consistent with revelation and which are not. And just as the theologian has to respect the tradition and explore it faithfully, so the bishop has to practice patience. Theology is a kind of foraging or scouting expedition into unknown territory, and it cannot be rushed. A theologian carries maps and guides and sends reports back home from stages along the way, but the theologian is not really sure where she or he will end up. Some explorations will result in dead ends, and some will be abandoned. But sometimes you get to the right place by following a more circuitous route than those with direct pastoral concerns find easy to understand. On the other hand, theologians do occasionally need to remind themselves that the objective of their work is a fuller appreciation of the Gospel for the whole community of faith, not just their professional confreres.

The Church and Political Life

What is the role of the Church in political life?

This challenge for the Church is a question that subdivides when we examine it. What are we asking here? Are we interrogating the role of the community of faith in the political culture wherever it happens to be in the world? Or are we asking about the role of Church leadership in teaching the faithful about appropriate political attitudes? That is certainly one way to cut the cake. But we might also be asking about how the whole Church or its leadership might intervene on a local, regional, national, or international scale. The parish or the diocese can be a major influence in the local context, and the Vatican surely exercises its role as religious leadership and its status as a nation-state to make its opinion heard and its influence felt on the world stage. And there is a third way to approach this issue, as a debate between those who believe the world would be the better for a more concerted religious impact and those who see the Church primarily as a body of people gathered to worship, moving through history rather than acting upon it. We might see these as the proponents of radical separation of church and state in a face-off with equally radical Christian activists.

Before addressing any of the questions we might ask in this investigation, and leading us toward one or another way of answering them, we need to remind ourselves of what we said earlier about the nature of the Church and especially of its mission. In discussing the mark of the eternity of the Church in chapter 1 we said that there is a Church *when* there is an identifiable community, however small, bound together by the common experience that the loving care of God for them is supremely available in their intimacy with the story of Jesus Christ. Obviously enough, over the centuries the Church acquired many more characteristics and a whole institutional structure that, while not strictly necessary, certainly identify the Catholic Church of the present day. But the simpler description maintains its importance in this way; if the Catholic Church could not recognize itself as a community bound together by the common experience that the loving care of God for them is supremely available in their intimacy with the story of Jesus Christ, it would not truly be a Christian Church. The simple description does not say everything, but it contains the essentials. It also issues a challenge to the complex religious institutions that have developed over the centuries, among them the Roman Catholic Church. No political involvement that is inconsistent with being a community fired by the experience of the love of God in Jesus Christ has any place in Catholicism, or indeed in any other Christian faith community.

The license for political involvement must come from the Church's mission. What is not part of its mission is, by definition, not part of the Church. As we saw earlier, mission is always evangelization, but "preaching the good news" is often something done indirectly and frequently more by dint of living a certain way than by proclamation in a narrower sense. We discovered in the discussion of mission in chapter 1 that the good news that Jesus is the sacrament of God's love in the world unfolds into the revelation of God's loving concern for each one of us, God's wish that creatures God has chosen to make in the divine image and likeness will find their way individually and collectively to a deeper and richer human existence in the world that is their home. The more like God we become, the more and more fully loving we will be, and the bonds of love that tie the human family together will be the stronger. Evangelization, then, is humanization and humanization is divinization. Our unity with God in Christ is directly connected to our solidarity with our brothers and sisters around the world, particularly with those who are poor or defenseless in any way.

God's love is fierce and abiding, not sentimental or fleeting, and the love of God's Church for the world God has created must demonstrate the same characteristics. While God is not fickle, human beings most often are. Yesterday's crisis is just old news, even if it continues, and the failure of nation-states to address anything not in the national interest is matched by our individual capacity to shut our hearts to pain and suffering that does not directly impinge upon us. If the kid next door breaks her leg we try to help if we can and we take her chocolate or a gift card. If there is a death in the family we grieve and we reach out to one another. But we live our lives cheerfully and to a degree generously against a background of worldly misery that, if we attended to it even a little, would spoil our appetites for the good things in life. Countless thousands of children die every day from preventable diseases and malnutrition, while we fuss about taxes or the difficulty of finding parking spaces. Even worse, most of the time we go to church we receive the Eucharist and leave with lightened hearts, though the world into which the Eucharist came as the symbol of God's love for all just hasn't made an appearance in the liturgy.

It is because we are weak and sinful people that we have to structure our solidarity with the world's afflicted. Without structures, sinfulness will always defeat love because love will be pure sentimentality. Marriage structures human partnership and family against the depredations of time. Ritual structures worship. Regularity that can at times seem stultifying orders the monastic life. The liturgical calendar gives shape to our awareness of the story of our salvation. Community organizing helps to make the good intentions of people more lastingly effective. And politics shapes and gives expression to the values of our societies, or so it is intended to do. Without political life, we would have well-meaning chaos at best, a dog-eat-dog power struggle at worst. Good political life rises above both these failures, while ineffectual political life illustrates both of them perfectly. When we are disillusioned with our political leaders, it is most usually because we feel that they are not acting for the good of the nation or the world. They fail not because politics is venal but because bad politics is venal. Good politics is hope and possibility for the world.

That the mission of the Church to bring the human community to a fuller sense of its own need to fashion a world of fundamental human dignity is inescapably political is evident in the fundamental principles of Catholic Social Teaching. We discussed these principles earlier in this chapter when we looked at how the young can be brought to a closer identification with the Church. Here we shall not repeat that discussion but simply point out that Catholic Social Teaching as a whole offers a consistent vision of the good society. It is not reducible to a set of policies or programs, and by and large the Church stays away from endorsing particular political initiatives or favoring one party over another. However, its social teaching is derived not so much from Scripture as from ethical theory, particularly that of the natural law, and this has two important consequences. One is that the teaching is open to debate in the public arena precisely because it does not depend on biblical authority. And the second is that for just the same reason, the principles are considered universally applicable. They derive not from revelation but from reason, and therefore they can be argued as universally binding on the whole human race. A belief in human dignity or the commitment to the common good are not for Catholics alone, or just for Christians or theists. They are for everyone. As a consequence, Catholics or the Catholic Church as political actors are really bound to argue and defend the vision of human society enshrined in Catholic Social Teaching. And this is where trouble can begin, especially in a society like the United States where constitutional separation of church and state is sometimes taken to mean that religious traditions as such have no right to involve themselves in secular affairs.

While the constitutional separation of church and state does not mean that religious bodies may not have a voice in public policy issues, it rightly suggests that the primary way people of faith should be involved in political life is as individual citizens rather than corporately. The Catholic influence in public life is in the first instance a matter for Catholic politicians and activists, who as citizens have just the same rights as others, but who as Catholics have a responsibility to give expression to the fundamental principles of Catholic Social Teaching. This teaching is a way of articulating a major component of the mission of the Church, to struggle against the antihuman forces at work in our world, and all Catholics in virtue of their baptism are charged with that mission in the world. The role of the institution qua institution is twofold: it has a responsibility to educate Catholics about the content of Catholic Social Teaching, and it must stand ready to intervene as a body when what is at stake is so important that the work of individuals threatens to be ineffectual. On the whole it has a done a poor job of education. It has a better record of speaking out on issues, usually managing quite successfully to keep them in the public's awareness and to be clear about the Catholic response to them. In a pluralistic society such as our own this is about as much as can be expected or desired. Individual Catholics should be educated on the principles that guide our social and political vision, and the Church should see to it that major issues remain in the public eye and that the Catholic position on them is clear and unequivocal. However, politics being politics, the Church as Church finds it difficult to engage in the debate and compromise that is the stuff of public life. Ethics is about principles, politics is "the art of the possible," and there are going to be conflicts.

The example of Catholic attitudes toward abortion in American society is illustrative of how complex it can be to mix ethics and politics. The ethical position of the Catholic Church is clear. Since it believes that human life begins at the moment of conception and since the Church is committed to the protection of all life, especially that which is defenseless, the Church is opposed to the termination of pregnancies. The political situation of American society is equally clear. Since Roe v. Wade was settled by the Supreme Court, abortion within certain parameters is legal. But once we get beyond these facts, things rapidly begin to unravel. All Americans are faced with the question of how they balance legal rights that all have against ethical values that all may not necessarily share. The Catholic Church also has to deal with the fact that while most Catholics would consider themselves pro-life rather than pro-choice (an ethical position), the majority seem not to favor efforts to overturn the legal protection of abortion (a political position). It is safe to say that the teaching Church has not figured out how to address this particular apparent discrepancy. The ethical issue is not the issue of abortion, on which a majority of Catholics take a pro-life position, but that of the right and wisdom of one sector of society to overturn a law that exists for the sake of the entire population. Of course Catholics or any other body within American society can and should speak up for positions on which they feel strongly, but it would seem wiser to lobby the American population to change its positions rather than lobby Congress or the Supreme Court to do something that the American people as a whole might not support. In the presidential election campaigns of 2004 and 2008 we saw the spectacle of selected candidates for Senate, House, or Presidency pilloried for their positions on abortion, which seems not to take into account the complexity of the roles of someone holding elected office, not to mention their duty to uphold the law.

For the teaching Church to take a backseat position and let the Catholic people as a whole lead the way in representing a faithful political ethic requires that the Church do an effective teaching job. The failures here are lamentable, and the responsibility has to be shared. On the side of individual Catholics, especially those with any public visibility, whatever their positions on particular ethical/political issues, they had better be able to articulate clearly what their Church teaches. This is the more important if they are going to take a position at variance with that teaching. But it is the teaching Church that in the end bears the responsibility, because of factors we have already encountered once or twice in the book. If there is a big discrepancy between what the teaching Church proclaims to be Catholic truth and what at least a sizeable minority of Catholics seem to believe, then *either* the Church is teaching poorly *or* it is teaching the wrong thing. While on particular issues it may be teaching the wrong thing, when we face—as we do—a faithful Church here in the United States in which frankly the people do not pay a whole lot of attention to the pronouncements of the teaching Church, then the more probable answer is that the pedagogy is at fault.

If pedagogical failure rather than erroneous teaching is the likelier cause of faithful Catholics' failure to know, understand, or follow the teachings of the Church, the problem is compounded by a decline in respect for the teaching authority. While this is often explained in these times as fallout from the poor episcopal performance in recognizing and handling the scandal of clerical sexual abuse, other factors play a part. One of them, rightly or wrongly, is a growing sense that the clerical state—especially the level of the episcopate—is a poor vantage point from which to appreciate the way in which most people in our society live and the pressures they face day in and day out. A second and related factor, which is probably not something of which most laypeople are aware but seems to be significant, is that those with the most extensive experience of the ethical problems at issue are rarely if ever involved in informal ways in the development of ethical teaching and never formally responsible for that teaching. There is no reason in principle that male celibate clergy living within a clerical culture should be considered disqualified to speak on issues of marital fidelity, the regulation of birth, or the challenges of being divorced and remarried. But a Church where being a male celibate is a requirement for teaching with authority on just such issues has a really uphill struggle to persuade people that it knows whereof it speaks.

Building on the Strengths of the Church

What are the strengths of the Church that it needs to build on?

Inevitably when we focus on the challenges to any community or organization the picture can seem too critical. No doubt this chapter about challenges to the Church has seemed that way at times, and so it is appropriate to end this chapter and lead into the third and final more constructive phase with a different kind of challenge. For all its difficulties and the challenges it faces, the Roman Catholic Church is one of the great phenomena of world history and home to more of God's people than any other religious body. One can be disturbed about this or that thing going on in the Church without it reducing one's sense of belonging. There is no guarantee that the feeling that this is my Church will never be eroded, and there is some evidence that younger generations do not share the same fundamental loyalties as their elders, even if they are participants in Church life. But on the whole, Catholics are happy to be Catholics. The surveys we have mentioned earlier show that overwhelming numbers of those polled, even if they are not frequent participants in the liturgical life of the Church, are proud to call themselves Catholics and want their children to grow up the same way. Indeed, one of the signs of hope in the Catholic Church today is the growing sense among the laity that they may have to fight for the Church more than they did in the past but that it is something worth fighting for. So what are the principal strengths on which the Church would be wise to build? We will list a few of them, and they will reappear in the final chapter of the book, where we shall sketch a vision of the Church moving forward.

First among the strengths of Catholicism must be its liturgical life. Even when, as is often the case, the weekly parish liturgy is conducted in a less than inspiring manner, it is the center of the spiritual life of the community. Access to the Eucharist is vital to the life of the Church, but even more important, it is the heart of every Catholic's spirituality. If

Vatican II was a little harsh on non-liturgical devotions and various traditional rituals and practices, it was so in the name of something more significant, to bring the liturgy of the Eucharist to life, and to do so by insisting on the active role of the laity within public worship. We have already noted once or twice that in our Church today the Eucharist is under siege in a number of ways, and we have to find the way in which we can ensure that whatever happens to the Church, we will always find the Eucharist at its center.

A second strength we need to recognize and affirm is the ministry of laypeople who are at work inside the Church, often in ministries that until recently were the preserve of priests or religious. At the present time we are in a process of great flux and development in our understanding of ministry, complicated and to a degree accelerated by the declining numbers of traditional clergy. In this exciting but troubling time the emergence and growth of what has come to be called "lay ecclesial ministry" has been astounding. Today there are around 35,000 lay ecclesial ministers in the U.S. Church, and the day is fast coming, if it has not already arrived, when they will outnumber the total of active priests. What we have not yet done successfully as a national or even a world Church is to reflect on the theological significance of this form of ministry and its implications for our understanding of ministry in general. As far as we can see most lay ecclesial ministers—though not all—do not have the desire to be ordained priest, but they and the Church as a whole have the right to a clear and assured statement of their position in the Church of the future.

A third strength to which we definitely do not pay enough attention in the United States is the catholicity of the Church, its reach across time and space. Our failure to attend to catholicity is to be expected of people who are myopic about geography and forgetful of history, but it is doubly odd when we recognize that the nature of American society reflects this catholicity. The American Catholic Church today is extraordinarily pluralistic. Many a downtown church in a major city that was once Irish or Polish or German is now in the hands of Vietnamese or Haitian Catholics, and much of the most vibrant theological reflection published in the United States today is written by Latino/a Catholics.[44] As for the value of history, the best historical scholarship about the U.S. Catholic experience

---

[44] Some examples include: Roberto S. Goizueta, *Caminemos Con Jesus: Toward a Hispanic/Latino Theology of Accompaniment* (Maryknoll, NY: Orbis, 1995); and Ada Maria Isazi-Diaz, *Mujerista Theology: A Theology for the Twenty-First Century* (Maryknoll, NY: Orbis, 1996).

provides us with enormous lessons for how we might strengthen the Church of today.[45]

The fourth strength we need to consider is one that is particularly the possession of the U.S. Catholic Church but could be of most value to the worldwide community of faith. Religion and culture always intertwine; in the United States this means that the Catholic community is imbued with characteristic American democratic values. We Americans have lots of failings and much to learn from other nations. But the vitality of our democratic traditions is a gift to the world Church and a resource for our own national Church. This, of course, is a much misunderstood value across the board. It does not mean that everything should be put to a vote. After all, we are a representative rather than a direct democracy. In our political life we do not put everything to the vote. But we do have a say in choosing our leaders, we do expect them to listen to us, and we do hold them accountable. These strengths of a democratic society are expectations that people do not entirely lay aside when they put on their religious faces. And so the challenge will be to figure out how the best of our democratic traditions can play a part in the Church without us becoming a people of committees, factions, and procedures.

A fifth and final strength on which we have to build is one that is the possession of all religious traditions: our hope. Our religious faith is in fact best understood as "fidelity to hope," and our hope as Christians is in the saving message of the Gospel, that Jesus Christ is the revelation of God in history and the Savior of the whole of humanity. Hope is not exactly optimism. The trouble with mere optimism is that it tends to go with not doing very much to make happen what you optimistically expect. "Oh, it'll all turn out fine, you know," is typical. Hope is more disciplined, a blend of work for the realization of that hope with the recognition that our hope ultimately is not in ourselves but in the God who loves us. Pray as if everything depends on God, but act as if everything depends on you. Simple realism about our world would logically lead us at this point in history to a profound pessimism. Like optimism, it is passive before the "facts." Lots of fine agnostic people and wonderful organizations that have no religious dimension do a great deal of work for good in the world. However, it is difficult for them to give an

---

[45] For example, the works of Jay Dolan, especially *In Search of an American Catholicism: A History of Religion and Culture in Tension* (New York: Oxford University Press, 2002); and the fine new book by James M. O'Toole, *The Faithful: A History of Catholics in America* (Cambridge, MA: Harvard University Press, 2008).

account of hope in the way that religions can. It would be a strange religion that was without hope about our final destiny. So our challenge is to become clearer about the relation between our hope in the Lord and the responsibility that is directly connected to that hope to work for the good of the world. Liberation theology has been the target of a lot of criticism in our Church, some of it quite unfair, but on one point it is beyond reproach: salvation, say liberation theologians, comes in the personal transformation that occurs in our struggle in history for the coming of the reign of God. It is not the reign of God and we cannot make the reign of God happen, but when we work for the reign of God, something happens to us. That transformation is possible not only for individuals and not only for liberation theologians, but for the Church as a whole.

Chapter Three

An Inductive Ecclesiology

When you do ecclesiology, there really are only two possible ways to go. You can start with a definition of the Church and use it to evaluate where the Church is and where it is not, where it is faithful to the tradition and where it is not. Or you can start by looking at all the places that claim the name "church," prepare a composite description of them, and then formulate your more theoretical understanding of Church. You can work from above or below, deductively or inductively.[1] You can be a Platonist or an Aristotelian. Like Procrustes, you can trim and stretch the living body of Christ's faithful with the surgical instruments of theological abstraction, or you can try to attend to the way in which the Spirit is at work among believers. The assumption that deductive approaches are rigorous and inductive methods are woolly headed romanticism needs to be challenged in the strongest possible terms. In this third and final chapter we will explore at some length the idea of an inductive ecclesiology and then examine some of the practical implications for treating ecclesiology this way.

---

[1] In his recent outstanding book, *Ecclesiology and Postmodernity: Questions for the Church in Our Time* (Liturgical Press, 2007), Gerard Mannion has written eloquently of the need for an ecclesiology from below, and has offered valuable proposals for a comparative and dialogical ecclesiology. Building on the work of Roger Haight and others, Mannion argues for a more pluralist starting point for ecclesiology in the experience of being church that can be found in many places, not only in Catholicism.

The Idea of Inductive Ecclesiology

Inductive ecclesiology has to begin from the Church that actually exists, that is, all the ecclesial groups around the world that claim the name of "church." But one can legitimately also do an inductive Catholic ecclesiology in precisely the same way beginning from all those communities that claim communion with the Roman Catholic Church, or an inductive Methodist or Orthodox or Episcopalian ecclesiology on somewhat similar lines. Here we are concerned primarily with the Roman Catholic Church, but the very idea of an inductive approach means that such a confessional ecclesiology cannot be conducted in isolation from the larger project.[2] Ecclesiology from above always excludes; from below, it seeks to include. This is not exactly a matter of sheep and goats; idealized ecclesiology is so clear about what the Church is that it can confidently and without any malicious intent declare who is "in" and who is "out," and seem genuinely surprised if the excluded take umbrage. Empirical ecclesiology has the opposite problem; it struggles to find criteria for inclusion beyond the claim to be part of the whole, in order not simply to be the big tent that admits absolutely everyone. To some degree this problem is moderated by empirical ecclesiology's necessarily local or contextual character. Although the end product of all ecclesial reflection is to arrive at some generalizable sense of what the Church is, inductive method approaches that point through reflection upon a definite local context.

The first step in this discussion is to get clear what we mean by the turn to inductive rather than deductive methodology, not only in ecclesiology but in theological reflection as a whole. A wonderful source for clarity on this point can be found in the work of the great twentieth-century Jesuit philosopher and theologian Bernard Lonergan, who underwent a kind of personal intellectual revolution in his thought around the time of Vatican II. This is laid out for all to see in the essays he wrote between the publication of his great philosophical work *Insight* (1957) and *Method in Theology* (1972). Lonergan argues an important notion of change in the opening essay of *A Second Collection*, "Transition

---

[2] Here is where the comparative ecclesiology project of Roger Haight is so valuable. See his *Christian Community in History*, vol. 2, *Comparative Ecclesiology* (New York: Continuum, 2005). There is a very useful collection of essays inspired by Haight's work, *Comparative Ecclesiology: Critical Investigations*, ed. Gerard Mannion (New York: Continuum, 2008).

from a Classicist World-View to Historical Mindedness."[3] The classicist mind-set, which deals in universals or essences, is not the only way to go. "One can begin," he writes, "from people as they are."[4] Human beings construct their lives out of all kinds of intentional acts by which they seek meaning, and human communities are formed out of "common meanings." These meanings are not some "stock of ideal forms subsistent in some Platonic heaven" but, rather, "the hard-won fruit of man's advancing knowledge of nature, of the gradual evolution of his social forms and of his cultural achievements."[5] We need to apprehend humankind "as a concrete aggregate developing over time," where intentionality or meaning is "a constituent component of human living," which is of its nature "shifting, developing, going astray, capable of redemption." Historicity, then, leads to "an exigence for changing forms, structures, methods. . . . [A]nd it is on this level and through this medium of changing meaning that divine revelation has entered the world and that the Church's witness is given to it."[6]

A further essay from the same collection, "Theology in Its New Context," originally delivered in the mid-sixties and first published in 1968, makes a more direct application of these philosophical insights to the history of religious reflection and the changes that occurred to theology in the mid-twentieth century.[7] Lonergan sees the changes in theology as a return to an earlier approach that had been supplanted by the emergence of a form of dogmatic theology at the time of the Enlightenment. Dogmatic theology "replaced the inquiry of the *quaestio*" that had been typical of scholastic method with "the pedagogy of the thesis." A dynamic form of theology had been moved aside in favor of one more static, which "demoted the quest of faith for understanding to a desirable, but secondary, and indeed, optional goal" and "gave basic and central significance to the certitudes of faith, their presuppositions and their consequences."[8] This kind of classicist theological thinking has now given way to one that, like scholastic thought in the Middle Ages, is "locked in an encounter with its age." The new theology Lonergan calls "empirical," but since he contrasts it to deductive thinking it is safe to say that he would accept

---

[3] Bernard Lonergan, *A Second Collection* (Philadelphia: Westminster, 1974), 1–9.
[4] Ibid., 3.
[5] Ibid., 4.
[6] Ibid., 6.
[7] Ibid., 55–67.
[8] Ibid., 67.

"inductive" as an appropriate synonym for empirical. He characterizes it as local and particular and evolving, and notes that new vocabulary and imagery has replaced the Aristotelian conceptual apparatus. Very quickly, he says, "the vacuum is being filled with biblical words and images, and with ideas worked out by historicist, personalist, phenomenological, and existential reflection."[9] The earlier dogmatic theology talks of human nature and analyzes the human person in terms of soul and body. The new theology "adds the richer and more concrete apprehension of man as incarnate subject."[10]

Lonergan's account of the new theological paradigm in which the human person is seen as incarnate subject, moving and shifting in response to all kinds of historical and psychological currents, has its analogue in the ecclesiological developments in the mid-twentieth century. If the human person lives a life of intentionality or meaning, and if communities are constituted by common meaning developing in the same dynamic process, this much is clear. We can think of the Church less as a static, unchanging, and "perfect" reality, and more as a sort of collective incarnate subject, moved and changed by the same forces that affect the human person. This is inherent in ecclesial imagery from Vatican II such as People of God or pilgrim, but it is also present in the idea of the Church as the Mystical Body, which was in so many ways the parent to the more recently developed models for the Church. In ecclesiology today as in Christian anthropology, the rigidity of the soul/body dualism gives way to much more complex understandings of the relationship between what can change and what abides. In the neoscholastic ecclesiology of the Church as a perfect society, the shape of the Church as we know it in history is part of its essence, is permanent, is that without which we would not be Church. But at Vatican II and beyond, the Church is always growing and changing in ways we cannot predict and that will surprise us. There is a core, a permanent reality, of course, but this permanent reality is located in the community of the faithful throughout history who, in the power of the Spirit, have the responsibility to preserve the tradition and to grow with the times.

In the same essay Lonergan offers some tantalizing remarks on "conversion" as the methodology of the new theology. He points out first that the shift to the new theological approach that he has sketched out remains as much in need of a foundation as did the more traditional

---

[9] Ibid., 60.
[10] Ibid., 61.

approach. Without "a critique of methods" we will be unable "to distinguish tinsel and silver, gilt and gold." The potential problem for the new approach is that it "can too easily be made into a device for reducing doctrines to probable opinions."[11] As we seek out a method appropriate to the more empirical or inductive approach, we are searching not for prescriptions but, rather, for "the grounds that governed the prescribing." Drawing ideas from scientific method, he suggests that the foundation of scientific method is the "subject as scientist," since the method is really the whole set of human operations that leads to discovery. Moving to an analysis of religious living, Lonergan suggests that its method is "conversion . . . a radical transformation on which follows, on all levels of living, an interlocked series of changes and developments."[12] Finally, since theology is reflection on religion it follows that it is reflection on conversion, and since conversion is fundamental to religion, reflection on conversion provides theology with "a foundation that is concrete, dynamic, personal, communal and historical."[13]

The idea of conversion is amplified and clarified in Lonergan's 1971 Marquette Lecture published as *Doctrinal Pluralism*.[14] The lecture explores the forms of pluralism in our modern world and the ways in which human consciousness has developed from naive realism to various blends of scientific, religious, scholarly, and modern philosophic forms. In his own lapidary and at times quirky way Lonergan demolishes any claim to the continuing usefulness of the classicist tradition and the scholasticism that is its theological face. We need a new theological approach more suited to our world in order to withstand the negative effects of pluralism, he thinks. But to get to this point we require a change of heart. Conversion is such an event that also ushers in a process. "It is not just a development," he writes, "but the beginning of a new mode of development." It is three-dimensional, involving intellectual, moral, and religious components, and to be successful all three are needed, though "relapses" in one or all three can occur.[15]

Lonergan's masterwork, *Method in Theology*,[16] takes all of this much further, but the peculiar language aside his vision is not a complicated

---

[11] Ibid., 53.

[12] Ibid., 66.

[13] Ibid., 67.

[14] Lonergan, *Doctrinal Pluralism* (Milwaukee: Marquette, 1971).

[15] Ibid., 34–39.

[16] Lonergan, *Method in Theology* (New York: Herder & Herder, 1972).

one. In essence even the changed Lonergan of these later years calls for the same four transcendental principles he consistently maintained to be applied to a world beyond classicism. "Be attentive, be intelligent, be reasonable, be responsible," and when you behave in this way you will see that we are beyond the days of classicism and into those marked by attention to historicity, pluralism, and so on. In *Method in Theology*, in fact, he offers a slightly altered version of the transcendental principles that makes just this point: "Be attentive, be intelligent, be reasonable, be loving, and, if necessary, change."[17] The application of the transcendental principles moves us to conversion on all three levels, intellectual, moral, and religious. Only all three together equip us for engagement with a pluralist world.

Lonergan's great work was methodological and that means that even though we are greatly indebted to him, we are on our own when it comes to the kind of analysis of the Church that we need to do. He gave us some important tools, but we have to get on with the job. Armed with his four transcendental principles and oriented toward what people are actually doing and saying in the Church, we need to engage in what anthropologists often call a "thick description" of the Church seen as a collective incarnate subject. For Lonergan, let us recall, the human person cannot be thought of any longer simply as possessor of an unchanging human nature. While "human nature" is not an entirely unhelpful notion, it must give way to understanding the person dynamically, as a historical human being living in a particular time and place, attending to all kinds of social and moral and intellectual currents, and to that degree different daily. This is what it is to be an incarnate subject and, though Lonergan did not explicitly say so, it seems possible to think of the Church this way too. It does not have a fixed and unchanging nature; while it is always the same, it is also always changing. The continuity in change that is the Church is a product of the fact that its reality is the countless millions of people, each of them an incarnate subject even in the days when the term would have been neither understood nor accepted. For this, if for no other reason, ecclesiological method today has to be inductive.

To choose to employ an inductive or empirical approach to reflection on the Church does not mean that we shall never arrive at pronouncements about what the Church *is* or that we shall never propose models for understanding it. In fact, if we think about the earliest years of the

---

[17] Ibid., 231.

Church we can easily imagine that what happened there was an inductive process that resulted eventually in statements about the nature of the Church. All that we know of the early Church suggests that it stumbled into its eventual structure, rather than planned or deliberately constructed it. The classicist may want to insist that the whole reality of the Church was in the mind of Jesus like some kind of blueprint, but serious scholarship does not look at it that way anymore. The gospels show Jesus moving toward a reformist movement within Judaism, and Jesus himself and his early followers both before and after the resurrection only slowly come to see the implications of his words and deeds. The Holy Spirit that guided the apostles was also subject to the limitations of their imaginations and their courage. When St. Paul declared the Church to be the Body of Christ, the power of the image had to have come from its explanatory potential, but what it explained was what was actually going on in the early Christian communities. Jesus, after all, had followers before there was a Church, and the first ecclesiologist wasn't even one of the Twelve.

The problem with inherited ecclesiology is not that its models and definitions are wrong but that over the centuries the models derived inductively have calcified and led to a deductive vision of the Church that, like all such deductive approaches, seeks to trim the really existing phenomenon—the Church today—to fit the images of the past. Sound theological reflection is always playing catch-up to the actual beliefs and practices of the Church. However, magisterial authority can sometimes give the impression that when it canonizes some development as the faith of the Church, it is necessarily for all time. To borrow from Lonergan's distinction about classicism, it is not that its insights are no longer true but that they are no longer useful. So we can even see the councils of the Church responding flexibly to these kinds of changes. The fathers of Vatican I in 1870 simply took for granted the vision of the Church as a "perfect society," an institution whose membership was entirely visible. In the hundred years that followed theologians who were uneasy with the adequacy of this definition of the Church gave great attention to Paul's image of the body of Christ, rechristening it the "Mystical Body." Pius XII gave his authority in 1943 to seeing this image of the Church as more valuable than that of institution, because it responded to the clear sense of people that "visibility" is not the sole criterion for membership of the Church.[18] Some Catholics are so in name only, and many who are

---

[18] In the encyclical letter *Mystici Corporis Christi.*

not Catholic are clearly close to God. But by the time of Vatican II the image of the Mystical Body had given way again, this time to an even more concrete expression of the Church as the People of God, which *Lumen Gentium* explicitly employs to express the universality of God's offer of salvation.

Of its nature, theology tends toward being an elite activity. The assumed need to know the history of the tradition and the fact—until recently—that theological learning and the clerical state belonged together, have meant that theologies have usually reflected the standpoint of a professional class. Until recently, too, these theologies have been produced for the most part by theologians whose public status and responsibilities involve the preservation of the institution's account of itself. Where others emerge to challenge the traditional narrative the institution tends to consider them suspect and to isolate them as dissenters. To a degree, of course, any movement for change is dissent, at least dissent from the status quo. But in Church circles as in revolutionary politics, the status quo is often canonized through the entrenched power of an elite leadership class, effectively rendering any dissenting voice "subversive." But there is surely room for theologians who are not so intimately tied to the forces of production.[19]

Much has changed in recent decades in the Catholic Church to place this ruling hegemony under stress. One factor is the emergence of liberation theology with its orientation to the religious reflection of the oppressed as the starting point for theology, and the many variations upon it produced by feminist, Womanist, gay/lesbian, environmental, and other theologizing communities. The Vatican moved quickly to stifle the threat of liberation theology, claiming in a 1984 document that it was overdependent on Marxist rhetoric and collapsed salvation into purely human liberation from oppression.[20] Needless to say, liberation theologians had trouble recognizing themselves or their work in this document.

Even where liberation theologies have not been consciously adopted, however, as is mostly the case within the institutional Catholic Church in North America and Europe, the rising educational level of the Catholic

---

[19] See Paul Lakeland, "For Whom Do We Write? The Responsibility of the Theologian," in *The Promise of Critical Theology: Essays in Honor of Charles Davis*, ed. Marc P. Lalonde (Montreal: Wilfrid Laurier, 1995), 33–48.

[20] See the Congregation for the Doctrine of the Faith, "Instruction on Certain Aspects of the Theology of Liberation," published in 1984 and available at http://www.campchabad.com/roman_curia/congregations/cfaith/documents/rc_con_cfaith_doc_19840806_theology-liberation_en.html.

laity has meant that more of them have been engaged in religious reflection, many of these with precisely similar professional credentials to those of the aforementioned clerical class. The emergence of the phenomenon of lay theologians in significant numbers has been frequently noted and is important for two reasons. First, it broadens the experiential base for theological reflection beyond the clerical class, which has been the only significant theological voice for at least a thousand years. Second, it has created a group of theologians whose methods and conclusions are not subject to ecclesiastical control in the same way that ordained theologians can be managed. Everyone ought to accept that broadening theological reflection is good for the Church. Most would probably also agree that it leads to a livelier theological debate, though some certainly do not have the stomach for the vigor of some expressions of disagreement.

Neither the emergence of liberation theology nor the new phenomenon of lay theologians, however, necessarily means the end of elite theologizing. As anyone who has studied liberation theology knows, the direct reflection of peasant groups in Latin America or the observations of black South Africans often undergo strangely complex transmogrifications before they reach a wider public in the multitude of academic books to which they have given rise. The peasants of El Salvador or Brazil surely did not know that they were sitting in a hermeneutical circle. And a lay theologian with a PhD is no less likely than the academic cleric of a previous generation to climb into the ivory tower and wrap him- or herself in the mantle of theological jargon. In fact, since lay theologians are more often than not citizens of the academy, the temptation to the arcane may be stronger for them than it was for the medieval schoolmen, most of whom did at least a little preaching.

The emergence of a more inductive theology requires in the first place consistent attention to the life of the Church at the grassroots. This is not therefore a development that coincides exactly with the rise of lay theologians, since they can be as elitist as the clerical class they are largely replacing. Moreover, theologians who are priests are just as likely these days to employ the tools of inductive method. Theologians, lay or clerical, will have to be what sociologists call "participant-observers" if they are to be close enough to the grassroots to gauge accurately the ways in which the Church is developing as a faith community. Standing and acting within the *sensus fidelium*, they will need to reflect on the way in which it is moving. Carried along by the currents of tradition, they must also help the Church navigate the shoals and rapids that lie in wait around the next bend in the river of history. But because there is no way to be outside history, no vantage point from which one can dispassionately address the changing Church without being oneself a part of those changes, inductive method is here to stay.

An initial example of the application of inductive method to ecclesiology is not hard to find. It is difficult to see how the actual, concrete, historical Church today can be satisfied with any exposition of the nature of the Church that cannot account worthily for the genuine holiness of Christian traditions and world religions beyond the Roman Catholic Church without subsuming their access to grace under some kind of Christian umbrella, however subtly expressed. While some theological positions leave room for this kind of flexibility—the ecclesiology of the People of God for one—some that should, like a communion ecclesiology, are consistent with maintaining that Protestant communities contain "defects" and cannot be called churches. Pope Benedict XVI holds both to communion ecclesiology and to this attitude to Protestant faith communities. However, much more important than theological differences is the clear sense, confirmed by the kind of sociological data gathering we will examine shortly, that Catholics today are for the most part not interested in wrangling about whose religion is the best, or whether Jews or Buddhists or whatever can achieve salvation through their own religion. This kind of conversation inevitably smacks of the schoolyard argument between second graders about whose dad is bigger or richer or stronger than the other. Moreover, while the theological argument is considerably more sophisticated than the plain insistence of good Catholics today in large numbers that people can find God perfectly well in their own religions, in the end that is what the council fathers are saying in *Lumen Gentium*.

The difference between classic expressions of Catholic and Protestant understandings of the Church actually illustrates the role of inductive method. The fundamental distinction between Catholic and Protestant ecclesiologies is usually seen to be that Protestantism sees particular historical churches as instantiations of "the Church" that is an invisible reality, whereas the Catholic Church makes a claim for the oneness of the invisible Church and the visible Roman Catholic Church. While this can and should be challenged on some grounds (e.g., by analyzing the notoriously difficult *subsistit in* of *Lumen Gentium*), in the Catholic claim that *this* Church was founded by Jesus we have sweeping testimony to an inductive ecclesiology nestling within Catholic theological abstraction. Jesus Christ sets the character of the Church that is to be not by thinking about what it might be but by calling the apostles. The Spirit at Pentecost quickens that particular apostolic community not by lecturing them on ecclesiology but by inspiring them to go out and preach the risen Christ. It does not matter whether we think it happened exactly this way or not. In favoring this founding story and in the claim to faithfulness to the apostolic tradition, the Catholic Church is at root arguing inductively.

But is ecclesiology also sociology? There is surely a measure of historical and professional sophistication that needs to be applied to the reports on the beliefs and values of actual members of the actual Church today, but equally certainly the Church is to a high degree what they say it is, though not necessarily what it ought to be. This is the formative component of the *sensus fidelium*. While the whole faithful people's living out the tradition has to be done in an attitude of respect for the tradition itself, the Spirit guides the community of faith not solely to obedience but, rather, in a much more complex dance, balancing what remains permanently valid and what is growing and changing even as we speak. When we discover through sociological data that the merely anecdotal has a good basis in fact, we are swimming in the great flowing river of tradition. We learn that the Church is far more culturally, ethically, and religiously pluralistic than any of our theological blueprints envisage. And we see any and every local initiative of God's faithful people, Catholic or Protestant, as a little piece of the story.

The principal tool of ecclesial reflection today is description, conducted by one who tries to be attentive, intelligent, reasonable, loving, and open to change. We cannot promise to use these requirements with the same discipline as Bernard Lonergan himself did, but the effort to do so will inspire us in the direction of a thick description of the community of faith at the present time in the North American context. To choose one particular context is not to abdicate responsibility for a comprehensive ecclesiology but, rather, to recognize that it is of the nature of a more empirical or inductive method to start from the local and build up toward the more universal. To begin in the opposite way, moving from the more general to the particular, is a characteristic of that classicist method that Lonergan so persuasively argued has had its day. The more inductive approach also differs from the classicist model in several other ways. It will reflect a more popular and less elitist vision, its contextuality will lead naturally to a more pluralistic picture, and it will inevitably be more concrete. Any such contextual theology, of course, will have to be careful not to canonize its own particularity. The ecclesiology of Catholicism is in the end the sum of the parts, not the triumph of one part—not even the Roman part—over the others.

Be Attentive, or Read the Signs of the Times

Any discussion of the importance of "reading the signs of the times" has to begin with the Second Vatican Council's Pastoral Constitution On the Church in the World of Today, where the term is introduced and the method is employed.[21] This document, which is customarily known by the first few words of the Latin text, *Gaudium et Spes* (GS), begins with a ringing embrace of the world beyond the Church and the assertion that for Christians, "nothing that is genuinely human fails to find an echo in their hearts" (GS 1). The council is clear that it is addressing itself "to the whole of humanity," consciously seeing this present document as an examination of the role of the Church in the world, "[n]ow that the Second Vatican Council has deeply studied the mystery of the Church" (GS 2). Having enunciated its purpose, the council turns to a lengthy introduction in which the challenges and hopes of the human race are described. The sentence of this introduction reads: "At all times the Church carries the responsibility of reading the signs of the time and of interpreting them in the light of the Gospel, if it is to carry out its task" (GS 4). After the descriptive introduction the document is divided into two parts of approximately equal length. The first enunciates theological principles about the dignity of the human person, the human community, the impact of human activity upon the world, and the nature of the relationship between the Church and the secular world. The second part looks at "some more urgent problems" for the world of the day, and the bishops select marriage and the family, culture, economics, politics, and international relations. Each section describes some contemporary features of its particular topic that seem to give cause for concern and proceeds to a careful application of Catholic ethical teaching.

Gaudium et Spes, both in its strengths and in its weaknesses, has important lessons for those who would adopt a more inductive approach to ecclesial reflection. On the one hand it makes a serious effort to begin each of its constituent discussions with a kind of description of the human condition in today's world. It does not start with theological a prioris, it is not judgmental, and it openly recognizes the ways in which Church and world are both teachers and both learners. The document clearly respects the world as not only in need of the light of the Gospel

---

[21] This document, *Gaudium et Spes*, is usually referred to as "The Church in the Modern World," but the present translation is both closer to the Latin and a more accurate rendering of the council's intention. "Modern" is not a word they use and it is a word that introduces all kinds of philosophical and political alarm bells.

but also possessed of other sources of wisdom from which the Church can truly learn. This kind of humility and openness before the world is highly instructive. But at the same time the document is a masterpiece of generalizations that simply does not recognize the import of local or contextual knowledge within the Church. Reading the signs of the times in the world at large, *Gaudium et Spes* is marked by enormous compassion and a strong sense of service. But nothing in the document recognizes that "the Church" itself is an increasingly diverse community of faith in which gender and race and ethnicity play an important role. It is as if the signs of the times are available only in the wider world and are absent from the Church. In the way in which the documents of Vatican II do not problematize the Church itself, they reflect that unchanging classicist vision that they had set out to overcome.

Being attentive in today's American Catholic Church will lead us to identify a long list of concerns, though attentiveness itself stops with the list and does not move on to the difficult process of analysis anymore than it censors the items of concern. Attentiveness is not ideological, because the selective attentiveness that would follow would be selective blindness and therefore, finally, inattentiveness. Just to give one example, when in 2002 the press and then the public became aware of the scope of the sexual abuse scandal and the deficient handling of the problem on the part of many bishops, both right and left were inevitably appalled by the same phenomenon. When it came to explaining the causes of clerical misconduct, right and left diverged widely, but that there was a problem to be addressed neither right nor left wished to deny. You didn't have to be terribly attentive to see that there was a problem. But the fact that there was consensus that there was a problem but no consensus on how to deal with it clearly shows that attentiveness is not sufficient. Intelligent attention to the problem is also needed.

Attentiveness to the current face of the American Catholic Church leads to the recognition that there are three major changes going on today that we need to recognize, analyze, and address. The first is the shifting profile of the Catholic community, evident not only in the growing number of Hispanic and Latino/a Catholics but also in the increasingly upper-middle-class face of white American Catholicism and the aging of the Church. Connected to these issues is the change in patterns of participation in Church life, especially the decline in regular Mass attendance and the loss of religious literacy. These two issues form a bridge to the second major topic, which is the developing understanding of the relationship between conscience and authority. We see this above all in the growing divorce between the teaching of the Church on ethical issues and the actual beliefs and practices of Catholics of all stripes, including those who continue to attend Mass regularly. Connected to this phenomenon and to some degree explaining it is a discernible change in the way in which people understand what it means to be Catholic, which is itself a further instance of a growing independence of judgment. And this brings us neatly to a third concern, the tension between the historical passivity of the laity and an emerging movement for a more participatory Church. Among more active and involved Catholics there are clear signs of a determination that in the future not all decisions about Church life should be made by the clergy but that in many ways laypeople should enter into the process of discernment and decision making. We need to be attentive to each of these issues before turning our intelligence loose upon analyzing their meanings and making some constructive proposals for addressing them.

Looking first at the changing face of American Catholicism, we can see that while the Catholic population in the United States is not shrinking, the percentage of those who attend church is declining and the membership of the Church is looking increasingly more pluralistic. Above all, the curious relationship between the claim to identity and the level of institutional commitment raises a lot of questions about just how we should count Catholics. Two sets of data help us to examine these and other issues. The first is the work of the four authors of the 2007 book we have made mention of several times, *American Catholics Today*.[22] To recap, these sociologists conducted a telephone poll, asking a series of questions of a randomly selected set of self-professed Catholics and dividing up the responses by age cohort and by levels of commitment to the Church. They also compared their data with three previous studies they had done at four-year intervals over more than a decade. The second is the even more recent book by Jerome Baggett, also mentioned earlier, in which he reports on and analyzes data collected in two-hour interviews of over 150 actively involved Catholics living in six quite distinct parishes in the Bay Area.[23] The one surveys the broader field of all those who consider themselves Catholic, the other looks more deeply into the lives and convictions of people who are known as active and involved

---

[22] William V. D'Antonio and others, *American Catholics Today* (Lanham, MD: Rowman & Littlefield, 2007).

[23] Jerome P. Baggett, *Sense of the Faithful: How American Catholics Live Their Faith* (New York: Oxford, 2008).

in their local communities of faith. There are lots of differences, some quite predictable. The more involved Catholics would be more likely to attend church more regularly and less inclined to contemplate leaving the Church under any circumstances. The less involved think in larger numbers that one can be a good Catholic and not attend church regularly or support the local parish financially. But there are significant similarities, particularly in the way in which both studies show Catholics negotiating their identity and their faith, in effect customizing them to match their needs and their experience.

There is an opportunity for a truly inductive approach to contemporary theology when the data collection of sociologists of religion is employed in tandem with the imagination of the theologian. If the social scientists are doing their work efficiently they accurately produce a picture of the ecclesial community as it actually is, regardless of what theologians or Church leaders claim it is or should be. They are being attentive in their own way, providing a background statistical picture against which individuals can set their own far more random and anecdotal thick descriptions. When individual perceptions seem to fit closely to the findings of sociologists, then there is a good chance that both are on the right lines. The significance of accurate social analysis and statistical findings is that while they do not exactly provide the stuff of theological reflection, they create a background factual picture that the theologian ignores at her or his peril. It sets out, to adapt words Bertolt Brecht wrote about science in general, not "to open the door to everlasting wisdom" but, rather, to "set a limit on everlasting error." Theology, as in some part a work of the imagination, must always be a servant of the facts. So, both the D'Antonio and Baggett volumes confirm the fluidity of American Catholicism and hence close the door on two common directions of ecclesiology. They give the lie to the "everything is fine" approach of the more Pollyannaish of the bishops and also the "everything is irretrievably falling apart" story told by alarmed conservatives, alarmed liberals, and the more pessimistic of ecclesiastics.

The American Catholic Church is no longer the preserve of the descendants of white immigrants that it once was. In 2008 there were over 64 million Catholics in the United States—considerably more than double what it had been in 1950 and up 5 million from the year 2000—comprising approximately 22% of the American population. In the U.S. Church 3% of Catholics are African American, 2% are Asian, 16% are Latino, 1% are Native American, and 78% are white, non-Hispanic. But by 2020 the U.S. Census Bureau expects the white, non-Hispanic populations to increase by only 5% while Hispanic/Latino and Asian/Pacific Islander Catholics will increase by 70% and 74% respectively. The Center for Applied Research in the Apostolate (CARA) reports that about 70% of American Hispanics/Latinos identify as Catholics, and since the growth in their numbers outstrips that of white Americans by a considerable amount you do not have to be much of a mathematician to figure out that the American Catholic Church is becoming much more racially pluralistic.[24] By mid-century the expectation is that roughly half of the U.S. Catholic Church will be of Hispanic descent. It is also the case that the growth in nonwhite and especially Hispanic immigration is mostly blue collar, and over time this may change the current situation in which Catholics are the most socioeconomically successful group among American Christians. When we turn to analysis by age cohort, it is immediately apparent that young adult Catholics are considerably less involved in the Church than older generations, and there are good reasons to believe that the decline in religious practice may not be what it once was, a temporary situation that would change once these younger Catholics married and had family responsibilities. Indeed, since these young people are only continuing a trend already established by their "post–Vatican II" parents of irregular or even sporadic involvement in eucharistic worship, they do not have role models for adult Catholic behavior that previous generations possessed.

When we absorb and digest the statistics about the Catholic population in the CARA reports, in the D'Antonio volume, and at least implicit in Baggett's book, American Catholicism comes into focus as an increasingly racially and socioeconomically mixed community of faith in which active Catholics tend to be older, members either of the pre–Vatican II cohort who came of age before 1960, or the Vatican II cohort (the older baby boomers born in the late 1940s or early 1950s). Measurements of institutional commitment by most normal methods suggest that there may not be much of an active Catholic community in the not-too-far-distant future. Added to this is the fact that constructive lay involvement in shaping the Church is also overwhelmingly the work of Vatican II and older folks, both on the more conservative and the more liberal ends of

[24] See the web site at www.cara.georgetown.edu. In his book *Catholicism in Motion: The Church in American Society* (Liguori, MO: Liguori/Triumph, 2005), Jim Davidson critiques the usual methods for establishing these numbers and suggests a somewhat different picture, with Hispanics numbering between 25% and 38% of the Catholic population (see esp. pp. 16–17).

the spectrum. And although it may be true that young adults today are "over" Vatican II or regard it as past history, the mix of interest in spirituality and personal growth with at best lukewarm liturgical involvement and minimal attention to Church teaching certainly does not easily translate into a vision of return to traditional parish life.

Our second major concern is that of changes in the attitudes of self-identified Catholics to Church teaching. These are frankly startling. The D'Antonio survey is where we have to start, since its methods produce a picture of the entire Catholic community rather than merely its most active cohort. The raw numbers reveal a mix of reassurance and concern. So, when asked to select from a list of twelve teachings and practices the four most important to them, they selected helping the poor, belief in Jesus' resurrection from the dead, the sacraments, and devotion to Mary. Clearly, these choices would warm the heart of the Holy Father. But the four items that were considered less important, by a wide margin, were perhaps not so reassuring: Church teaching on abortion, Vatican teaching authority in general, teachings against the death penalty, and, last in importance, a celibate male clergy. The highest scores for "not at all important" went to the celibate male clergy, again, and to teachings that oppose same-sex marriage. When asked about the rights and wrongs of particular issues, 61% said that individuals should make the final decision on the use of birth control, closely followed by engaging in homosexual activity (46%), extramarital sex (47%), advocating pro-choice positions on abortion (44%), and a divorced Catholic remarrying without getting an annulment (42%). Only 18% strongly agreed that "Catholicism contains a greater share of truth than other religions," and 68% strongly agreed that how a person lives is more important than which religion they belong to. When asked about the place of women in the Church and whether they would support or oppose their exercising certain roles, 81% thought women deacons were just fine, 93% considered they would make good parish administrators, and 63% supported their ordination as priests. While only 23% thought you could be a good Catholic without believing in the resurrection of Jesus from the dead, 36% were comfortable with the idea of a good Catholic who did not believe that the bread and wine at Mass become the body and blood of Jesus, and larger numbers saw no necessary connection between being a good Catholic and helping the poor (44%) or the parish (58%).[25] Whatever conclusions we come to about the state of the Church as a result of statistics like these,

---

[25] *American Catholics Today*, 173–83, provides the raw data from the 2005 Gallup Survey on which this book's findings are based.

it is evident that they show a mixture of sound priorities, ignorance, and confusion about the tradition, and a far greater level of tolerance for change than that evidenced by Church leaders.

The third area concerns how much involvement the Catholic laity should have in the decision-making processes that have been in the hands of the clergy alone for a very long time. While only 40% were ready to withhold money until they were assigned a greater role in financial decision making, a whopping 89% thought that the Catholic laity should have the right to participate in decisions about how parish income should be spent, how diocesan income should be spent (84%), deciding about parish closings (80%), and selecting priests for their parish (71%).[26] Data like this explains the depth of feelings about the lack of a real say in church affairs, though it raises the question why, if opinion is so strong, lay people as a whole do not turn their feelings into actions. Activist lay Catholics on issues of church governance remain a small minority.

All these statistics and the many more with which the D'Antonio volume provides us include items that will please or disturb both more and less conservative Catholics, but that only make sense as a whole when we think about the research method of the team. Their telephone poll began with asking if a person was a Catholic or not, only later identifying how important their Catholicism was to them and how committed they were to the institution. This not only provided the useful information that overall Catholic identity was strong while institutional commitment was relatively weak but it clarifies the data somewhat. Many of the respondents probably hadn't thought a lot about some of these questions and some of the answers might have been motivated either by nostalgia or by a sense of what it was appropriate to say. So while large numbers selected the Eucharist in particular and the sacraments in general as "very important" to them personally, the majority of those asked attended Church only infrequently.

When we turn to Baggett's conclusions, his somewhat different approach both qualifies and confirms the D'Antonio findings, particularly since he deliberately chooses many of the same questions that the earlier team had developed. Indeed, he quotes the D'Antonio study to make many of his points about the fluidity of American Catholicism and how many Catholics "defect in place" rather than actually leave the Church when they are dissatisfied with one or another aspect of Church teaching. But his preference for conversation rather than polling and the much

---

[26] *American Catholics Today*, 105–22.

lengthier amounts of time he spent with his subjects mean that his work is lighter on statistical analysis but replete with anecdote and personal history. His sample is also smaller though still considerable at around 250, and in line with current life in the Church, it is skewed toward those over 40 and about two-thirds women. Nevertheless, his point that there is no one such thing as American Catholicism is nicely illustrated, and he comes to a conclusion with which the D'Antonio volume would be in agreement: that American Catholics like other people of faith actually negotiate their own relationship to their religion. They treat the tradition with respect but they expect it to aid their faith and to conform to their experience. Baggett's conclusions suggest that "one iteration of American Catholicism has clearly ended, but another has begun." Those 250 Californians he interviewed "caution us against writing them off as less Catholic than their predecessors" because even in their more critical stances they employ the symbol system of Catholicism to call it to account.[27] They may be more interested these days in questioning the answers than an earlier generation's predilection for answering the questions, he writes, but they remain staunchly loyal to their Church, especially to their local parish community.

These and other social critics[28] help empirical theologians by assembling data and observations, and they provide a convincing picture that the Church is changing, not necessarily ending. However, what the Church is can never entirely be settled by a description. There remains the theological moment itself, when the difficult question of meaning is raised. If these things and those things are going on in the Church, if we are becoming a community more loosely connected to rituals and practices, more independent in our relationship to the teaching Church, less Caucasian, and definitely older, what does this say about how we should today answer the question, so what then is the Church? Theology is about trying to understand the fruits of our attentiveness.

Be Intelligent, or Practice Discernment

Intelligence is what we bring to bear upon the data that we have, but it is no guarantee that we will get it right. It is intelligence that can look at apparently random numbers and see a sequence or a pattern, and it

[27] Baggett, *Sense of the Faithful*, 239.

[28] See, for example, Michele Dillon, *Catholic Identity: Balancing Reason, Faith, and Power* (New York: Cambridge University Press, 1999); and Andrew Greeley, *The Catholic Imagination* (Berkeley: University of California Press, 2001).

is intelligence that can take a few facts and weave them into a story. Sometimes, of course, the same set of data might lead two individuals to entirely different conclusions. If they are storytelling it may simply be a tribute to human creativity. If they are looking for *the* answer then one of them (at least) is wrong. Intelligence is what makes us human, the skill that leads to understanding, but arriving at the correct answer or understanding that there is no one correct answer requires that intelligence be applied with a particular kind of awareness, that we not just be intelligent, but be wisely so.

Discernment is the wise application of human intelligence. Armed with knowledge, our practice of discernment brings us to the point of judgment, of a decision about the meaning of the facts or situation and, perhaps, of the actions to be taken in consequence of this judgment. But the crucial wisdom involved in discernment is the awareness of the need for humility before the facts, particularly if these facts affect me personally. Understanding filled with discernment is as much about eliminating the subject from the discernment as it is about focusing on the facts. It is not an easy skill to learn because we are programmed to see ourselves as the center of our universe and to understand the world around us as it is relevant to us and our own needs and concerns. Understanding, discerning the truth, often requires us to bracket our own subjectivity, and inadequate understanding is frequently marked by the kind of defensiveness that turns into personal attacks on those who think differently from the way we think.

While humility and the bracketing of our own concerns is not the mark of the grown-up world in which we live, it is definitely a characteristic of adulthood. Ah, if only our grown-up world were truly adult, what a place it would be, marked by wise discernment and a longer-term, other-directed sense of what needs to be done. That it is rarely this way is one of the best arguments for the truth of what the tradition has called original sin. Eating the fruit of the tree in the Garden of Eden was at once the most obvious act of short-term gain and the most horrendous in long-term consequences. Often enough the sin of Adam and Eve is thought of as pride, but it might equally well or even better be seen as putting themselves first and breaking their intimacy with God. It is a childish adult who is given almost everything and then insists on having more, and a wise and discerning one who can live contentedly with limitations. Our world so often chooses the former disastrous course and repeats the sin of Adam and Eve on a daily basis. Our challenge is to undo that sin by living within the plenty of our God-given limits and finding ways to ensure that everyone else can do the same.

The same tension between original sin and true adulthood that infects our world can be seen sadly enough within the Church itself. The glaring and obvious example is that of the scandal of clerical sexual abuse of minors, not only the evil behavior of the abusers themselves but also the evasion of responsibility that has marked the behavior of many bishops, brother clergy, and even not a few laypeople. The way in which Church leadership ignored the problem for decades is a textbook example of lack of discernment. Fear of consequences, a misplaced sense of loyalty, and an unwillingness to tackle a difficult issue led many bishops to hide their own poor judgment behind a specious self-justification that they were "protecting the reputation of the Church." However, beyond this terrible burden with which the whole Church now has to deal there are a multitude of other examples, less immediately horrifying but just as corrosive to the life of faith. One such is a style of teaching and leadership that displays no nuance, even when dealing with enormously complex questions. Whether the issue under consideration is the use of contraceptives or premarital cohabitation, abortion or end-of-life issues, the death penalty or homosexual relations, the place of women in the Church or the significance of celibacy to the priesthood, the genuine values that the tradition seeks to uphold are made much harder to hear because the teaching does not take account of the complexity of the lives of the people whom they address. Contraception is not just license or selfishness, abortion is not just murder, euthanasia can be motivated by compassion, same-sex couples love just like heterosexual couples, and so on and so on. None of this is to criticize a particular teaching, but to make the somewhat different point that teaching has to be heard to be effective and that simple answers to complex questions may not carry conviction. When teaching is not heard or "received," as they say, the fault does not always lie with the recipient.

The American Catholic Church is alive and well and increasingly composed of true adults who, as adults should, take their responsibilities to their community of faith very seriously. While many Catholics look askance at their coreligionists who do not accept this or that aspect of Church teaching, it cannot be denied that dissent, even unwise dissent, is often an intellectual struggle with conscience in the face of conflicting data and one's own experience. Few better descriptions could be offered of how an adult, not a child, negotiates her or his life. However, for a much less contentious symbol of an adult American Catholic Church we could look to the enormously significant rise in numbers of what are usually called "lay ecclesial ministers." While there are some reasons to think that the descriptor is not accurate, the phenomenon is enormously important to the Church on a number of levels. In the first instance, it represents a lay movement emerging to do the work that declining numbers of priests and religious used to do and no longer can. Second, it demonstrates beyond doubt that laypeople are capable of doing this work. It may even suggest that what is "properly" lay activity is much more than what we once thought it was, or even that what we have always called "the clergy" is a group designation that needs to be expanded. But finally and above all, each of the 35,000 or so lay ministers in today's Church (approximately the same number as clergy) is an adult and responsible Catholic who has chosen to work for the Church they love. Now this certainly does not mean that adult Catholics choose to be lay ministers and the rest are still children or otherwise less responsible. In fact, there is a lot to be said for Karl Rahner's argument that a lay minister is not really a layperson at all, and that the truly lay mission is to be the Church wherever they happen to be in the world.[29] But it is harder to count these individuals, to distinguish intentional from accidental Catholicism in the lives of those who do not hold some particular responsibility inside the Church, and so the lay ecclesial minister makes for a better symbol of the discerning adult Catholic.

As we examine the growing adulthood of American lay Catholics it can sometimes be hard to remember that the clergy too have their growing up to do. There was a time in the Catholic Church when the clergy exercised an obviously parental role to a laity mostly made up of the unlettered. Until relatively recently, perhaps as little as fifty years ago, clerical relationships to laity were on a spectrum between harsh authoritarianism and benevolent paternalism. Laity were not treated as equals. There were always exceptions, of course, those whose education or money or power placed them in positions that made it impossible to treat them as children, but laity as laity were not the equals of the clergy. Remember the words of Pius X, "the one duty of the multitude is to be led, and like a docile flock to follow their pastors." However, when the laity have shaken off the role of hapless sheep, the shepherd must either be left looking foolish or retool for a different occupation in a different world. And if the agricultural imagery has had its day, so too has any analogy to parent/child in the clergy/lay relationship. Or at least it is

---

[29] Rahner, "Notes on the Lay Apostolate," in *Theological Investigations*, vol. 2 (Baltimore: Helicon, 1963), 319–52.

the vastly changed relationship that parents must develop with their mature adult children if they wish to retain their respect.

If the adulthood of the laity means that they expect to be treated as equals, then an adult clergy is going to be a clergy that is not discomfited by a laity that treats *them* as equals, and that can return the favor. In the ranks of the American clergy we see a strange shift taking place. The clergy now approaching retirement are by all accounts less conservative and less cultic in their approach to priesthood than those more newly ordained.[30] This means that those clergy who have presided over the period of the Church's life in which lay Catholics have begun to claim their ecclesial status as adults are beginning to give way through death or retirement to clergy who are in many cases wedded to an older notion of the priest/layperson relationship. What we have so far seen does not suggest to us that their impact will reverse the laity's claim to adulthood but, rather, that these younger clergy will be faced with their own challenges. Some of them go through an uncomfortable period of adjustment, others leave the priesthood disillusioned, and still others are either "lucky" enough to be in a diocese in which the bishop supports the cultic image of priesthood and so provides them with comfort, or they find a pastoral bolt-hole in situations like high school chaplaincy, where they have replaced life among lay Catholics claiming adulthood with the more impressionable world of the adolescent.

On the whole, parochial clergy are well positioned to reconfigure their relationship to the laity because they are in daily proximity to them, a situation not shared by most bishops. For the most part, this has been happening almost unnoticed in the last few decades, and all American Catholics either belong to or know parishes where the pastor and people have easy and productive relations marked by mutual respect. The problem with younger clergy is troubling, however. To a degree, it must be the case that the types of individuals feeling called to priesthood today are different from their immediate predecessors, and it is hard to see how they can find the model of the priesthood they aspire to in the face of the contemporary Church. They are often referred to as "restorationist."[31] Their calling is somehow connected to dissatisfaction with one

---

[30] See William L. Portier's prize-winning essay on this new phenomenon, "Here Come the Evangelical Catholics," which can be found at http://www.communio-icr.com/articles/PDF/portier31-1.pdf.

[31] The term "restorationist" is usually used to refer to those individuals and groups in the Church dissatisfied to some degree with postconciliar changes, usually because

aspect or another of the postconciliar Church. But it must also be the case that current seminary education either does not teach them to see that the Catholic Church is as fluid a reality as D'Antonio and Baggett have indicated, or it does not care if they do not get the message. A challenge that has to be faced, then, is that of determining how best to select and educate candidates for the ordained ministry so that they are comfortable with the actual community they will face, in the pews and out of them, and not simply bent on reshaping it toward some theoretical image of what the Church *should* be.[32]

Closely connected to the growing adulthood of the Church is its call to accountability. One of the distinguishing marks of adulthood is a willingness to be accountable for one's words and actions, and being attentive to the American Church today rapidly reveals both the determination to be accountable and the demand for accountability. Whatever we make of the less than docile approach to Church life of more active Catholics that we see in Baggett's book and that we can infer from polling samples, it is at the very least a call for the right to be heard and listened to. There are several places where Vatican II writes eloquently about the rights and responsibilities of the laity to speak out for the good of the Church. Unfortunately, the "proper channels" through which it imagined this would happen do not, in fact, exist. When the desire to take responsibility on the part of adult Catholics meets an institutional culture in which that desire is not truly honored, then we have a Church that, intentionally or not, infantilizes its laity. "Infantilization" means refusing to treat people as adults and instead maintaining an ecclesial institutional culture in which they are effectively treated as children. So long as the Church does not develop avenues through which laypeople and for that matter the "lower" clergy can have public and effective input into the daily life of the Church, the adult wish to be accountable will be frustrated. The consequences of this situation can be seen in the many contented ex-Catholics taking highly active roles in Episcopalian,

---

they believe them to be distortions of the message of Vatican II, and hence committed to restoring those features. The papacy of John Paul II is sometimes described as restorationist, and that of Benedict XVI may come to be seen in the same light. The younger cadre of priests we are discussing here are also sometimes called "John Paul II priests," in part because they share this same restorationist attitude.

[32] In addition to the work of Donald Cozzens mentioned earlier, see two books by Paul Philibert, *Stewards of God's Mysteries: Priestly Spirituality in a Changing Church* (Collegeville, MN: Liturgical Press, 2004); and *The Priesthood of the Faithful: Key to a Living Church* (Collegeville, MN: Liturgical Press, 2005).

Lutheran, and United Reformed Churches. The damage to the Church is not inconsiderable, though it probably makes for a quieter life for Church leaders.

If the determination to be responsible for their own Church is a mark of adult Catholics today, then it is not surprisingly accompanied by a call for the clergy—priests and bishops—to show the same sense of accountability. Like lay Catholics, the virtue of clerical accountability divides into personal and "professional" or, more properly, pastoral accountability. Personal accountability is much more difficult for celibates than it is for married or partnered people, who sit at breakfast every day across the table from their accountability. Marriage and family responsibilities are a wonderful check on personal irresponsibility, and broken marriages are usually if not always a result of immaturity or irresponsibility on the part of one or both spouses. Whether the issue is balancing the family checkbook or paying the mortgage, drugs or alcohol or sexual misbehavior, married life is a protector against these failings and, when they occur, marital breakdown is often a tangible and tragic consequence. Clergy vowed to celibacy have financial needs and are called to the same self-discipline as laypeople where money, alcohol, and sex are concerned. Yet they do not have the support system that the family provides, and if they fail, the consequences are not always so dramatic in their immediate personal lives. It is a fearful and precarious thing for lonely people to be responsible only to God and themselves, and the extent of sexual abuse or plain sexual misconduct, on the one hand, and alcohol abuse, on the other, is a real problem for the Catholic clergy and their Church. It is not only reprehensible and regrettable in itself, it may also point to the need to take another look at the whole issue of clerical lifestyle and culture.

When we turn from personal to pastoral or professional accountability, we should expect to find weaknesses in the one area to be accompanied by challenges in the other. Accountability builds accountability. Someone whose personal life is responsible and disciplined is likely to behave in the same way professionally, and to want to operate in a professional context that supports and rewards accountability. Such practices of accountability do not, however, distinguish the Catholic institutional Church. There is some bottom-up accountability, though not as much as one might imagine, and the only top-down accountability there is can be found among bishops and clergy who choose to insist upon it in their own diocese or parish, not because it is mandated but because they think it important. So senior clergy at least are relatively impervious to the demands of their bishop, and bishops operate pretty freely relative to Rome and with total freedom relative to their brother bishops within the regional or national hierarchy.[33] Given the shortage of clergy, even relatively young priests who do nothing to bring themselves the unwelcome attention of their bishop can count on quickly achieving the considerable independence that goes with being a pastor of their own parish, especially if they do not see it as a trust they must make work in cooperation with an adult laity. There is, without question, periodic use of the language of affective accountability, but there are no structures of effective accountability. So, for example, a pastor may say and indeed think that he is the servant of the people of his parish, but where is the 360 degree evaluation system that would enable him to discover how good a job he is doing, just as it would allow him to have a say in his bishop's performance at the diocesan level? A pastor may run his parish pastoral council as democratically as he wishes, but canon law makes clear to him that all lay opinion is "consultative only."[34] A bishop may want and indeed probably should want to hand over all diocesan financial affairs to an independent board of qualified lay Catholics, but canon law ties him to decision making in an area that has little or nothing to do with his pastoral duties or, in all probability, his personal skills.

Our attentiveness to what is going on in the Church today has revealed another layer of the issue of adulthood and accountability in the way in which Catholics make ethical choices and the kind of attention they pay to the teachings of Church leaders. The point we need to attend to is not that laypeople make better or worse decisions than bishops, or that episcopal teaching is out of touch, or that laypeople are victims of sloppy thinking, but that laypeople simply assume that they will be the court of final appeal on matters of their own ethical standpoints and values. It really does not matter to them what the bishops say about this, or whether their teaching is superior to the consciences of the laity, the turn to the subject—as Lonergan might have put it—is unlikely to be reversed any time soon. On the whole the laity give respectful attention to the words of their Church leaders, but they treat what they have to

---

[33] For an insight into how the institutional Church in the United States actually works there is still no better book than that by Thomas J. Reese, *Archbishop: Inside the Power Structure of the American Catholic Church* (San Francisco: HarperCollins, 1989).

[34] The best discussion of this problem is to be found in Bradford E. Hinze, *Practices of Dialogue in the Roman Catholic Church: Aims and Obstacles, Lessons and Laments* (New York: Continuum, 2006).

say as advice, not instruction. Clearly, this is not true of all or perhaps even most Catholics, but it seems to be characteristic of more active Catholic laity in general and of young people in particular.

If it is correct to characterize the changed attitude of the community of faith to Church teaching as a dimension of the growth in adulthood and accountability, then it suggests a shift in that teaching away from instruction on particular issues and toward conscience formation in general. For the Catholic population to take more ethical responsibility on its own shoulders is undoubtedly a good thing, but it does not automatically mean that they do not need help in figuring out the process by which good decisions are made. The adult catechetical movement in the Church saw this coming some time ago and has moved in exactly that direction, attempting to refocus education in the parochial setting on adults rather than children.[35] Instruction in theology and religious studies in Catholic colleges and universities is also on very much the same path, helping people to learn to make good and informed decisions rather than simply telling them what they must do or think. But the challenge of ignorance not only remains, it grows every generation as the old "Catholic culture" continues to dissipate. We cannot turn back the clock, but we would not be wrong in seeking ways in which the Church might restore the knowledge of the history of the Catholic tradition to a people who have largely lost touch with it.

Be Reasonable: Ecclesiological Models and the American Experience

The picture that sociologists, theologians, and other analysts paint of the changing American Church is the material of a more inductive ecclesiology. As we try to move from attentiveness through understanding toward being reasonable and responsible (or loving), and to contemplate change, we are being invited to make sense of the whole. Human beings make meaning by drawing the data of their experience into patterns that enable them to order, grasp, and so "understand" the raw information that would otherwise be sheer chaos. This is the moment at which modeling becomes an important activity. What models suggest themselves out of the welter of the data itself as potentially fruitful ways to make sense of what we see before us? What should we make of this

---

[35] See, for example, Jane Regan's book, *Toward an Adult Church: A Vision of Faith Formation* (Chicago: Loyola Press, 2002).

American community of growing and changing people of faith, maturing in their sense of responsibility for their Church and reaching out for greater scope for their adult awareness of the need for accountability and authenticity? The answer is surely not to be found by simply opening up the treasure house of history and looking around for something that might fit. Explaining the Church to itself today might be a little bit like costuming a client. Off-the-peg stuff never looks as good as bespoke tailoring. Still less is it likely that someone outfitted in whatever we can find in that old chest in the attic will look anything other than thrown together. For a costume ball, perhaps, but not for a suit of clothes for living.

The ecclesial models that emerge naturally from the shape of American experience and its current forms of expression will be dynamic, not static. In the pages that remain in this book, we will explore four such images. Each of them suggests itself to us from the sketch we have provided of American Catholicism today. Consistent with our resolutely inductive approach, each can only be explored as provisional, perhaps enlightening for the moment but definitely of human rather than divine origin, and so probably destined to be replaced as times change and we move ever on. These images are historically conditioned and context dependent, but that does not mean they have no relevance beyond the shores of America. The internal pluralism of the American Catholic Church is only the local expression of the much richer pluralism of global Catholicism. The inductive ecclesiological investigations currently taking place in other parts of the world need to be attended to and learned from, just as our experience may have something to offer to others. For example, we have a lot to learn from Asian Catholic reflection on the Church as a tiny minority community in cultures dominated by equally ancient world religions. While this kind of thinking has sometimes unnerved Rome, it has much to offer to European and North American cultures where the dominance of Christianity in general and Catholicism in particular is giving way to a much more pluralistic religious and cultural environment.[36]

The Church as Hospice

Our attentiveness to the American Catholic Church makes it clear that in terms of traditional understandings of institutional commitment

---

[36] See Richard R. Gaillardetz, *Ecclesiology for a Global Church: A People Called and Sent* (Maryknoll, NY: Orbis, 2008).

and religious literacy, it is to a high degree an aging community that shows many signs of entropy. We need therefore to consider the arresting possibility that the best ecclesial model for our times is that of the Church as hospice. This observation builds upon an address given a few years ago by a distinguished Catholic priest to his fellow clergy in the Diocese of Milwaukee. Father Bryan Massingale, a moral theologian who teaches at Marquette University, proposed to his clerical brothers that the best model for pastoral care today was that of the hospice.[37] He did not develop an ecclesiology from this proposal, though it is not unlikely that there is one lurking under the surface. His concern was to help aging and overworked clergy, some of them no doubt despondent or depressed, to make sense of a Church in which their work seemed to be a matter of running very fast in order, at best, to stay in the same place. Massingale's point is surely that the Church for which traditional pastoral care is still required is one that is passing. But the model of the hospice reminds us that care and respect for the dying person, continuing to celebrate that life up to the moment of death, providing comfort and love, is just what pastors are there to do. At the same time, neither the caregiver nor the dying patient hides from the fact that death is coming close. Equally important, Christian reflection on hospice is always filled with the creative tension that exists in all Christian theology between death and resurrection. Death is the moment of entry into new life for the individual. The dying that the historic community of faith must do and that is evidently going on in the American Church today is simply one side of the coin. On the other, new life is emerging, and for this to happen, some dying has to take place. In Massingale's words, the distress of clergy and laity alike at the ills of the American Catholic Church, if we only look at it with the eyes of the prophet, is something "aided and abetted by God's own self." Eschewing the extremes of nostalgic wallowing in the past or despair at the present, "the prophet announces: 'Look! Pay attention! God is doing something NEW,'" and helps out the old so that the new may emerge.

Some pages back we considered the possibility that we might think of the Church as a "collective incarnate subject" along the lines of Lonergan's historicist transition from nature to subjectivity. Massingale's reflections on dying and rising add a dimension. For the individual Christian, death takes place in the confident hope of resurrection and

---

[37] Massingale's presentation can be found at http://www.jknirp.com/massin.htm.

new life. But the dying and rising of the Church as a collective incarnate subject in history is a metaphorical application of Christian death/new life dynamics, and the new life that is to follow the death of the old will emerge within history, at least this side of the eschaton. The model of hospice is very helpful as a way of explaining much pastoral care at the present time, and also of suggesting that we look beyond death to the new life that is coming. But in itself it does not give, nor is it intended to provide, an outline of the emerging new life. For that, we need to supplement the hospice image with others that grow directly out of the American experience.

The Church as Pilgrim

The model of "the pilgrim Church" refers any contemporary theologian to the pages of *Lumen Gentium* in which the Church is described in this way, but American Catholics would likely think at least as quickly of the pilgrim fathers who crossed the Atlantic on the Mayflower. Here we can suitably join the two ideas together. Vatican II's pilgrim Church is primarily intended in the document to relate the community of faith on earth to the heavenly community toward which it is oriented. However, subsequent theological reflection has extended the application of the term to stress the imperfect but hopeful progress of the Church within history. The pilgrim is always on the way, sometimes taking a wrong path and having to get back on track but, because guided by the Holy Spirit, the pilgrim Church travels in confident hope of finally arriving at its destination. The image is particularly useful because it finesses a difficult ecclesiological challenge: how to recognize the historical imperfections of the Church with the divine origins that make it difficult to ascribe error to the Church itself. The presence of the Holy Spirit with the Church until the end of time is perceptible in the ways in which we are periodically nudged back onto the right path, not led by the nose or frog-marched toward the eschatological banquet.

Employed inductively, the model of the Church as pilgrim is appealing because it grows out of the history and culture of America and forces itself upon the imagination because of its explanatory potential. The pilgrims who arrived at Plymouth Rock were on an adventure, escaping from a more restrictive religious and political reality into a new world in which they would be free to worship and organize themselves according to their own convictions. Or so they thought. Of course, this was only a part of the truth, because they soon found themselves dealing with native inhabitants, trying to tame an unkind and unrelenting wilderness while benefiting from its bounty, and before long, interacting with other settlers who did not share their religious or political culture. Survival in the new reality, for the pilgrims as for all others in similar situations, depended upon their adaptability. Without abandoning the distinctive way of life they had traveled here in order to preserve, their prosperity and security required that they find within themselves untapped and perhaps unsuspected reserves of flexibility and creativity to go with the courage and faithfulness that was already well established.

Courage, faithfulness, flexibility, and adaptability in a new world in which not everyone shares your religious beliefs or your political convictions and in which some would likely welcome your disappearance and do not want to hear your opinions. Does this sound familiar? Isn't this in fact a pretty good description of where the American Catholic Church stands today? Like the pilgrims of old we have a venerable and honored tradition that helps protect our continuing identity. But our future requires us to find all kinds of resources within the tradition to transform ourselves into a community that will thrive in a pluralistic and constantly changing environment. We need to be able to speak with authority when ethical values are challenged or misunderstood, we need to find ways to maintain a vibrant religious identity at a time when institutional commitment is not a high value even among those who consider themselves Catholic, and we need to be so comfortable in an environment of a pluralistic and at times secular democracy that we can admit elements of that democracy into our own ways of governing ourselves as a community of faith.

The Church as pilgrim connects nicely to the image of the Church as hospice. The pilgrims who arrived on these shores were leaving the old world for the new. For them, Europe meant the death of their hopes and perhaps of their very selves. They set out on a voyage that in the short term was considerably more perilous than the situation they left behind. So Plymouth Rock was for them God's gift of a new life to replace the old one they left behind, and the Atlantic Ocean a definite symbol of passing through death to life, emerging from the baptismal waters onto the shores of America and beginning again, full of hope in the great gift that God had given them. It did not mean that their future was guaranteed; it meant simply that God had provided them with a new situation in which to work out their salvation. The Bible and the community's traditions came with them, the world in which they had to reflect upon them was radically different, and the old ways just weren't going to work anymore. Today those pilgrims are absorbed into the fabric of American culture and history, still alive but probably not in the ways they had anticipated or even wanted. But God makes of our futures something that grows out of our past and present but is not finally in our control. So it will be too with the Catholic Church.

The Church as Immigrant

The image of the Church as immigrant requires even less imaginative transposition for American Catholics than does that of the pilgrim. Anyone who knows even the smallest amount of our history knows that we were "an immigrant Church." Those with a little more historical sense may well add, "and we still are." Beyond the indisputable historical accuracy of both assertions the image of the immigrant has more riches to offer our reflection. Immigrants are people who are never entirely at home in the places in which they live, but whose project is to make a home in this place. An immigrant is someone whose presence enriches the place they call home by bringing to it those other things in the immigrant's memory and culture of birth, but whose happiness and lasting contribution to their new home depend upon finding resources to shift allegiance without abandoning allegiance. In an obvious illustration of this, Italian immigrants to this country, like the Irish and the Jews and the Germans and the Poles, had to become American but did not have to stop being Italians. Think of all that American culture would have lost if Italians had just become homogenized Americans. Precisely the same task lies before current waves of immigrants, mostly Hispanic or Asian. The truly successful immigrant and the one who contributes most to the host country is the one who manages the difficult process of being bicultural.

The idea of the immigrant suggests a way of being Church that is truly American while no less Catholic and Christian. American Catholics—perhaps all people with strong religious identities could say the same—have to be bicultural. We have to be equally at home with our Christian religious identity and our sense of ourselves as American. While this is true in the sense in which it was a major preoccupation of American Catholics in the first half of the twentieth century to be accepted in a dominantly Protestant culture as "real Americans," there is a deeper meaning to it today. Today, when acceptability is largely not a problem, we have to find a way to be both religious and secular. For individual American Catholics in the past that probably meant a cautious appropriation of some American cultural values—perhaps religious tolerance—but no dilution of their strong religious profile. Today it more commonly means the opposite, namely, to reappropriate their Catholic identity as a strong challenge to some distortions of our society without abandoning anything truly valuable in American culture.

But for the Church as a whole and especially for the institutional Church, we still in so many ways seem to be at that earlier stage, looking on American society with deep suspicion and appropriating only some elements of the culture—perhaps religious tolerance—while resisting a more holistic embrace of the American religious and political genius. And here perhaps is the internal problem for American Catholicism: that the people and the institution are in different places vis-à-vis the culture in which they have made their home and to which they owe allegiance. The internal challenge of the Church today is in large measure a matter of Catholics who are thoroughly and healthily American trying to deal with an institution that is modeled upon very different assumptions, drawn not from the Bible but from human cultural and political preferences for imperialism, benevolent despotism, and paternalistic patterns of governance.

The history of early American Catholicism is one of a struggle between a nascent truly American model of church and the impact of huge waves of immigrants who, in their sheer numbers and in the very European vision of church they brought with them, simply swamped the indigenous church.[38] Eighteenth-century American Catholicism was a small and delicate phenomenon, bearing two marks of its moment in history. The small numbers and the almost complete absence of priests had meant that it was in large measure a lay-led Church, and its more educated members were imbued with the same Enlightenment tolerance and relative liberalism as their non-Catholic counterparts. The distance from Rome allowed the young Church to grow in its own way, with a system of lay trusteeship of parishes employed in Maryland, with the first Catholic bishop of Baltimore, John Carroll, elected by his fellow clergy, and with the creative experiment of a bicameral diocesan legislature under the far-sighted Bishop John England in Charleston, South Carolina, in the 1820s. These distinctly American developments disappeared once the successive waves of immigration began and the pressure to conform to a Roman model of Church became stronger. Bishop England's model for diocesan administration worked well but was never

---

[38] See Jay Dolan, *In Search of an American Catholicism: A History of Religion and Culture in Tension* (New York: Oxford, 2002); and James M. O'Toole, *The Faithful: A History of Catholics in America* (Cambridge, MA: Harvard University Press, 2008).

tried anywhere else. Lay trusteeship gave way to autocratic bishops, and bishops were appointed without much say on the part of clergy, still less laity.

The nineteenth-century demise of the pre-immigrant model of Church that was developing in the new America was a missed opportunity for Catholicism and for ecclesiology, and a lesson for today. It is a warning about how not to be an immigrant, since it showed the profound contempt for an indigenous model of Church. Many who encountered that model were too narrow to contemplate its merits. This should suggest to us today that as we rightly see ourselves in part as immigrants to a new world of religious pluralism in which we have an important voice but no monopoly, we should be ready to learn from the virtues of the society and of the other religious families among whom we live. The Church as immigrant is always learning, always a little off center, wanting to belong without discarding its identity, and wanting to contribute to the vitality and plurality of the new world. The Hispanic immigrants who are changing the face of American Catholicism can be for all of us a symbol of the immigrant mentality we should always carry with us.

How, then, do we address in this immigrant Church the tension between the eagerness to be American Catholics, which marks active Catholics today, and the reluctance to be anything but Roman Catholics, which seems to be the distinguishing characteristic of the hierarchical position? We should all want to be both Roman and American, of course. But we are "Roman" Catholics only in the sense that we are participant members of the Roman communion, sharing a history and a theology and recognizing the pope, the bishop of Rome, as the leader of the global Church. We have no responsibility to be "Roman" in any other way at all, and culturally and historically it is far more likely and arguably more important that we should be American. But there are some points of real and potential conflict between the two faces of American Roman Catholicism, most notably in the American expectation of democratic process and an open society as it comes into occasional conflict with the sometimes comically obsessive secrecy of the Vatican. In fact, thinking of it as comical is a good way to avoid becoming too angry with some of its features and helps us to recognize that the papal teaching authority and the Vatican bureaucracy are by no means the same thing.

In the end, the immigrant model of Church reminds us of the provisionality of much of the baggage we carry as a historical institution. Like any immigrant we possess ideas, habits, and practices that have their origins in times long past but that we tend naturally to assume are fixtures of what a human being or a human society must be. And then we meet another culture, one in which we are going to have to find a way to be at home, in which cultural expectations are not at all the same. Moreover, to be the immigrant Church is to be "always immigrant," living constantly with the sense of provisionality and flexibility, always ready for a new turn in the road along which we will always be the People of God, always called to spread the good news, but by no means always called to do it in the same way. We will probably always carry with us at least some of the marks of our origins, and our genetic makeup will indicate our continuity with the Catholics of the fourteenth century and the fourth. But as successful immigrants we simply cannot always be looking back over our shoulder for reassurance. The Holy Spirit that guided the Church in the fourth and fourteenth centuries is no longer in those past times, but in this present time, coaxing and guiding us toward the next bend in the road.

The Church as Pioneer

Of all the images that resonate with Americans, the mythic power of the pioneer must be the strongest. The Conestoga wagons heading west, forging a new life in a new Eden, is an image that is instantly recognizable to almost everyone. The people in these wagons travel lightly and travel in hope, not sure what their exact destination will be but knowing that they plan to settle somewhere in the setting sun. They have left the relative familiarity of the land "back east" to head into an uncertain future, filled with hope and not a little fear. They know that the people and the places they have left behind they will probably never see again. As pioneers they are building a new life for themselves, and they are fashioning a new country for their children and their children's children, even though many of them will die before they see it come to fruition. Pioneers, we can see, are adventurous, determined, courageous, resourceful, and—if not entirely foolish—aware that success depends more upon the grace of God than it does upon sheer good fortune or unaided human energies.

When we apply the image of pioneer to the Church we uncover an additional important element that is not so apparent in the pictures we have drawn of the Church as pilgrim or immigrant. There is a shadow side that accompanies the mythic power of the pioneer image that the original pioneers were mostly unaware of but that with the hindsight of history we can and must learn from. The descendants of these hardy pioneers despoiled the virgin land even as they farmed it, and harmed its native inhabitants and much of its wildlife. They not only tamed a wilderness, they also destroyed portions of it in their ignorance and sometimes greed. The lesson of the pioneer experience is that with all their virtues, they needed judgment, temperance, and humility before the vast new world into which they were entering. Successfully building a new life worthy of respect requires learning the ways of the world you encounter and finding how best to unite the old and the new, the indigenous and the imported, the tried and true and the newfangled.

The image of pioneer adds to our images of hospice, immigrant, and pilgrim a note of more protracted fortitude in the face of the elements, natural or of human origin, and a welcome call for humility in the face of our encounter with the new. The future is always almost with us, and even though we cannot anticipate it we have to be on our toes and ready to deal with it. The pioneer Church will have gritty resolve and joyful hope in equal measure. Its success will depend on being able to distinguish between what it needs for the journey and what it would be wise to leave behind, and the knowledge that what it can take along it may need to jettison along the way. The pioneer image calls on us to think about what we do and do not need to cling onto. The heavily loaded wagon may be more comfortable in the short term but is not likely to make it over the next mountain pass or through the next swamp. Just as the Church as pioneer is always on the way, so it is also always about to begin the next stage of its journey, always needing to ask itself what to discard and what to pack, in the knowledge that it will never return to this precise spot again, unless of course the journey is abandoned. The pioneer Church that abandons the journey is eternally fixed in the past, and the past moment in which it is stuck is not the living point in history that it once was but a kind of wax effigy in which no blood flows.

In his classic work *Models of the Church*, Avery Dulles made two general observations that are relevant to our consideration here of these images from the American experience.[39] The first was that we should distinguish between images and models, recognizing their differences but being appreciative of the value of both. A model is different from an image because of its heuristic potential; its internal structure corresponds to that which it is being used to explain so that deeper understanding can occur. An image may provide a flash of insight but does not go further. So People of God is a model, but "sheepfold" is an image. The

[39] Avery Dulles, *Models of the Church* (Garden City, NY: Doubleday, 1974; New York: Doubleday, Image Books, 1991).

second observation Dulles made was that when we are dealing with models (and presumably with images) it is important not to focus on one to the exclusion of others but, rather, to seek to keep as many as possible in play. So the ecclesiologist becomes a kind of theological juggler, one might say, and richness of ecclesial reflection corresponds to how much success she or he might have in keeping as many balls as possible in the air at the same time.

These observations suggest that it would be a mistake to pick out one image as the single image or model that explains the Church. Mystical Body and Communion and other venerable images from the tradition will continue to shed their light on the mystery of the Church, though they may do so in different ways at different times. They are in play, as are pioneer and immigrant and others from the American experience. In fact, we could easily go beyond the four we have briefly examined and enrich our ecclesial reflection still further. What help might we get, for example, from the image of "the New Deal," in which the masses were put to work to build the American infrastructure and in the process to recover the dignity that hard times had threatened to overwhelm? The sorry story of America's treatment of African Americans has its parallel in the subordination of black Catholics in the Church, but it also can be applied analogously to how the Church treats women. Formal emancipation may come with the declaration that all have equal dignity in virtue of their baptism, but women still have their own version of Jim Crow laws that formalize a "separate but equal" story of complementarity behind which lurks continuing discrimination. A similar set of reflections on how the Church treats Catholic groups of its own people who are distinctive for one reason or another could be stimulated by reflection on the irony of the Declaration of Independence's ringing claim that "all men are created equal." Just as America has had to learn the deep truth in that statement, so must the Church explore further what it means to say that we are all created in the image and likeness of the one God.

Beyond the Images:
From the Local to the Global

The multiplication of images and models that the foregoing discussion suggests is a distinct feature of the inductive approach to ecclesiology. It is not only that the American experience throws up for our consideration all sorts of creative possibilities but also that every other society in which the Church is present can do the same, and all the reflections thereby generated—here and abroad—enrich the global understanding of catholicity. In fact, they *are* catholicity, which thrives upon the tension between the local and the universal. So it would be a serious mistake to think that inductive method cannot support a global ecclesiology. On the contrary, it supports an ecclesiology of constant reformation, one in which regional and even local cultures feed religious practice and stimulate the imagination to make better sense of what the Church is and does here or there, now or then. The cultural and liturgical variations that were encouraged in the immediately postconciliar period almost half a century ago were signs of this nascent empirical approach to what it is to be Church. Their restriction, if not suppression, in more recent decades is not so much a result of distaste for cultural variation in itself as it is a by-product of the restoration of a more centralized Church and its accompaniment, deductive ecclesiology.

The vision of the global Church as one of constant reformation is not quite enough because it does not offer grounds for determining which reforms or which culturally influenced ecclesial movements are legitimate. Bernard Lonergan saw this problem clearly when he wrote that the "new largely empirical approach to theology can too easily be made into a device for reducing doctrines to probable opinions." He feared that without a foundation the inductive approach would become "the dupe of every fashion," and it is obvious enough from our foregoing discussion how this could happen if we have no method by which "to distinguish tinsel and silver, gilt and gold."[40] Relying as we must on the constant flux of ecclesial experience at the grassroots, it can seem a huge challenge to distinguish the tinsel from the silver, but it is necessary if we are to make the case for inductive ecclesiology.

Lonergan's solution, which we have already discussed above and which we adopt here, is to identify the method of inductive ecclesiology as reflection on the ongoing conversion of the Church, which we understand as a collective incarnate subject. Inductive ecclesiology is a process of discernment of the movement of conversion or change that is a constant feature of any historical community. What makes it ecclesiology is the object it discerns, which is the *ekklesia*, the community of faith called together by Christ as a witness to God's saving love for the world. And the activity upon which the discernment is focused is "conversion viewed as an ongoing process, at once personal, communal and historical,"

---

[40] Lonergan, *A Second Collection*, 53.

which "coincides with living religion."[41] The theology of the Church, then, is that intellectual activity that watches over the community's faithfulness to its historical mission. The Church's mission is one of dynamic discipleship of Christ, where ongoing conversion is the method by which it renews its sense of how to be a sign of God's saving love for the world, here and now.

The Church is a communion because it is a communion of communions, all of them in a process of constant conversion to Christ. Each local community of faith is a body of people in communion with one another and with the larger Church because, in the first instance, it partakes of communion with Christ. The Eucharist expresses and cements all those facets of communion, and energizes the community in its primary mission, to be an effective sign of the love of God in and for the world. It is communion with Christ in the Eucharist that gives the people of God the strength to be converted anew every day to the challenging mission to be God's presence in the world, agents of its continuing progress in humanization. Eucharist without mission is sterile; mission without Eucharist is mere activism. The importance of the eucharistic liturgy lies, therefore, not solely in the real presence of Christ but also in the living community in this time and place. The one sacrifice of Christ is remembered in all times and places, but only so that the grace of God will strengthen and inspire the community to be what it needs to be in this particular historical moment to be faithful to its mission. Christ calls us to conversion, undoubtedly, but our conversion is not to some static memory. Rather, it is conversion in the Spirit to the living Christ in the here and now, the Christ present in all of us but especially in the poor and downtrodden.

The Church is the communion of the converted and the communion of conversion. While this is not a concrete image, it is a very concrete process that underlies it. For the Church to be the Church most faithfully it always has to be asking itself what the Gospel call to mission demands of us *now*. Our faithfulness has to be to the Gospel call, not to the forms or practices that were appropriate to that call in times past. This does not mean that we have to jettison the past for the sake of jettisoning it, or out of some predilection for novelty, but it does mean that we cannot be slavishly bound to what worked in the past. When the Church was the driving force of medieval European society, or when the Church was

---

[41] Ibid., 66–67.

in a struggle with the Protestant reformers, or when the American Church was trying to find a way to be both Catholic and American, these times called for certain historically conditioned courses of action. Today in the United States and in many other places around the world, we are not in anything like these situations. We are a vibrant religious community coexisting with others, Christian and non-Christian alike, in a secular and pluralistic state. As citizens we are shaped by American culture and history. As Catholic Christians we are also shaped by another related but distinct history and culture. Ongoing conversion calls for courageous, Spirit-driven discernment of the changes we need to make in order not only to be attentive, intelligent, and reasonable but also—and above all—to be loving. If the Catholic Church is not evidently a loving community of faith, then it is failing. If we are loving—and love must be other-directed—then, imperfect as we will be, we are doing something right. It is the response to the call to dynamic love that make us the same Church the world over; but it is how we incarnate that call in our own particular time and place that finally makes us faithful to the logic of conversion.

It is at this late point in the book that it is finally appropriate to say a little about the "Rome" in Roman Catholicism. Obviously enough, the papacy is the symbol of unity of the worldwide Church. It is the papacy, both as an office and as a symbol, that precludes the centrifugal movement of local churches, spinning off and away from unity with the larger Church. The papacy and the Eucharist together are the twin foci of Catholic unity, all in the service of mission. Without the Eucharist, there is no Church. Without the papacy, there is only the local Church, though there could of course be some free and purely human association of local churches, such as exists in the World Council of Churches. But that is an organizational convenience for the sake of Christian solidarity and good works, not an organic unity.

There is little danger that the papacy will forget its role as symbol and focus of unity, but it will exercise it successfully only if it recognizes the legitimate pluralism of local churches. This is a difficult balance, because too little leadership and the Church will fragment, too much and the truly catholic character of the Church will be endangered. In the terminology we have used throughout the book, there will be friction and even more serious problems if leadership acts too deductively or top down, when the Church as a whole is becoming more inductive or bottom up. If we have an Aristotelian Church and a Platonic papacy, there will be tensions in both directions. If the Church is Thomist and the papacy is Augustinian, then we are going to need a form of internal ecumenism if leadership is not to lose its credibility and endanger the unity of the world Church.

Be Loving . . .

If we are committed to the idea of the Church as the communion of the converted and of conversion, then the need for change will come as no surprise. A community of conversion is constantly in process of change; the challenge is to make the right changes, and these are dictated by the aims of conversion. As we have already said, conversion in the Church is to a more faithful attention to the mission to be an effective sign of the love of God in the world. Fired by the Spirit and shaped by the life of Christ, we are moved to a mission of loving the world for God. While discernment of what is and is not appropriate change in the service of this end is indispensable, ongoing conversion to Christ *is* "living religion," as Lonergan would say. Personal and institutional change is of the essence of the community of faith, because the changing times will always require more of us in the service of our mission.

There are many things in the Church that active and involved Catholics from one end or other of the spectrum would like to see changed. More conservative or traditional Catholics rightly stress the centrality of the liturgy to the life of the community and seem dissatisfied with its present form. The changes they would like to see would bring the liturgy back much closer to the liturgical forms that only the very oldest Catholics now remember. Some want to keep the present shape of the Mass but restore at least some of the Latin language. Others are unconcerned about the Latin but would like a Mass that makes clearer the respective responsibilities of priest and people in its celebration. They are unhappy with what John Paul II used to deplore as "the clericalization of the laity and the laicization of the clergy." Still others, though fewer, will be happy with nothing less than a return to the preconciliar form of the Mass in all respects. These same conservatives also see the changing shape of Catholic identity that we witnessed in the sociological data to have been occasioned by a decline in personal discipline, both that of people and clergy. Obedience, they feel, has slipped from the pantheon of Catholic virtues. This leads them from liturgical concerns to the whole list of what they would consider liberal hot-button items like birth control, same-sex unions, celibacy of the clergy, ordination of women, and on and on. All of these have become issues, they argue, only because of the failure of attention to the teaching authority of the Church, especially as symbolized in the pope, which provides strong and clear teaching to those with ears to hear. In their heart of hearts, conservative Catholics probably do not expect a return to the packed Churches of the 1950s, but they look to a Church that while smaller will be what they would consider more faithful to the tradition, more truly *Roman* Catholic.

Among active and involved more liberal Catholics, the emphasis is less on making the Church more *Roman* Catholic and more on developing it as an *American* Catholic Church. It is always easy to caricature such a wish as a lack of respect for the pope or Vatican, but most liberal Catholics would not see it that way. Their probable response to such an accusation, one frequently made, would distinguish between a Roman Catholicism in which all local color and variation is homogenized away, and a Roman Catholicism that is a global communion of Christians united under the pope as the focus and symbol of their unity in the ancient tradition of the apostolic Church. Preferring the latter on historical and theological grounds, they would insist that they remain Roman but distinctly *American* Roman Catholics. And if you were to ask in what exactly this "American" piece consists, it would be explained in terms of culture, history, and—frankly—style. To a degree, "style" is an obvious and innocuous issue. All cultures and therefore all local churches are going to have their own styles. Clergy in one country dress and live one way and clergy/lay relationships are partly a product of local culture. How people dress for church and what they find when they get there, how they greet one another and how much dancing and foot tapping they do varies widely among African or Hispanic or Anglo-Saxon Catholics.

The concern for national style as an ecclesial issue is distinctive of liberal Catholics. While it can be as inconsequential as what you wear to church, style can also be more substantive. In particular, the political style of a national community is often different in many ways from that in another. American political culture in its ideals and best practices is intensely democratic and extraordinarily participatory. Public opinion is frequently determinative of national policy on important issues, sometimes even when it arguably should not be. When public opinion is ignored, Americans' satisfaction with their political leaders plummets. They are suspicious of Washington insiders and sometimes want to "throw the bums out." Every four years they get an opportunity, and many Americans would also like term limits to curb lifelong political influence. In electing an African American to be president in 2008, Americans signaled a willingness to address the ancient wrongs of their own culture and history. In an elementally pure act of American cultural life, the election of Barack Obama as president demonstrated the priority of pragmatism over all other considerations. It's what works that counts.

In contemplating change in the Church nationally and in measuring the value of the American Church to global Catholicism, the question of the role of participatory democracy and the associated issue of the value of pragmatism may well be where the battle lines are drawn between different perspectives. Within the American Church, more conservative elements see little if any need for democracy and eschew pragmatism in the name of long-established patterns and practices. More liberal Catholics take exactly the opposite position, openly arguing for more democracy in the day-to-day doings of the Church, a greater say for the whole people in the selection of their bishops and pastors, and lay control over financial affairs. Significantly, they rarely if ever extend their demands to doctrinal issues, where they evidently sense that some things are best left to the experts. But of course the changes they argue for are also based on the same principle; it is just that they themselves are the experts. Lay Catholics in particular can lay claim to a whole range of expertise that does not belong to the clergy as a class but which for historical reasons is reserved to the clergy in Church life. Finance is only the most obvious example. Parish administration, counseling, and even the skills of theological reflection or biblical and ethical scholarship no longer belong with the clergy as a class.

On one level, the choice between the liberal and conservative vision is just a gamble. If the conservative assessment of the state of Catholicism is correct, then to go down the liberal line will mean the further weakening of Catholicism as a distinct and living Christian Church. If the liberals are stymied in their call for further change in the Church, for more democracy and participation, they believe that the claim to Catholic identity on the part of those with little evident institutional affiliation will mean the reduction of the Church to an anachronism, a museum-piece testimony to a vanished time. But if both assessments of the other's program are very similar, envisaging a weakened Church as its consequence, their respective visions of what would happen if their own diagnosis were to be accepted are subtly but significantly distinct. The application of the old discipline, say the conservatives, would probably produce a smaller but more faithful Church. More democracy and more participation, say the liberals, will lead to a less passive, more adult and accountable Church that will be more attractive to the young and their disaffected elders. This Church, they think, will grow.

To move beyond the impasse over the future of the Church we need to return to the ecclesial image of hospice, since both liberal and conservative solutions are like so many friends and relatives in denial over the impending death of their loved one. Each in their own way sees a remedy that will restore the health of the patient. Latin liturgy or married priests, liberally applied, and the patient will be up and about in a matter of days. Both are in denial, and until we restore the Christian dynamic of death and resurrection to our consideration of the current face of the Church our solutions cannot be sufficiently radical. We do not need life support; we need new life.

If the situation of the Catholic Church is as dire as all this, how then to explain the extraordinary vitality of many American parishes? It was John Paul II's belief that only in the United States had the vision for renewed parish life that stemmed from Vatican II actually come to something like fruition. Seeing the local community at its best, it is hard to disagree that the high-functioning American parish is a poster child for the vision of *Lumen Gentium*.[42] There are very many local faith communities distinguished by wholesome adult relationships between ordained and lay members, good liturgies with sensitive homilies, genuine sharing of ministry, and a deep concern for the needs of those in and around the parish. There is a working parish finance council that removes the pastor as far as possible from dealing with the money. A good parish has a support group for everything, people sometimes joke, but there is a kernel of truth here. And the whole is cemented together by a functioning pastoral council in which the health of the community is symbolized. If there are problems to be addressed they are dealt with openly, as adults do, each taking her or his share of the responsibility. It is an adult and accountable community of faith.

The problem the Church faces is certainly not with the current state of the better American parishes, which are after all the local communities with which active Catholics most closely identify. The problem is with the future of these parishes in a national Church that is entering hospice care. All the challenges to the life of the community that we have discussed above, like the demographics of the ordained and changing responses to ecclesial authority, indicate a Church approaching severe crisis. The good parishes are wonderfully healthy for now, but they are not increasing in number. Who will staff them in the future, and what will the people do who find that the community that gave them life is changing for the worse or being closed down or amalgamated with another local parish? Sometimes these reorganizations are necessary, but

---

[42] For a sampling of these see Paul Wilkes, *Excellent Catholic Parishes: The Guide to Best Places and Practices* (Mahwah, NJ: Paulist Press, 2001).

however we dress them up, they are not signs of life. The living parish is fine for now, probably destined to decrease in number, and helpless in the face of larger problems with the Church that cannot be satisfactorily addressed at the local level. The good parish may very well suggest solutions to the national Church, but it cannot implement them beyond its own confines, and often not even there, since so many of them come up against the "consultation only" clause that canon law makes clear governs almost all forms of lay participation.

To create structural changes in the Church that will result in a greater likelihood of increased participation and a fuller life of faith for a larger community, mixed by gender, ethnicity, race, age, and sexual orientation, we need to be more loving, and that means above all that we need to listen better. We certainly need to listen to one another, both across ideological or theological differences and between laity and clergy. But most of all we need to listen to the Spirit as it speaks through what is actually going on in the living, daily Church. The attitudes, convictions, and practices of people of faith, even and perhaps especially when they do not comfortably fit the templates we have inherited from the past, are one way in which the Spirit may be speaking to the Church. Not automatically and always, of course, but the test of authenticity is not simple conformity to the past. Obedience is not the only virtue. Rather, the Spirit is speaking when the movements "from below" are oriented toward more effectively being a missioned community, charged with the task of reflecting the love of God in the world.

So what are the things that we can legitimately do to prepare for the new life that the Spirit brings? What will we venture that will prepare the Church for a new springtime? All our discussions thus far leave us with one remaining task, to offer some concrete suggestions for structural change in the Church that grow out of the changes that are continually going on in the community of faith. The Church is a collective incarnate subject, always changing. It is the community of conversion and of the converted. But it has a bureaucratic and institutional side that can simply become outdated. The institution is the wineskin, and the work of the Spirit is the new wine. We all know what happens when you put new wine in an old wineskin.

. . . And if Necessary, Change

There are some dramatic changes in the Church's future if it is to continue to be a strong voice proclaiming the good news. In what follows here we will consider some constructive proposals for change. They may seem impossibly unrealistic or even ridiculously idealistic. No matter. They follow from the serious discernment we have engaged in throughout these pages of the state of American Catholicism today. The American Catholic Church is only one voice in global Catholicism, and it may be that some of these ideas speak most clearly to the national context. But the catholicity of the Catholic Church is reflected at least as much in the variety of ways of being that it demonstrates worldwide as it is in the uniformity that sometimes seems to be pressed upon it. We have much to learn from others; for now, what does our experience suggest we might offer to the Church?

Democracy in Church Life

The single outstanding feature of American Catholicism is that people expect to have a say in the shape of their own Church. The Church is not something simply given from above, to be put on like a suit of clothes. The Church is created and re-created among us, as if we were constantly refashioning the clothes handed down to us, altering them so that they fit a changing body, and even adapting here and there to new fashions. But this cannot happen effectively if the process of orchestrating change is not conducted intentionally and in the open, with voice for all.

The initiative for democratization of the Church begins in the local parish, and the single biggest obstacle to its success is not the intransigence of the clergy but the passivity of the laity. Here is where people and their pastors will have to negotiate their way around the obstructions to full voice, but it cannot happen if it is only the vocal few who show any interest. Nothing will change if the minimalism that has so affected lay life for centuries does not come to an end. The roots of lay passivity lie in ignorance of the responsibilities of Christian discipleship incurred in baptism. Historically, the blame for that goes to Church leaders, who did not tell the full story about baptism. Today, the blame goes to all of us, because being better educated carries additional responsibilities. What was once the invincible ignorance of an uneducated laity has become to a high degree the culpable ignorance of an educated people who should know better.

Step one in bringing true democratic activity to the Church is for the pastoral council to initiate a pastoral plan with three objectives: better education, better liturgy, and more focused mission. The emphasis in education should be in the first instance not on spirituality or on doctrine but, rather, on history. Sometimes, whole towns or cities read a book together, and parishes could follow that example. Let us say that a parish community made a commitment to reading together James O'Toole's *The Faithful*, a recently written history of the American Church of considerable merit, both attractive and informative. This would generate a conversation within the community about how and why we are where we are, which could be conducted both formally in meetings and informally in all sorts of ways. Whether or not all agreed on the merits of the book, and the chances are good that there would be some differences of opinion, the process of engaging with it and with one another would be genuinely empowering. At the end, the community would know more and be more confident about itself than it was at the beginning. History is empowering and to a high degree escapes the hidden agendas that can infect both theology and spirituality.

From the first step in educating ourselves that a joint reading might represent, more structured procedures would need to be developed through which the community would come to see the linkage between liturgy and mission. This is a critical step that is often missing even in some of the best of situations. The priestly character of the whole people makes them mediators between God and the world, and the liturgy is the communal drama in which this mediation is most intentional. The priestly people bring the cares and concerns of the world before God in worship, and carry the grace of God from the liturgy out into the world where they are charged with the responsibility of being God's agents. Consequently, good liturgy cannot just be a matter of a dignified ritual studded with good music and a homily that inspires. It must also be an expression of a missionary Church. Somehow, the cares and concerns of mission must be made central to the liturgy, and not just in the intercessory prayers that usually occur immediately before the offertory. Worship is not a respite from the workaday world or a recharging of the batteries. It is in a symbiotic relationship with mission.

All of this does not make the Church more open to the voices of regular people, but it might empower regular people to work for more democracy. That indeed is the hope, and it is certainly likely to be the case that the call for greater voice in Church matters beyond the parish will come from those who already have voice within the parish. Moreover, since it is a fact of life that inductive ecclesial reflection rapidly comes into confrontation with a profoundly deductive (that is, top-down) institution, in the end real change will require real institutional change, and this is simply unlikely to happen without sustained pressure from the community of faith itself. The life of faith is not empowered by the doings of Church leaders but by the power of the liturgy, the wisdom that comes from education and prayer, and the courage that is expressed in engaging in Christian mission.

In an appropriately energized local community of faith a model for Christian living will be on display where the Pauline ecclesiology of charism clearly balances the Petrine insistence on order and hierarchy. A hierarchical institution is not at all one in which everything is top down but, rather, one in which everything and everyone has its place.[43] This in practice is going to mean that the ordained are freed to do the work of sacramental ministry and the rest of the community take up the challenging tasks of administration, education, and many elements of pastoral care. The most pressing issue here is the separation of the pastor and deacons from the financial affairs of the parish (and, correspondingly, the bishop from those of the diocese). Not only is money unrelated to sacramental ministry and the charism of orders without connection to financial acumen. Placing the finances of the parish in the hands of the laity empowers them further, makes financial solvency and transparency a little more likely, and—most important—begins to drive a wedge between orders and jurisdiction.

The "consultation only" clause in canon law that bedevils all efforts to wrest inappropriate authority from those in holy orders exists partially as a reflection of and partially as a support to the historic association of orders and jurisdiction in the Church. Whatever may have been the historical circumstances that justified this in the past, they do not exist today. Authority in almost all walks of life is shared either by an elected group of individuals or in some complex system of checks and balances. Either you have a parliament or you have a clear constitutional separation of powers between legislative, executive, and judicial branches of government. In this regard the Catholic Church is a historical anachronism that has evidently not yet come to terms with democracy, and the principal sign of this is not so much the figure of the pope as it is the identification of an undemocratic model of jurisdiction with orders. This is where the logjam can be found.

To separate the responsibility for administrative rule from pastoral ministry frees up the minister to exercise genuine spiritual leadership.

---

[43] See Richard R. Gaillardetz's discussion of the notion of hierarchical "ordering" in his essay "The Ecclesiological Foundations of Ministry Within an Ordered Community," in *Ordering the Baptismal Priesthood: Theologies of Ordained and Lay Ministry*, ed. Susan K. Wood (Collegeville, MN: Liturgical Press, 2003), 26–51.

This could have healthy consequences for the Church at all levels. In the parish, responsibilities would be shared based on the skills that people possessed and their willingness to put them at the service of the community. In other words, the parish would be a truly vocational enterprise. At the level of the diocese, offices other than that of bishop would be assigned according to capability and have nothing to do with ordination. The same goes for the Vatican. There is no connection whatsoever between holy orders and the ability to lead a Vatican congregation or be a cardinal. Either can be done equally well by the ordained or the non-ordained. The only argument to the contrary is effectively one that says, "the ordained make every decision." This begs the question of the relationship between orders and jurisdiction; it does not answer it.

The Reform of Ministry

The most concrete sign of the crisis in American Catholicism is the dramatic decline in the number of priests serving parishes, but this in itself only points to a larger issue, one of the need to rethink ministry in the Church. Far too often in today's Church the crisis in the priesthood is explained as a failure of people rather than of the structures. There are far fewer men in the United States offering themselves for ordination than there were a generation or two ago. There are many reasons for this, but there is no way to blame it on a lack of generosity or some other spiritual malaise, anymore than the enormous number of priests, religious, and seminarians in the Church of the '40s and '50s meant that people were better then than they are now. Much of the bulge was explicable socially and culturally, and much of today's dearth can also be understood in cultural terms. Moreover, it seems beyond doubt that many more men would be willing to consider priesthood if the Church did not require celibacy, and there are countless women who would like to serve if they were not excluded solely because they are women. In this situation it is particularly difficult to explain why the Holy Spirit should be staunchly supporting the Western Church's exclusion of women and married men from the priesthood while some other Spirit— whatever we name it—is misleading good people into thinking they may be called to serve the Church, though the institution does not want them.

Inductively speaking, the Catholic Church in America sees changes in patterns of ministry to be long overdue. The statistics were provided in earlier chapters of this book. The facts are clear: very few Catholics seem to believe that male celibate clergy are the wave of the future, a large majority are ready to have a married man as its pastor, and a somewhat smaller majority are ready for women pastors. Significant numbers of priests and bishops agree with this judgment, though not many bishops speak openly about it, at least until after retirement.[44] This amounts to a large-scale reimagining of the Church under way among rank-and-file Catholics that their leaders either will not countenance or cannot allow themselves to admit is a possibility. Theologically speaking it is the *sensus fidelium* at a particular moment in its history, undergoing rapid change.

While the hot-button issues of celibacy and women in ministry are not going to go away, there are several other steps that could be taken right now to confirm the emerging structures of ministry today. First, we need to make a clear separation between the thriving office of the permanent deacon and the increasingly irrelevant "order" of transitional deacons, those who will serve for only a year or even just a few months as deacons before being ordained priests. The United States has more permanent deacons than the rest of the Church put together, and obviously many of them do valiant service. Equally obvious, there is some ambiguity about their roles: are they practical assistants to the bishop (as they mostly were in the early Church), or are they primarily there to take the heat off overworked priests by doing many of the things the priests alone used to do, administering many sacraments and preaching occasionally? Second, it is becoming obvious that the future of much ministry in the Church is with the clumsily named "lay ecclesial ministers," and yet they serve without any clear, formal structure of commissioning or ordaining to what are frequently full-time responsibilities. Ministry to the community of faith needs to be dignified by more than a contract; some ceremony of commissioning should be standardized. In both the cases of lay ministers and permanent deacons, the defects in their formal situations could be solved largely by serious theological reflection on their offices in the Church. Third, there perhaps ought to be a reinterpretation of some of the minor orders that mostly became defunct after Vatican II in order to dignify the occasional ministries of reader and eucharistic minister. It is most important that in any restoration of any of these offices they be made equally available to women and men.

The most radical change we could consider in ministry in the Church would not be any of the above, certainly not the end to mandatory celibacy and not even the admission of women to ordination. No, the most

---

[44] For a sample, see Bishop Geoffrey Robinson, *Confronting Power and Sex in the Catholic Church: Reclaiming the Spirit of Jesus* (Collegeville, MN: Liturgical Press, 2008).

radical step would be a comprehensive rethinking of the theology of ministry so that all forms of ministry, from the full-time leadership responsibilities of the bishop to the occasional voluntary activity of the layperson who reads at Mass one Sunday a month, would be placed on a spectrum and within a common understanding of ministry. In this process of renewal it would be absolutely critical to take a close look at the long-standing theological assumption of "substantive ontological change" occurring in priestly ordination.[45] Some of the best work being done in this area today proposes rethinking ministries "relationally."[46] If a calling to ministry involves a reshaping of the person's relationship to the community of faith, then we can certainly see some ministries involving more dramatic reordering (bishop, pastor) and others less, without creating the chasm of substantive ontological change and perpetuating the clerical class. With this would come a whole range of possibilities for temporary or part-time "priestly" ministry, team ministry of pastoral leaders, and many more options.[47]

Teaching with Authority

The teaching role of the bishop is more important and more difficult today than ever before, but it can no longer be conducted along the lines of past generations. There are two reasons why significant changes need to take place. The first is that all that needs to be known in order to grasp the field of knowledge well enough to speak authoritatively vastly exceeds the capacity of any single individual. Popes and bishops have of course always relied on the help of trusted associates to advise them and to draft the documents that they will eventually sign. Today they need that help much more, and they need it from a far wider range of theological and pastoral opinion than they might have sought in previous times. Though teaching, especially ethical teaching, needs to be clear and unequivocal, it also has to respect the legitimate range of expert opinion that surrounds the topic under consideration. This is the case both because today most ethical issues are not answered easily and also because teaching that does not take account of what responsible people actually do in complex ethical situations will simply not carry conviction.

---

[45] Wood, *Ordering the Baptismal Priesthood*.

[46] Edward P. Hahnenberg, *Ministries: A Relational Approach* (New York: Crossroad, 2003).

[47] A full discussion of the many possibilities here can be found in Paul Lakeland, *The Liberation of the Laity: In Search of an Accountable Church* (New York: Continuum, 2003), 266–82.

This brings us neatly to the second reason for significant change, that the audience for ethical teaching is no longer what it was a generation or two ago. Then, it was more evidently obedient than it is now, though silent obedience might also have been a cover for just getting on with your own life according to your own conscience. Now, teaching that does not fit the complexity of responsible human behavior is simply ignored, which means that it is disobeyed.

Reshaping the teaching authority of the Church in a way that will garner it greater respect requires placing it in the context of pluralistic debate familiar to American Catholics in their daily lives. Just as the nation is a forum for formal and informal debate over our values and the practices that follow, so too should be our Church. We are not adults in the secular world and children in the Church; in both, our willingness to accept the vision of the common good—if we are not simply passive before the currents of the times—is directly connected to the degree that we feel we have been included in the process by which the decision was made. Moreover, the creation of such a climate of debate within the Church will have inestimable value in building up Catholics' sense of their responsibilities as citizens to bring more closely together their secular lives and their lives of faith. This would also be one more important way to assert the importance of making our Church more adult and more accountable. Owning the teaching of the Church is a whole lot easier if we are called to be responsible to positions that in part we have been responsible for creating.

The resources for energizing open public debate in the Church are not difficult to find. Almost every parish in the country and certainly each diocese include people with skills and qualifications in medicine, psychology, social work, theology, and so on. These, today including even theology, are things that some Catholic laity have become experts in, but in the present climate much of that expertise is shut out of the process of ethical discernment and formal teaching. Many dioceses also have the extraordinary tool of a Catholic college or university within their borders, part of whose mission is to help the Church think. At the present day, partially because of John Paul II's initiative in his letter on higher education, *Ex Corde Ecclesiae*,[48] and in part because of the felt need to offer some resources to help the Church overcome the crisis engendered by the sexual abuse scandal, the best of these institutions of higher education devote a large portion of their energies and resources to

---

[48] This can be found at http://www.ewtn.com/library/PAPALDOC/JP2UNIVE.HTM.

educating the Church itself. Additionally, the American taste for "joining" has meant that special interest groups have proliferated in the Church, whether they are the old standbys like the Knights of Columbus or newer organizations such as Call to Action or FutureChurch or Voice of the Faithful or even Faithful Voice.[49] The important thing here is not whether one agrees with the particular agenda of any of them, but the mere fact of their lively existence offers testimony to the vigor of our public ecclesial forum. Finally, there are countless books, magazines, newspapers, and reviews that reach many Catholics and stimulate their reflection, together with online resources and the extraordinary proliferation of Catholic bloggers, the best of whom make a real contribution to debate and even the worst of whom show that difference of opinion is alive and well in the Church.

While the resources are plentiful, making good use of them is not so certain. The place for debate and discussion, as in so many things, is in the local community of faith. It is also the case, therefore, that the battle for the future of the Church is largely being conducted at the grassroots level. Given the present top-down ecclesial organization it is inevitable that public debate about the Catholic Church will focus on the upper reaches of leadership, but you do not have to be particularly observant to notice that the vigor of the Church is in the local community, nor an especially good theologian to know that this is exactly the way it should be. And while there is little doubt that one charismatic pope could advance the cause of Church reform almost overnight, he could only do so by letting an adult and accountable Church have its head. If our Church leaders could only see that they themselves are not the players. Bishops are at some times referees, while at others they are coaches. They are there some of the time to see that the action of which they are a part respects its own rules, and some of the time to offer support and advice to the players. If they are wise, they know that the most skillful and creative plays on the field are such that they themselves may be incapable of performing. The Holy Spirit guides bishops and the rest of us alike, but while all the baptized—including the bishops—are guided by the Spirit to play the game, bishops as bishops are guided by the Spirit to let the game play out. As anyone who has ever watched a football game knows, too much whistle is sure to spoil it.

---

[49] Faithful Voice is a small conservative organization whose name riffs on the liberal organization Voice of the Faithful.

Leadership and the Life of Faith

While all institutions have to have a measure of bureaucracy and a set of rules, the depth-structure of the Church is patterned according to the divine life and not the Ford Motor Company, and its daily life ought to follow that pattern. The ancient Cappadocian Fathers imagined the three persons of the Godhead entwined in a dance of mutuality in which their differing responsibilities did not translate into different levels of importance. The Trinity is not a hierarchy but a community; as goes the life of God, so should go the life of the Church. Love, mutuality, account-ability, respect, and shared responsibility all trump the more mundane concerns of order, organization, obedience, and hierarchy. The institution is important, but it exists to protect the freedom of the community of faith to worship God in spirit and in truth, not to restrict it or to put fences around it. The large heart of Pope John XXIII showed that perfect love casts out fear. In his absence the Church needs to live by the Spirit, not by the letter.

In global Catholicism it is the responsibility of national or regional conferences of bishops to mediate between the local Church, colored as it is by the local culture, and the Roman authorities whose knowledge of the local Church is mostly dependent on these very bishops them-selves. It is not the responsibility of Rome to determine how the local culture can internalize Roman teaching. That is the prerogative of the local Church, and the bishops' conference is the natural conduit between the two, though more often than not in today's Church it is bypassed. This means that the first challenge for the national bishops' conference is to reassert its proper responsibilities. Over the past forty years Rome has worked very hard to restrict the role of national episcopal confer-ences, arguing that they have no proper theological status and hence no teaching function in their own right. This judgment is certainly question-able, not least because bishops' conferences seem to reflect the synodical structure by which the early Church governed itself very well before Roman centralization set in. But leaving this contentious issue aside here, to recognize the national Church's role in helping the local Church to digest and apply Roman teaching is not at all the same thing as asserting the right to teach in its own name. So, for example, U.S. bishops have produced in recent years a series of helpful reflections on the significance of lay ministry.[50] In these booklets the bishops help the American Church

---

[50] The latest is *Co-Workers in the Vineyard of the Lord* (Washington, DC: USCCB, 2005).

to digest John Paul II's letter *Christifideles Laici*,[51] while also drawing upon the particular American experience of lay ministry to enrich that teaching. Here we can see the U.S. bishops engaged collectively in their proper task of mediation between local and global Church.

Where the U.S. bishops acting collectively seem not to be so effective is in representing to Rome the legitimate cultural values of American society that rightly and properly have some shaping influence on how Catholics see their Church. First among these and foundational to all other issues is American expectations that all the baptized should have some voice in the Church, which follows directly from adult participatory democracy. The democratic spirit, genuine if not always highly functioning in American political culture, drives most of the issues over which American Catholics take issue with their Church. Statistics clearly reveal, as we saw earlier, that Americans think they should have a say in how their pastors are chosen and who will be selected. They evidently intend to form their own moral consciences, at their best paying attention to episcopal or papal teaching but not letting it dictate to them. They will not be told how to think of other religious traditions. They are increasingly insistent on a more equal role for women in the life of the Church, including its ordained ministry, and there is good evidence that the refusal to follow papal teaching on birth control will be followed by a similar refusal to think about same-sex unions as "gravely defective."

All the issues that follow from the American Catholic wish for a greater voice in the Church, and the attachment to democracy that grounds that wish, can be represented as problems or as calls for renewal. There are currently many voices in the American hierarchy who see them simply as signs of disaffection or disobedience. In consequence, these issues are not represented to Rome in a way that has behind it the weight of authority of the American bishops. No wonder that Rome does not hear these cries from the American Church as anything other than problems to be dealt with. But what would happen if our bishops explained to Rome that the collective concerns of active American Catholics as a whole were actually a call to conversion, to preparation for the new life of the Gospel that is always being prepared by the Holy Spirit? They emerge, after all, from the national Church whose parishes John Paul II

---

[51] *Christifideles Laici* was the papal response to, or summary of, the Rome Synod on the Laity that took place in 1987. The 1989 document is available at http://www .vatican.va/holy_father/john_paul_ii/apost_exhortations/documents/hf_jp-ii _exh_30121988_christifideles-laici_en.html.

identified as those that were most reflective of the reforms of Vatican II. The American Catholic Church, despite all the challenges we have discussed, is in fact functioning quite well at the local parish level, though how long that will last is far from certain. It has much to offer to the world Church.

Faced with the likelihood that the present U.S. episcopacy has neither the convictions nor the stomach to insist on more local autonomy for the American Church, the grassroots Church will have to dig deep in its reservoir of eschatological hope, praying as if everything depends upon God but, of course, acting as if everything depends upon us. It sometimes seems as if Church leaders are sitting in denial around the deathbed of the old Church; if so, the rest of us need to comfort them but also to call them to the practical consequences of their belief in resurrection. John Henry Newman wrote eloquently of the way in which it was the laity, not the bishops, who saved the early Church from the Arian heresy through the depths of their faith.[52] If the *sensus fidelium* came to the rescue there, it can do so once again. Far too often, movements for change in the Church are dismissed as faddy or off-the-wall liberalism, and it has to be admitted that sometimes advocates of change make their cases in ways that encourage this reaction. Behind the apparent anger or occasional clumsiness of most activists, however, you are far more likely to find a deep love of the Church and equally deep hurt at the damage it is doing to itself. Channeling anger is not easy, particularly when structures through which it can be somehow made effective are missing, but it is essential if it is not to be destructive.

It should come as no surprise that the necessary, constructive confrontation between Rome and the leaders of the American Church is unlikely to happen without pressure from below. An inductive ecclesiology will surely expect just such a relationship between the base and the superstructure, because creativity is far more likely to be found in the Church's living heart—in the local community of faith—than it is in the bureaucracy. The challenge for Rome is quite similar to that which faces Washington DC. Get out, meet the people, listen to them before you speak, go home and think about what they have to say and about your call to serve them. The better you know the people you serve and the complexity of their lives, and the more successfully you have incorporated what they have told you into your worldview, the more authority

---

[52] In *On Consulting the Faithful on Matters of Doctrine*, ed. John Coulson (New York: Sheed & Ward, 1961), 110.

will your teaching have. The more divorced you are from the lives of the faithful, the less will your teaching carry conviction. Today the Church is at its healthiest at the grassroots. That should be a lesson for all of us.

Turning to the role of the U.S. bishops relative to the national Church, it is ironic that a culture of participatory democracy like that of the United States should be served by a group of bishops who collectively seem to be allergic to the democratic process. "The Church is not a democracy" trips off many tongues so easily—by no means simply those of bishops— and while it is true as a statement of fact, it is not self-evident that it ought to be. Auxiliary Bishop Brady of Sydney, Australia, was even clearer when in the spring of 2008 he reportedly responded to disgruntled parishioners with the phrase, "the Church is a dictatorship, not a democracy."[53] Bruce Russett of Yale University has helpfully pointed out that democracy by plebiscite is not a worthwhile objective, though some critics of democracy in the Church often assume that exactly that is being called for. But even the minimum, the requirement for a "decent consultation hierarchy," a step that is not truly democratic, is resisted.[54] The idea of a decent consultation hierarchy was explained by John Rawls as what was appropriate to a society committed to the idea of the common good. It would be marked by there being "an opportunity for different voices to be heard," and that at some point in the process of consultation they would have the right to express dissent and be listened to by their leaders. Leaders "cannot refuse to listen, charging that the dissenters are incompetent and unable to understand, for then we would not have a decent consultation hierarchy, but a paternalistic regime."[55] While Rawls was thinking of political society, the transposition to the Church is an easy one, since the notion of the common good is so central to the Catholic tradition.

The first and best thing that American bishops can do for their Church, then, is to listen, even to listen to what sounds to them like dissent, but this will require an altogether different understanding of leadership than they have been led to apply, and an appreciation of power that is a long way from the arbitrary exercise of authority. It is not clear how much

[53] From an April 2008 story in *Australian Catholic News*, available at http://www .cathnews.com/article.aspx?aeid=6809.
[54] Bruce Russett, *Governance, Accountability, and the Future of the Catholic Church*, ed. Francis Oakley and Bruce Russett (New York: Continuum, 2004), 196–202.
[55] John Rawls, *The Law of Peoples* (Cambridge, MA: Harvard University Press, 1999), 49 as quoted in ibid., 200.

genuine listening can be done across the divide that separates clerical and lay life at the present time. The job of a bishop is an unenviable one, but it is made well-nigh impossible for him to really understand the lay life of faith in the world if his place in a clerical world insulates him from at least some of the same stresses of family life, finances, the struggle for meaningful employment, and so on. Whatever we may individually think about the mandatory celibacy of the clergy, it has to be admitted that one downside is that the clergy are to a high degree removed from the stresses of ordinary life.

To help overcome the challenges that the bishops cannot themselves remove, such as that of celibacy or a clerical culture, they might do a great deal for their churches by creating avenues of contact and interchange between bishop, priests, and people. They could certainly break with practices that seem unduly to separate laity and clergy, and just as they can promote more vigorous pastoral and financial councils, so they can also initiate conversations on issues of importance in Church life. Which bishops would not be better prepared to teach by exchange or listening sessions with laity on sexual ethics, end-of-life issues, Church and money, political choices, same-sex relations, and so on? Only fear or willful ignorance could lead a bishop to think that he is better off with a narrower range of advice or no advice at all. What the bishop teaches might be no different, but in all likelihood it will be taught with more sensitivity to those to whom it is addressed—and heard more clearly— the more completely its recipients were involved in the discernment process of which it was the result. Include people. There is nothing to lose and much to gain.

The diocesan synod is one structure the bishops might use to establish their commitment to a different way of governing. Canon law allows for the bishop to call such a synod whenever in his estimation the time is ripe, and it indicates the process by which all sectors of the Church shall be represented at the synod.[56] As the law now stands, it is clearly stated that the role of all involved in the synod is consultative to the bishop, and that a synod should be seen in the context of the bishop's teaching office. This is no different from the legal situation of finance and pastoral councils; and while at the present time none of these are anything but consultative, the style and convictions of a bishop or pastor can make

---

[56] Canons 460–68. See also the Vatican Instruction on Diocesan Synods of 1997, available at http://www.vatican.va/roman_curia/congregations/cbishops/documents/rc_con_cbishops_doc_20041118_diocesan-synods-1997_en.html.

such consultation either vital and energizing or pro forma and irrelevant. A decent consultation hierarchy would obviously expect the former.

In the end, it is at the level of the local Church that the battle for the future of Roman Catholicism is being fought. Catholics living in the world in faithfulness to the mission to bring the love of God to that world are the principal players in the game. Vatican II was in itself an enormous step forward on the part of the institutional Church toward recognizing that fact. It was unlike all previous councils in its clearly pastoral intent. Its theology of the Church prioritized baptism, the role of the Spirit, and the work of the laity. What the Church has so far failed to do with the council's message is, on the one hand, to change structures and style to match the vision and, on the other, to reflect in depth on a theology of laity. On the former count the revision of the Code of Canon Law, promulgated in 1984, was an effort to bring law into line with conciliar teaching, but it did not go far enough. As law, perhaps it could not go further, because law awaits theological reflection, and the "merely consultative" clauses that shore up the clerical estate cannot be removed until the theology of laity leads us to a firmer understanding of adult responsibility in the Church. The roots of solid ecclesiological reflection lie there, in the life of the local community of faith and the ecclesial responsibilities of the baptized Christian. This, in the last analysis, is why ecclesiology today must be inductive.

Epilogue

Living Communion

Ecclesiology often seems to take for granted, if not ignore, the liturgical life of the Church. As I draw this book to a close I do not want to be thought guilty of this charge, so let me say unequivocally that without the Eucharist we have no Church. In these days of declining numbers of traditional vocations to the priesthood, it is curiously often the so-called liberals who make the claim for the centrality of the Eucharist. Facing a future in which we must choose between making changes in who can be licitly ordained and settling for less frequent opportunities for eucharistic worship, the so-called conservatives have an interest in playing down the easy availability of the Mass. Perhaps we will be told that the Eucharist is not a right, perhaps that absence makes the heart grow fonder, and we will be more fervent when we can no longer take it for granted. I am not so sure that Pope St. Pius X would have welcomed this turn away from his promotion of frequent communion, but then he did not have a shortage of priests to concern him.

To speak of the absolute necessity of the availability of the Eucharist is not to make an argument that at the center of the Catholic religion there is a pious act. By no means. The sacrament of the Eucharist is the ritual bridge between the dead and risen Christ on the one side and the call to mission on the other. It is the moment when the worldly concerns of God's people are placed on the altar and put it into perspective. It is the time when we smother our worries and our fears with a blanket of praise and thanksgiving. But above all, in the hackneyed words of the hymn, it is "bread for the journey." For all its holiness in itself, the Eucharist, like the Church, is oriented beyond itself to the mission of God's holy people in the world. When Jesus celebrated his last supper with his friends it was not just a good-bye; it was about the future beyond Calvary, both his own rising to new life and the life of the Church in his Spirit.

When we think about the close connection between the Eucharist and the call to mission, we are the heart of what it is to be the Church. Gathered together in his name, the two or three or five hundred of us recall Jesus Christ in word and sacrament, share in his body and blood and go forth in his name to spread the good news that God loves and cares for the world. In the end, this is all it is. Sublime, and yet so simple. Everything else is secondary and instrumental to the proclamation of God's love in word and by example. Over the course of two millennia Christians have struggled to be faithful to their mission. The many ways we have found to be church are both a testimony to our collective sincerity and a witness to our failure to be tolerant with one another. We are alive alright, the Catholics and the Baptists, the Orthodox and the Pentecostals, but our communion with one another is imperfect, which means our capacity to be the loving presence of God in Christ in the world is fragmented and less than it might be. The ways we have to heal this brokenness are many, but surely they are primarily matters of love, tolerance, and unity in the common purpose with the rest of humankind to heal the human heart.

This book is intended to help the Catholic Church take a step in the direction of being more what we are called to be. For that reason, it is at times a little controversial, perhaps even a little abrasive to some ears. It is hard for the largest Church to be humble, but it is something we must learn to do better if we are to lead the family of Christian churches through the difficult times that undoubtedly lie ahead. At Vatican II the bishops talked of reading the signs of the times, by which they effectively signaled their conversion to the inductive method that we have employed throughout these pages. History is our best teacher, both world history and local history, ancient history and the history we are making in the present moment. The mistakes we as a Church made in the past are lessons from which we have to learn now if we did not learn then. The way we are perceived today by other Christian churches, other religions, and the children we are raising in our own families are lessons of history in the making, which we must not ignore.

The future of the Catholic Church cannot just be the clerical church of the past, nor should it be thought that a kind of lay-led palace revolution will solve all our problems. In the end we may need to turn back to the humble and brilliant French Dominican friar, Yves Congar, and his conversion late in life from a clergy/laity vision of the Church to one of different ministries. Some ministries may be more central to the needs of the Church than others. We do not all possess the gift of leadership or preaching but then, again, not every great preacher can teach first-graders their catechism. In the past we have as a Church insisted that ordained ministry is a calling from Christ, not simply a commissioning by the community of the faithful. While the stridency of our claims for the special character of ordained ministry may have been occasioned by the fires of religious controversy, it is in itself quite true. But what our focus on the special character of ordained ministry has obscured is the realization that every ministry in the Church is a calling from Christ. In the Christian community there is no such thing as a calling that is not simultaneously from Christ and by the community in the power of the Spirit. If this is so, then we have to stop thinking about clergy and laity as a fundamental division in the Church; there are different ministries, and the default Christian, so to speak, is someone who is baptized to witness to the love of God in the world, whether ordained, commissioned, or just doing the best they can.

The Church is a living communion, and in this communion we live and move and have our being, but its reach extends to the whole world which it serves and to which it witnesses. What we are for mission we must also be in the Eucharist. This requires the availability of the Eucharist, as we have had occasion to note in the preceding pages. But it also means that the eucharistic ritual itself must be an exercise of the whole community gathered around the altar. If you want to know what someone thinks about the Church, look at what they have to say about the Mass. Vatican II saw it rightly as the work of the whole Church and for that reason promoted the use of the vernacular, the restoration of the elements of the sacred meal to what had become the simple reenactment of a sacrifice, participation of the whole community in responses and liturgical gestures, and the liturgical adulthood of all the baptized through their involvement as readers and eucharistic ministers, through the reception of Communion in the hand and under both species of bread and wine. When we find our Church seeking to roll back some or all of these developments since Vatican II, we would be mistaken if we think this is just about "the dignity of the liturgy" or "the beauty of the Latin." This is about the nature of the Church. Here in the liturgy is where our worship is focused, here is where we see the bone-structure of the Church, and here may be where we have to take our stand on what it means to be a living communion. If we can get this right many other details will fall into place; get it wrong and we may be neither living nor a communion.

Further Reading

Baggett, Jerome P. *Sense of the Faithful: How American Catholics Live Their Faith.* Oxford and New York: Oxford University Press, 2009.

Cozzens, Donald. *The Changing Face of the Priesthood: A Reflection on the Priest's Crisis of Soul.* Collegeville, MN: Liturgical Press, 2000.

———. *Sacred Silence: Denial and Crisis in the Church.* Collegeville, MN: Liturgical Press, 2002.

D'Antonio, William V., James D. Davidson, Dean R. Hoge, and Mary L. Gautier, *American Catholics Today: New Realities of Their Faith and Their Church.* Lanham, MD: Rowman & Littlefield, 2007.

Dulles, Avery. *Models of the Church.* Garden City, NY: Doubleday, 1974; New York: Doubleday, Image Books, 1991.

Gaillardetz, Richard R. *By What Authority? A Primer on Scripture, the Magisterium, and the Sense of the Faithful.* Collegeville, MN: Liturgical Press, 2003.

Hahnenberg, Edward P. *Ministries: A Relational Approach.* New York: Crossroad, 2003.

Haight, Roger. *Christian Community in History.* Vol. 2, *Comparative Ecclesiology.* New York: Continuum, 2005.

Hinze, Bradford E. *Practices of Dialogue in the Roman Catholic Church: Aims and Obstacles, Lessons and Laments.* New York: Continuum, 2006.

Johnson, Elizabeth A., ed. *The Church Women Want: Catholic Women in Dialogue.* New York: Crossroad, 2002.

Lakeland, Paul. *Catholicism at the Crossroads: How the Laity Can Save the Church.* New York: Continuum, 2007.

———. *The Liberation of the Laity: In Search of an Accountable Church.* New York: Continuum, 2003.

Mannion, Gerard. *Ecclesiology and Postmodernity: Questions for the Church in Our Time.* Liturgical Press: Collegeville, MN, 2007.

———, ed. *The Vision of John Paul II: Assessing His Thought and Influence.* Collegeville, MN: Liturgical, 2008.

Oakley, Francis, and Bruce Russett, eds. *Governance, Accountability, and the Future of the Catholic Church.* New York: Continuum, 2004.

O'Toole, James M. *The Faithful: A History of Catholics in America.* Cambridge, MA: Harvard University Press, 2008.

Robinson, Geoffrey. *Confronting Power and Sex in the Catholic Church: Reclaiming the Spirit of Jesus.* Collegeville, MN: Liturgical Press, 2008.

Rush, Ormond. *Still Interpreting Vatican II: Some Hermeneutical Principles.* Mahwah, NJ: Paulist Press, 2004.

Schreiter, Robert J. *Constructing Local Theologies.* Maryknoll, NY: Orbis Books, 1985.

Wood, Susan K., ed. *Ordering the Baptismal Priesthood: Theologies of Ordained and Lay Ministry.* Collegeville, MN: Liturgical Press, 2003.

Index